THE LAST JOURNEY OF MARCUS OMOFUMA

AN ACCOUNT OF PRISON EXPERIENCE

BY

EMMANUEL OBINALI CHUKWUJEKWU

iUniverse, Inc.
Bloomington

The Last Journey Of Marcus Omofuma
An Account of Prison Experience

iUniverse books may be ordered through booksellers or by contacting:

iUniverse
1663 Liberty Drive
Bloomington, IN 47403
www.iuniverse.com
1-800-Authors (1-800-288-4677)

ISBN: 978-1-4620-4617-1 (sc)
ISBN: 978-1-4620-4618-8 (ebk)

Printed in the United States of America

iUniverse rev. date: 11/30/2011

THE LAST
JOURNEY OF
MARCUS OMOFUMA

CONTENTS

CONTENTS

This is the story of a Black African immigrant in search of greener pasture in Europe. The book also reveals and describes experiences of other African nationalities who became victims of the hostile Austrian asylum policy in their attempt to migrate.

It is also the account of one African asylum seeker at the mercy of the Austrian police, and the effect it has on his fellow asylum seekers. The story also deals with the various dilemma faced by both Africans and their European hosts. It is also about the basic truth that Austria and most European nations do not welcome foreigners as immigrants, especially Blacks. It further deals with the problems of Africa, its history and its hope as seen through the eyes of its troubled emigrant citizens.

The story begins with Marcus Omofuma and his fellow detention inmates having a lively discussion of African politics in the prison. Marcus has a premonition of doom and discloses it to his comrades. The premonition came true while he was being deported back to Nigeria on board a Balkan Airline flight. He was killed. His fellow inmates enter into series of civil disobedience actions within the deportation prison camp—including a collective hunger strike. During these actions, through the discussion and dialogue among the Africans, we got a deep insight into problems of Africans in both Africa and Europe.

The Africans are as critical of Africa as they are of Europe. The dialogue between the Africans is illuminating, and in its subtle brilliance; manages to be an entertainment mixture of tragic-comedy and drama. In particular the story of Jean Kanombe, a former Rwandan child soldier brings us closer than ever to the African experience. The drama is heightened by the resistance of the Austrian authorities to the detainees and their eventual cave to releasing the prisoners when an Australian born journalist, John Nelson writes an exposé on the murder of Omofuma and the hypocrisy of the Austrian immigrant policy.

The action culminates with the mass demonstration for Omofuma in Vienna and the massive arrest of African asylum seekers in a police action code named 'OPERATION-SPRING'. Over two hundred and fifty Africans were initially swept off the streets and from their homes in the politically charged atmosphere of Austrian national election, as an action against alleged drug dealers. All the heroes of the story were re-arrested and some of them suffered up to ten years imprisonment.

The author of this book is one of those prisoners and he wrote this novel while in prison.

"Did you ever feel as though you have something inside you that was only waiting for you to give it a chance to come out? Some sort of extra power that you could be using if you knew how? I'm thinking for a strange feeling I sometimes get, a feeling that I've got something important to say and the power to say it—only I don't know what it is and can't make any use of the power.

If there was some different way of writing or, else something different to write about, I'm pretty good at inventing phrases that wake you up even if there about something that everybody knows already. But that doesn't seem enough. It's not enough phrases to be good; what you make with them ought to be good too. But what's the good of that if the things you write about have no power in them"

Helmholtz speaking to Bernard in "BRAVE NEW WORLD"
By Aldous Huxley

> "It is strange the way the ignorant and inexperienced so often and so undeservedly succeed when the informed and the experienced fall."
>
> Comedian Bob Newhart.

God has made this possible in the sense that He magnified His name; and blessed His servant by making this dream of mine come true.

I'll praise His name all the days of my life.

Obinali.

In memory of Marcus Omofuma

ACKNOWLEDGEMENTS

This book was inspired by an opportune meeting of the author and Marcus Omofuma and conversation they had together. Though other characters in this book were fictitious and purely author's imagination, the story could not have been written without the help of Dr. Lennart Binder, an Austrian based 'Human Rights' lawyer, who made it possible for me to have the first writing materials while in prison. To you sir, I could only say thank you and more grease to your elbow.

I wish to thank Gundula Ludwig in a very special way for her tremendous and relentless efforts towards making this dream of my a reality. I'm forever grateful for all your help, selfless contributions and constant supports in my endeavours.

I want to also appreciate my Austrian Godmother, Ute Bock, who is well known within the entire immigrant communities, especially by the black African community in Vienna Austria, as Mama Africa. To you Mama, I pray God to continue to bless and protect you and all the members of your charity organization, the SOS Mitmensch, as you continue to render your tireless and selfless services to humanity.

To my mentor and big brother, Dr. Chigbo Onyeji and family, I express my profound thanks and gratitude.

With much respect I would like to extend my greetings to all my brothers and sisters, mostly to all those prisoners of conscience who had been imprisoned during the great 'Operation Spring' trials. May the Almighty

God replenish all of us whatsoever we might have lost during those years we spent in the hot and cold Austrian prisons.

Also of great help to the author, mainly during his long prison days— almost five years— in the 'Landesgericht' detention prison Vienna, were all the members of the defunct 'Association For Human Rights Of Immigrants (GEMMI).

To Evangelist Chi Benedicta Okonkwo, I so much appreciate your selfless contribution.

I would like to extend my profound thanks and appreciations to Reverend Fathers C J Ibeanu, Joseph Orji, Joe Ben Onyia, Joseph Bantega to name but a few, for your prayers, advises and contributions towards my spiritual life.

I hereby extend my humble greeting to Mr. Basil Okafor for his support and kindness.

Thank you also to DR. Festus Afamefule for your fatherly advises to me all these years I've come to know you.

To Mr. Godwin Nzewi (Akwanga), a great debt of thanks is owed. I would never forget your moral and financial supports to me.

With high esteem and profound gratitude to Mr. and Mrs. Emmanuel Oguegbu (Edom) and family, I express my humble appreciation. I must not forget the goodness you have shown me as a friend.

Also worthy to be mention are Mr. Emeka Obi, Miss Merscedes Tonda and Mr. Casmir Okezie Nolisa. You all contributed in one way or the other towards the success of this book.

Of very great important to the author were, Mr. C C Chukwujekwu, Mrs. Ann Chukwujekwu, Mr. Azuka Nwaolise and Mrs. Stella Favour Nwaolise, Mr. and Mrs.Keneth Chinyere Ugokwe, Mr. and Mrs. Chubi Rose Ozuruoha and family, Mr. Vitus Nwachukwu and Mrs. Chinwe Nwachukwu, Mr. and Mrs. Charles Nzeribe and family, Mr and Mrs Eze

Priscila Obizue, Mr. Lawrence Onyemaechi, Mr. Tony Onyemaechi, Dr. J P Ifeanyi.

With high esteem to my old parents, Mr. and Mrs. John Jane Chukwujekwu, for bringing me to this world and inducting me into good Christian and home upbringing. To dad and mum, I pray God to continue to guide and sustain you. Both of you are my greatest heroes and precious jewels.

I want to appreciate the following persons for their constant supports and benevolent dispositions towards me all these years I have come to know them; Mr. and Mrs. Ben Franca Ibegbulem and family, Mr. and Mrs. Mathew Nnodim and family, Mr. And Mrs. Longinus Ebubechukwu and family, Mr. and Mrs. Emeka Chi Okwegba and family, Mr. and Mrs. Chinedu Darlington Igbokwupute and family. Mr. and Mrs. Justin Okechukwu and family, Mr. Eugene Nsobundu and family, Mr. and Mrs. John Okechukwu (Echibe) H R H Chief Bob Eze and family.

Last but not the least, the author wishes to thank all my friends and well-wishers, both Whites and blacks for their persistent prayers during my trial periods.

Thank you all and God bless you all, Amen.

DEDICATION

I specially dedicated this book to all my family and extended family members, especially to Chiawolamoke, Chiagoziem, Chizitere and Somtochukwu.

INTRODUCTION

Through the past centuries European governments have done well in exploiting the resources of Africa, including its people in the slave trade. When African citizens due to economic conditions, dictatorial regimes and political wars at home have sought refuge in Europe, their first experiences of Europe have usually been prison. "Wow, what a welcome!"
Even the European government asylum policies are designed to almost ensure the failure of the Asylum candidates. In other words, it is a humanistic looking paper policy with no concrete social and financial system built in for the asylum seeker. The asylum seeker is not allowed to work or have job that would provide him or her with a decent income. Instead, he or she is forced to beg for handouts or engage in illegal activity. Everyone, even if he or she is not European must eat to survive.

There is no question that the African refugee is at a disadvantage (as are other third world and Eastern European people) in diplomatic representation. Their embassies are as much their enemies, as their host state otherwise they would not be political refugees. Many Africans for that reason carry different African identity papers other than their real country of origin. The African has another disadvantage—his or her colour. He or she is so obviously recognizable unlike a White person from Russia, he or she cannot blend in the indigenous population. In Austria, his or her colour automatically makes him or her vulnerable to the charge of 'drug dealing'.
In a country like Austria that has never come to terms with its massive 'Nazi past', an influx of Black people is sure to arouse attention and hostility.

Africa has failed its citizens in Europe as it failed its citizens at home. Africa's disorganization and political systems as well as tribal wars and economic chaos, have left its citizens in Europe open to persecution by European governments.

Euro-Africans could, if they were allowed to be productive individuals in Europe, benefit both continents. Imagine the financial remittance that would be sent to Africa to boost their home economy. The returning Euro-African could contribute to the creation of new African businesses and institution. What are Africa's political and business muscles?

Africa is a continent of huge natural resources (oil, gold, gas, etc.) not the least of which is its human population. This gives Africa huge diplomatic muscle with which to defend its citizens. However, without viable diplomatic institution to harness power. African citizens in Europe are cannon-fodder for European Immigration and police authorities. The African refugee in Austria, for example, is open to massive racist judicial abuse and manipulation because there are no diplomatic consequences for such actions. On the contrary, catching these helpless 'imaginary' drug dealers can lead to the promotion of the career of these police officers.

There is no American State Department, British Foreign office, or French QuaiD'Orsay screaming bloody murder for their abused citizens. For Africans there need to be the creation of an independent African State Department or Foreign office which acts as one for all of African citizens. This body could be part of the African Union (AU) . . . with real political and economic teeth. Those countries that are thought to be singling out citizens of African origin for racism would be subjected to 'sanction' . . . . that is banning their companies, citizens and governments from competing for Africa businesses and contracts. Though this sounds far fetched at the moment, it would radically improve the treatment of Africans around the world. Even the African governments individually would benefit as it would strengthen the current power structures and political hierarchy vis á vis Europe, the US and the Third World.

It is utterly—heartbreaking to see an African man murdered in cold-blood or having his soul crushed by judicial authorities because he knows there is no one out there diplomatically to protect him. There are no detrimental consequences for his abuse, only political and career reward.

However, for a country like Austria, the benefits of an integrated African population would be the best guarantee against a return to 'Nazism'. Of course, that is assuming they want that guarantee to build a non-racist society which is not at all clear at this point as far as extreme racist regime sometime have been favoured by the electorate. This will never happen until the 'Great Continent' of Africa learns to flex its muscles diplomatically for its own citizens.

Imagine if the Black population of America were by the N.A.A.C.P. via the African Union Foreign office to boycott European goods and lobby the US government to put pressure on the European governments in favour of oppressed Africans in Europe. One could believe there would be a chain reaction of events diplomatically that would stretch from Washington to Brussels. Europe (Austria) is incredibly vulnerable to diplomatic and economic pressure whether they choose to believe so or not.

Sharing prison time with many African brothers, one learns of the great and magical values in African culture, the warmth and love they share with those around them. One learns how they could make hardship and deprivation tolerable through their endless optimism expressed through the pride of the African people and the strength of their heart.

If only African governments know how to protect and harness the power of the Great African people. Please Africa, stand up and defend the greatest resources you have.

LONG LIVE AFRICA

CHAPTER ONE

At this moment, then the Negros must begin to do the very thing which they have been taught that they cannot do. They still have some money, and they have needs to supply, they must begin immediately to pool their earning and organize industries to participate in social and economic demands. If the Negros are to remain forever removed from the present discrimination continues, there will be nothing left for them to do.

===Carter G. Woodson (1875-1950).

The normal early spring morning sun had set as usual. Everybody puts on his light spring jacket. The time exactly 9:15; the prisoners of 'illegal entry' were out just for 15 minutes. Now as some of them were sitting together, some walked around the 40 by 40 square meters (which had been their permanent get together centre), talking and chatting. Some of them had already lit their cigarette. To them it was another bright day, one that needs to be enjoyed in full. They all seemed to be looking forward to this particular 'Tori section' . . . of all the things that mattered to them. It was the most gratifying.

As expected, Marcus Omofuma opened up the discussion, but today in an unexpected and exasperated 'mother' of all question.

"So, Gentlemen why, have we all left the African soil if we all insisted we 'LOVED' her?" Omofuma asked, smiling in his usual welcoming smile.

1

All eyes turned and fixed on him. The thought in those eyes seem to be. 'And what about this interrogating question'

"Oh! Guys," laughed Omofuma, waving his right hand in a calm gesture, "I'm not being rude, I thought about this particular question overnight. And, you know what, I couldn't really convince, myself about my answers. I knew it might look boring, or kind of an odd question to raise, but let us start discussing realities and not fantasies anymore."

"And what are your answers?" interrupted Koso Osei irritatingly.

He always took it monotonous whenever one wants to introduce another subject other than woman's affairs, especially when any of them will mention the Bible or Christianity (which he believes is the White man's original spying tool against Africa and its people) or on the contrary, when one tries to discuss about Africa as a whole, with its present day predicaments.

"I mean, can't we discuss something else on this beautiful spring morning than trying to while away boring hour on 'mother Africa?'" Koso suggested dully, nodding his head to others for support.

"So, which means Charlie, you don't love Africa? Or can I say, you're like a hateful lover who doesn't want to remember his affairs with his former fiancée any more? Like you're afraid to recount why you left Africa?" asked Marcus, this time directly to Koso, his face grinning, as he tapped him on the shoulder.

"But, Marcus, for God's sake tell us your own version. We are all ears as you can see," Koso grinned back.

"Are you a Nigerian?" enquired Marcus jokingly.

"No, but why,? You know I'm Ghanaian," Koso retorted.

"Because, I thought it is only Nigerians who use to answer questions with questions," said Marcus assertively.

He went on to give them an anecdote of one British man who once boarded a plane to Nigeria, mainly because he wanted to conduct research about the allegation that Nigerians answer questions with questions. So on arrival at the Nigerian airport, he accosted a Nigerian Immigration officer. After exchanging greetings; the British man said to the officer politely . . . .

"Please, don't be annoyed, but I have a little thing to ask you?"

The officer replied that he is free to ask anything being a tourist.

"Is it true that Nigerians answer questions with questions?" the British man inquired.

"Hm naa, who told you, that?" replied the Nigerian officer inquisitively.

"Yeah that is absolutely true. That's that" confirmed the British man "Now, I know for sure you NIGERIANS use to answer questions with questions."

"So, you see Charlie. You must answer my question straight, if you don't want to become a Nigerian. You got what I mean," asserts Marcus, happy that the other prisoners were getting interested too, because of his anecdote.

"Well, if that is the case, I better . . . because no one argues with you and wins" Koso quipped. "I think we all love Africa and we all would've loved to be in Africa and not desert her . . . so the question should not be why do we abandon Africa if we really loved her, but rather, why did the African Leaders fail Africa and her people? The Western countries had always been the cause and still remain the cause." Koso opined

"In my own opinion," begins Hyman Otta, who had been relatively quiet all this while, "to tell you guys the truth I would be the first person to go back to my continent Africa and my country Sudan if the war ends today. I wouldn't have in the real sense of it chosen to come to Europe in this manner . . . in a manner one is presumed a criminal because of one's color or race. Where the first culture you learn as a Black man is the prison culture. Where one is treated as a criminal on first sight without being a criminal or having committed a crime . . . only that one is really seeking to save his or her life. Yes. The authorities always think that all of us are economic immigrants" Hyman was saying in his preacher man voice.

He was dressed in blue jeans trousers and a black leather jacket, a pair of black loafers, with a matching facing cap. He was a very polite, well-mannered and sympathetic person who normally goes straight to the point because of his trainings. He went on.

"Listen, few of us might be the economic types as they thought, but what they don't know or do not want to know is that many of us are only fleeing from wars and dictatorial regimes. So they must not take the grain as the chaff."

"Hi man! I think you run better, but outside the track" interrupted Koso, who was getting more and more interested in the topic. "Look, there is nothing bad if the grains and chaffs find themselves in Europe or in any other place in this whole world. After all, it was the Europeans that taught Africans what migration is all about in the first place. We wouldn't have been coming if the Europeans had not come to steal the African wealth away thereby pushing 'mother Africa' to poverty-stricken and starving condition she found herself in today. Yeah, man, the Europeans sowed the seeds of poverty in Africa and they have been 'moistening' it since the days of Adam. Having come first, I think it is the right time Africa visits back. Whether they like it or not" Koso maintained

"Make no mistake. I agreed with all you said. Yoo, Charlie, some of us must have been the economic migrants which I bet I'm happy to be one of them. Yes, we've the right to migrate in search of works in Europe, America, Canada etc. to provide better life for ourselves and our families. That is never a criminal offence and should not in anyway amount to be so." Peters asserted, his big eyes pops out like they wanted to fall down. He was always in that mood when he speaks with bits of annoyance.

"Coming to that," said Marcus Omofuma, who was the initiator of the topic, and had been enjoying the argument immensely, "I think, the first thing the Westerners must do is to try and tell themselves the gospel truth about the flows of immigrants and immigration to the West. What can they know of the background of these people and why they wanted to reside in Europe? I'll like to outline my own view in this way. Firstly, Africa is a continent every African must have loved in one way or the other. Either for its geographical and tropical position or for its relatively peaceful co-existence before our WHITE MASTERS came to scatter the African way of life, thereafter sowing their wars and hatred oriented ways in us. This of course had been in Africa since then and had been the order of the day in that 'EUROPEAN FORSAKEN' continent. You will agree with me, my brothers that it's easier to learn than to forget, most especially when you have to learn from 'hard way' like the Europeans indoctrinated into Africa as Hyman rightly pointed out before. I, as well believe that the problems of all the ethnic wars must either be resolved or at least largely reduced through the efforts of Europe and the US and every other country that deals in arms to prevent the over-militarisation of Africa" Marcus declared, smiling and at the same time revealing his perfect sets of white teeth, using his left hand to brush at his punk hair style.

Koso Osei smiled a wild and bright smile.

"That's a very good point you made, *the wizard*" he uttered, stroking at his chin. He always respected Marcus opinion and adored him much. He had nicknamed Marcus *The wizard* because of his great brilliance. "You hit the nail at the head always."

"Secondly", continued Marcus, cutting Koso off his compliments, "the West cannot afford to overlook Africa now having perpetrated series of perditions against her, which resulted sometimes in flows of immigration. They must not intend to push the immigration problems into abyss . . . not really trying to find a constructive way of solving them and getting it off its patch. Europe and their Western brothers must live up to its responsibilities by accepting us and these problems of which they remained the prime culprits and not rejecting us."

"But, Marcus, was this the real situation we expected to find ourselves in, when we came over here?" inquired Hyman seriously.

"Brother, men! I mean, can a cushite change his skin? Or a leopard it spots?" asked Omofuma, flashing a smugly smile at Hyman. "We didn't expect it to be rosy, did we? We all knew about the history, don't we?

The Europeans don't want us to come because probably they were afraid of the past. But remember, one must confront the past before he must confront the present. We couldn't forget that they're all part and parcel of the 'HOLOCAUST'; especially Austria, where, Hitler actually came from. However, what they have not really understood is that they will never run away from their sins and their responsibilities so far as Africa remains poor and at war, the West will never know peace. You can't eat your cake and still have it."

"That is what you mean, Omoba," interjected Peters rivetedly, "is that a world perspective must be developed. No individual can live alone; no nation can live alone; so the Westerners and the Africans must teach each other how to live together as brothers and sisters or we are all going to perish together as fools."

"*Genau*" Marcus agreed. "As the saying goes, 'when one hand washes the other, the other washes back' after all, they have many things to learn from Africa, than Africa has to learn from them."

"Agreed" said Koso happily. "The Austrians could easily argue that they were never part of the Europeans that invaded Africa during the 'Great African Scrambles', *the wizard*, what could you say about this?"

"Nonsense, that's absolutely nonsense" replied Marcus promptly. "Austria was part of Germany which invaded Africa during the Second World War. And as far as Africa is concerned, since Europe is trying to come together or has probably become one bloc, every one of them must take the responsibility. Africa cannot wait any longer. Have you ever imagined what it's like? I mean the differences between the life conditions of the West and that of Africa?"

"Oh! Charlie, it's really shit. It's like comparing day and night" Koso murmured as his char-coaled face glowered. He is a typical Ghanaian with a tiny 'Ashanti tribal mark' on his round face. "Now, you come to terms with me. Was it the 19th century transcendentalist Ralph Waldo Ermson who said that 'what lies behind us and what lies before us are tiny matters compared to what lies within us'" quoted Koso.

He spread his hands deprecatingly and went on.

"By God, Africa is like a paradise that has been sliced up and manipulated by Europe and America, a place where HIV (Aids), oppression, unnecessary wars (being sponsored by the West) and the last but never the least 'POVERTY' were killing millions on monthly basis. Brothers, was Africa born to suffer?" he asked desperately.

"No, not really when she was not actually the cause of her problems. More than anything else, I think what Africa needs urgently now is a real political and economic power. And she must work for self-liberation. Africa must be motivated by hope, not fear. It must be now or never. It is a struggle for liberation she can and must identify with. Like John F. Kennedy once said: 'The time to repair the roof is when the sun is shining' and now is the time." Omofuma suggested.

"And like they say," added Hyman hopefully, "the first thing a doctor learns is how not to sleep. So, we Africans must as well start learning how not to be weak much more, sleeping."

"C`est la guerre" rejoined Koso, with a grateful smile on his face. "If the Europeans carried on with what they're doing to Africans now . . . by putting every one of us in prison instead of finding a way to welcome us, then it means they did not want to admit their past. How they exploited mother Africa. How many they've killed . . . they suppose to be welcoming Africans with an open and sympathetic mind to atone for their atrocious past on us."

At that very moment, there was a loud shout from a prison warder, who was standing in front of the widely opened green gate: "*Hey Leute, Spazieren ist fertig! Und alle . . .* " (Hey guys, the walk is over, and all . . .)

Immediately Marcus, Hyman, Koso, Peters and many other African and various 'illegal entry' prisoners of Chinese, South Asian, and Eastern European origins started marching out one by one back to their various cell rooms.

CHAPTER TWO

"The king said to him 'I am troubled by a terrible dream I had' which none of my counsellors can interpret . . . for my dream and attempted to find its meaning"

===Seder Ha Doros. Jerusalem ed.pp.174-176.

It was early morning of Friday the 30th of April 1999. Mild spring weather was at its full course. Marcus Omofuma finally woke up at about 5am. To him it seems anomalous. He usually finds it even difficult to be awake by 7am, a mandatory time, set by the prison authority for the prisoners to get out of bed. Yet the previous night had been different. He had been somehow wakeful all the night. When he eventually woke up he came down from the double-decker bed, tired, he headed towards the toilet stepping gingerly on the floor in order not to awake his roommates. After finishing his morning routine of washing his face and teeth brushing which never varied, he came back to the room; read a portion from his Bible and said his morning prayers. He was agitated and edgy to delineate himself from his fellow roommates and 'illegal entry' prisoners what had been haunting his mind for the past two weeks or so, especially this morning. He was not the type of person who believes in superstition, nor was he a phantasmagorical believer. However, over the past weeks he still found it hard to reason accurately all the things that had been happening to him. Sometimes as a human being, his instincts reminded him that things had not been moving fine for him since he arrived in this country and that danger was coming his way. Whereas he was not the only prisoner being threatened by the ministry in charge of immigrants to be repatriated

8

back to their countries, his own case to him was traumatic. He had tried many times without success to be optimistic in convincing himself that everything will come to pass and that things will become normal again. Hysterically it seemed to him that he would be fully involved in the coming danger, and whenever he remembered this, like this morning, he would be paralysed with trepidation. 'How on earth', he thought, 'will he escape this imperilment he felt these days?' He had written often and on to many human rights associations in the past weeks since this issue of repatriation was rejuvenated with several of his letters of appeal to them for help, but till then none had done anything sustainable to warrant his release from the prison. He wondered if these organizations did not receive his letters. Or, are they waiting for damage to be done before they will come to his rescue? Having spent more than five good months in solitary confinement, for as the authorities alleged 'illegal entry' into Austria, he strongly believed that he was supposed to have been released, because as their illegal entering law says six months is the maximum and no one has ever spent all the six months at once according to what he heard and what he has been experiencing since coming here.

A considerable number of other prisoners he met when he was initially brought to the deportation camp or even some that came after him had been released; many of them spending only two or three months, while four months seemed to be the maximal period spent by the majority of them. Yet, there is no hope for him to be freed soon. 'But all the same, as a Christian' he thought, 'he is expected to abide by the teaching to always be in a buoyant mood, believing that with God all things are possible, that sooner or later everything will come to pass and he will be a free man again.'

All this made him uncomfortable and have been ruminating in his mind that morning, as he sat near the iron protected window of their cell room, when suddenly he heard someone greeting in a languorous voice.

"Good morning Omo."

"Morning, my brother," Omofuma replied wearyingly, without turning to know which of his roommate that greeted him.

"Did you sleep well?" Hyman inquired curiously.

"Hey, okay!" Omofuma gestured with his head still without turning, deeper in his thoughts.

Hyman had infallibly slung to the belief that his fellow inmate was a jovial man. But within the preceding weeks, things had not been the same. Not only that, Omofuma's behaviour has become abnormal, he doesn't feel happy anymore. In fact his recent curious behaviours bored him; most especially, since, he didn't want to discuss whatever that had been troubling his mind with anybody. 'Nevertheless, this is prison. It is not every time one is supposed to be in a happy mood' Hyman thought, as he left for the lavatory.

However Hyman was not a good mind-reader. It was Koso, who fired the first notice that their fellow inmate and friend think much these days; and who heard Omofuma shrieked with pain while he was sleeping.

"I don't know how we can help ourselves, Marcus? But I presume that you can share with us what had been disturbing you. Why're you unusually distressed nowadays, Omo? It seems you're under increasing stress. Is anything the matter?" asked Koso sympathetically as he approached Marcus and held him on the shoulder, "I heard you screaming yesterday night something like 'Ooh! Ooh!' Like, you're struggling but when I woke up immediately, you were soundly asleep again like a new born baby" Koso smiled with as much confidence as he could muster and dragged a chair and sat beside Omofuma.

"Marcus is trying to take these situations too personal this time around, forgetting that we all had been in this messy prison together for a long time" Hyman shouted emphatically from the toilet.

Omofuma turned toward Hyman as he came out of the tiny lavatory, his face blunt.

"My brother, it's not as if I don't want you guys to interfere. Or trammel in my affairs, but truly, I don't know how to explain my recent predicaments. I had a very terrible dream last night, and was pondering over what it might mean. I haven't felt so frightful about dreams for long, yet this is different. You know I'm not concerned with my dreams normally, Hyman.

But this one is convoluted in nature. It made me feel unease since the early hours of this morning." Marcus stuttered mischievously.

"Then, tell your dream and I'll elucidate it for you" suggested Koso jokingly. "I wasn't . . . they called me 'Joseph the interpreter' for nothing. And for the fact that we're in prison like Joseph and the Egyptians then were, will make my interpretation come true. Now for starters . . ." he begins, flashing a gap-tooth smile, but was rather interrupted by Hyman's intolerable laughter.

"When did you become a 'dream wizard' Charlie, you haven't mentioned that before."

"Wait until I have finished my story, then you will be convinced" Koso said with a hectoring tone. "And then, you would've known whether or not 'Saul has become a prophet also' . . . ."

Once upon a time, back home in Ghana when I was a little lad of ten, one morning my elder brother Akota, who was almost two years older than me spurned eating, persisting not to do anything until our father explains his dream which he had dreamt the previous night for him, you know, my brother was kind of being pampered. A spoiled-child you could say, always making use of his youthful exuberance. Our father and our uncle Amoa tried all they could to persuade him to at least eat his food explaining that his dream has no meaning at all.

Koso narrated as he stared at Marcus sensing that he was paying much interest to what he was saying, and somehow hoping his magic is already working. He continued.

Not even a promise from our mother that if Akota eats his food she will take us to the zoo for sightseeing to see if this could change my brother's unshakeable egocentric stand, Akota being an animal enthusiast, but alias, my brother remained constant like a northern star.

He looked at Omofuma again and saw that this time he was buried with interest. He nodded his head in agreement, cleared his throat and went on.

So, my fellow prisoners of conscience, as you could see, all their tricks in coaxing him to eat proved abortive. Not until everybody was tired of the situation and my father about to loose his anger. I told Akota that I've the power to tell and interpret his dream for him, but under one condition. Immediately Akota's face which he had scowled like that of the animal called idiot. Do you know the animal? He asked committedly.

"Of course, I know it" Marcus replied interestingly, smiling for the first time that morning. "Don't forget I'm African like you, a 'bush' one for that matter!"

"Charlie, I too . . . I know and have seen one." Hyman said as he saw Koso staring at him with guileful smile on his face. He had known Koso to be a wily fellow, but he had come to admire his cunning scheme this morning at least for making Marcus to be so interested in his story and even making him laughed. And he added.

"Please Mr. Dream Wizard, I'm with you . . . don't try to cut this story, I'm . . ."

"Oh! No! It's just . . . I'm happy you guys know idiot, so as I was saying before, Akota's face brightened up and he asked me what my condition was" Koso related.

I told him if he is willing to obey my proviso, I would in turn consummate my own bond . . . my only condition is 'you must eat and freshen up'. You couldn't believe it, Akota without hesitation started to eat. Everybody in my family was astounded as my brother turned to his food and ate every damn food in his plates, licking hurriedly like a hungry wolf in anticipation of my interpretations of his dream.

"Then, what happened?" Hyman asked unconcernedly, discerning what the answer would be.

Koso regarded Hyman with a cold and scornful stare, yet with wistful smile on his face.

A moment later as Akota went and washed his plates, our father demanded that we have to give them a chance to discuss their business. We obeyed and went outside to play 'hide and seek game'. My brother after some minutes of playing with me was very happy to the extent he could not remember or didn't mention anything concerning the dream anymore. This prompted everybody within my family and from the extended families nicknaming me 'Joseph the interpreter' if you know what I mean?

Koso finally decleared triumphantly.

"Guy, but you didn't actually interpret your brother's dream?" Hyman snapped. "You only used your 'Machiavellian' scheme to manipulate your brother."

"Well, that's true . . . quite true" answered Koso thoughtfully. "Nevertheless, you must remember that every other person had tried and failed . . . So, they were all grateful, you know" he asserted.

Koso stared happily once again at Omofuma, who had been enjoying the story and the argument between his charactered friends, whom he had known for some months now. He was happy that his main aim which was to bring Omofuma out of his somber-state has been achieved, if not for anything else.

"So, *The wizard* would you please tell the interpreter your dream and wait for what the 'gods' has for you?" Koso joked.

"Concerning your recent awkward position, Omo" said Hyman, who was still somehow tongue-tied with the magic Koso's story had worked because he couldn't have known how to approach him and his problem this morning, "I think we've to be open to ourselves, having find ourselves in this same 'Austrian frying-pan'. After all, why are we friends if we can't share our problems among ourselves. There's a saying that 'when a man feels scratching at his back he looks for a fellow man to assist him, while the monkey turns to the tree to scratch itself."

"Hyman, you're right in your assessment, but, it's not as if I'm being too weird about my recent predicaments, my brothers. The fact is, I always perceive it's kinda exacerbating other people's problem, when especially we seem to be in the same footing, please don't misunderstand me" Marcus pleaded solicitously, glancing at the faces of his friends with concern.

Koso stared at Omofuma resentfully.

"That's exactly why we are supposed to heed for each other all the time. We're all involved in this law of racial discrimination and blatant menacing of immigrants by the Austrian government. We can only commiserate with each other as a mere formality. Sometimes one could feel so confused and dispirited in this 'dungeon' that 'he' wants to question God, why he was created at all? As far as I know 'this is nature and remember', nature must always take its course . . ." Koso prompted propiliatorly.

"Charlie, it seems you're as well a psychologist," suggested Hyman, laughing delightedly at Koso. "Are you a meteorologist also?"

"You can call me whatever you choose" Koso replied sharply. "But, don't forget 'the Prophet is not always being respected in his own village' he quoted.

And to Marcus he turned looking up at him and smiled smugly.

"Omo boy, don't forget to depict your dream to 'the dream Guru' but prior to that let me fix up coffee for us."

"Please, remember no sugar for me and I would prefer cappuccino" Hyman beseeched.

"And for me, precolated coffee," said Marcus with a grin. "And, I thank you both for being so good to me this morning."

"You're welcome" Koso murmured pleasantly and left.

+++

Ten minutes later, the coffee was ready and Koso brought it to them. Marcus Omofuma, 25 years old, about 5fth7 in height, dark-brown eyes with dark hair, cut in a punk-style. He had earlier on, partaken in a hunger strike policy the other prisoners observed to force the authorities to release him from his bondage, but to no avail. Twice he had done the hunger strike and twice the authorities had refused to release him, whereas the majority of other detainees had been released after the prison doctors had interceded on their behalf. On different occasions in the last few weeks he had been taken to the *Schwechat Airport* by the *Fremdenpolizei* to be deported back to Nigeria and on those terrible occasions he had resisted vehemently with them—at the end of which the police officers would bring him forcefully back and throw him back to his cell room. On a number of occasions, he had beseeched the authorities not to repatriate him, making an allusion to the fact that his life is in danger in Nigeria and that he would be decapitated immediately on arrival in Nigeria if they forced him back on the contrary, he always argued, that they should better release him and even ask him to leave Austria.

Just yesterday afternoon, the prison reference officer attached to him, Dr. Wolfgang Linkner had invited him into his office to say that the prison authority were 'cogitating on releasing him' as he put it . . . Hence, it turned out to be a 'Herculean' task to deport him since he declined to be deported voluntarily. Now barely twenty hours after the reference officer promised him that he would be released from this prison camp, Marcus Omofuma still finds himself in the state of utter confusion, owing to this turbulent dream he had.

"You guys, could remember what I told you yesterday after my meeting with the reference officer? But, this dream I had . . . I'm afraid seems to be a complete contrast to what the officer meant" Omofuma affirmed conspicuously, pacing slowly around the heavy iron-door-partitioned cubbyhole which was their cell room, still holing his coffee cup in his hand.

"So, what you're trying to tell us is . . ." questioned Hyman Otta mysteriously, as he sipped his cappuccino. "By the virtue of this latest dream, which in the real sense are ubiquitous with you these days, has now entirely altered your optimism of being released? And you still want us to believe you're not a superstitious proselyte or that you don't believe in dreams?"

"Honestly I'm . . . not . . ." Marcus stammered as he shook his head. "Nonetheless this dream in particular is petrifying. I don't really know why? I . . . mean . . ."

15

"Look, Marcus my coffee is getting colder . . . what's your dream?" demanded Koso, who all the while has been funny. "Or do you still want to 'proselytize' about, if I could borrow a word from our English teacher."

Marcus stared back at the faces of his cellmats, revealing the tremendous fears that had overshadowed him. He emptied his cup of coffee and walked towards the sink to was his cup and hands.

I dreamt I was released, but on my way back to the city, I noticed abruptly three sturdy men coming directly opposite me. At first I couldn't recognize their faces, whether they're Whites or Blacks and if they were coming for me or on the contrary, if they were patrolling on their own" Marcus lamented apprehensively. Until they were very close to me, I then saw their white faces and immediately had the notion that they were literally coming for me. Subsequently, I decided to retreat, but before I could do that, they've all besieged me.

He asserted, as his hands started to tremble. He paused and went back to the sink and fetched a cup of cold water and drank to calm the shivery which appeared to have overcome him as tears dropped down his cheeks.

"Behave yourself. Be a man Omo! Then, what happened next?" Koso asked anxiously.

He also felt tensed and startled, a loyal and tender-hearted friend, thence he lit his sixth cigarette of the day.

"Didn't they say anything to you before attacking you? Nay did you ask them why?" he queried, as he blew a series of smoke rings upwards.

Marcus stuttered convincingly, shivering.

Oh! Yes, I asked, and No they didn't say a word nor answer my questions. I asked them, what was the problem and, why they are in pursuit of me, assuring them that I wasn't absconding from the prison, instead, that I was duly released. I even showed them my releasing papers, but one of them collected it from me and tore up the papers. The worst part of it is, before I could wound up whatever I was saying, which in actual fact

I can't commit to memory, one of them, the most muscular churned out from the side of his roomy jeans trouser a commando knife and pointed it straight to my throat. At that point, I shut my eyes and started to shout for help but was gripped by a huge hand that enveloped my mouth and nose in attempt to stop my breathings. I still managed somehow to continue my shouting.

"Perhaps, that was when I heard you screaming" propounded Koso, who himself was by now noticeably upset.

"Maybe," he shrugged.

"Then, this might have been a very demonic dream indeed," Hyman agreed. "One can see why you're so frightened about it all . . ."

"My greatest problem is," murmured Marcus, enfolding his two hands across his chest, "who on earth are these people? Yes, I remember, they were dressed in complete black jeans, with a pair of black boots and black 'Kangaroo' caps that go with the attire, or, on the contrary why bringing out the knife and gripping my throat? What are these for?" he asked to no one in particular.

"Omo, to tell you the truth I don't either believe in dreams" said Hyman haughtily, as he sipped again from his coffee and puffed at his cigarette, nodding his heavily creasing face. "But considering the plights in this prison now and our own individual snag, I can only recommend continuous prayers and if you can cope, with at least three days fasting to confront this very dream . . . for as I know, the Bible has advised and warned us on this type of situation when it said according to the Book of Ephesians 6:11-13 . . . I quote:

'Put on the complete suit of armour from God, that you may be able to stand firm against the machination of the devil; because we have a wrestling, not against flesh and blood, but against the governments, against the authorities, against the world rulers of this darkness, against the wicked spiritual forces in the heavenly places.' . . . . And so on, you see what I mean" Hyman admonished as he ground his cigarette stub into the ashtray.

"And the Austrian government is one of these world rulers of darkness!" snapped Koso.

"I concur to what you've said" Marcus uttered. "But my problems are that I couldn't decipher what this dream or any of the dreams I'm having recently meant" he said uncommittedly.

At the same time, the doubled iron door of their cell unfastened and they were served 'fruit tea and four loaves of *Semmel*-bread for their breakfast by two prison warders, a wardress and two prison workers, who are also prisoners. They finished serving the breakfast and jammed and locked the door back.

"In continuation of our conversation" said Hyman Otta, a slim tall man in his thirties, very dark in complexion and with pointed nose; who was once a third year Theological student at 'St. John's Theological Seminary in his native southern Sudan (A school exceptionally built by the Roman Catholic church in the aspirations of preparing many young men for the priesthood). He has been preparing and looking forward to his ordination with great hope, before the recent outbreak of civil war (which since 1983 when it fully started, had claimed millions of lives and was between the national government dominated by Muslims from the north mainly Arabs, and the rebels from the south . . . the Southern people's liberation army (SLPA) led by John Garang, and was dominated by Africans predominantly Christian and traditional tribal believers). The SLPA insurgent's constant threatening had pressurized Hyman to escape from his country after he had lost his father and his two remaining siblings in the same day at the hands of the rebels. He had been earlier imprisoned, and tortured by the SLPA officers for alleged sabotage and conspiracy with his entire family against them. "I always found courage in God wherever, whenever and in whatever situation, both, good or critical, Omo try to believe in God and believe in his mercies. Our God is good all the time. He will never fail us. He said He will have mercy on us wherever and whenever we confess our sins, forsake them and call upon his name in truth and in spirit, believe me!"

He took Marcus by his hands and consoled him.

"Be assured only God knew why we're in this condition. He alone can count the hairs in our head. And most importantly He understands our individual problems easily much more than we think. That's why He admonishes us to always believe and trust in him, when He says . . ."

Hyman continued, as he glanced at Koso, who was already feeling annoyed.

"Yes, according to Isaiah 41:10, our merciful and kind God said:

'Do not be afraid, for I am with you. Do not gaze about for I am your God. I will fortify you. I will really help you with my right hand of righteousness.' . . . .

"Why is it that, in everything you must always preach about this God of yours?" asked Koso amazingly. "Where was this God when we're being arrested and imprisoned for illegally entry into Austria?"

A self-styled atheist who used to argue always with Omofuma and Hyman about God and his existence, asserting there is nothing like God or Allah as the Christians and their Muslim counterparts believe. One day he had told them outrighty that he doesn't believe in God because if he exists, he was a partial and unjust God, for leaving Africa to die in her poverty and diseased oriented culture. Instead, he was rather, an advocate of gods, like the one in his native land 'Ashanti Bosun' (god of river).

"In as much as this dream looks prodigiously fearful," Koso went on in his jovial manners, "yet, I saw nothing special in them. This is a usual dream to me, and as a guru master I would only say that Omo is in a self-destructive state these days. He was too distraught, and in state of confusion or can I say, hysteria."

"You're a hypocrite," Hyman shouted at Koso accusingly, "even if you're not a Christian to believe in God, aren't you African enough to believe in the adage that 'the cry of the owl at any village was thought to pretend the death of someone from that village'. Can´t you use your common sense to know that it's not every-time one plays."

"Koso, you take every single thing for a joke" Marcus chipped nonchalantly. "I agree, I dreamt but this is a different ball game. I haven't been in this state of mind after dreaming before. You never saw me complaining, have you?"

"No not at all . . . but . . ."

"There's no but, take it or leave it, there's imminent danger coming" Marcus said.

"Omo, I'm not joking, as promised by the reference officer they'll release you maybe by Monday or even before then. No matter how perplexed you may be, by the spate of dreams you're having recently, I don't agree that it has anything to do mystically nor spiritual as you want us to believe" Koso affirmed a bit gloatingly.

The door abruptly opened and a warder shouted.

"Hyman Otta!, *Bitte* (Please) . . ."

"Yea this is me" Hyman replied as he stood from where he was sitting approaching the door-way.

"What is it, sir?"

"You're wanted by the reference officer and I think you've visitors also . . ." the warder, whom they all called O.C. Nico said, politely reading from the papers at his hand.

"Oh! Sir, please let me take my jacket" Hyman pleaded and moved towards his cupboard.

"And, how are you today? I believe you guys are enjoying the Austrian prison systems?" O.C. Nico asked Omofuma and Koso, as he locked the door and left with Hyman.

"Of course, he knew that his country's prison conditions are very hard. Believe me, he even told me the other day that he's considering resigning from this *Beamten*-work because of the way foreigners are being threatened here. Could you imagine that? I swear . . . and I believe he was serious, you know he always has sympathy for us" Koso told Omofuma later.

"I knew he was a good man, yet, I don't expect him to speak like that. I mean, saying he would resign, that would be out of proportion. It would be a slap on the face of the government if he does it for our sake." Omofuma agreed.

"But you agree with me, few of them are really good, but their work is very hard. Would you rather be a warder if you have the choice?" Koso asked.

"Of course no!, Warder and police work are generally believed to be the worst work a reasonable human being would choose as first option. Don't you know that warders and policemen and policewomen were being compared to the biblical tax collectors," Marcus asserted with a great laughter.

"Well, for me I can do any job expect pastor's work, because I consider some 'pastors' (especially many Pentecostal church pastors) to be dubious businessmen and women, always trying to defraud poor parishioners their last penny in the name of God, 'stealing in the name of the Almighty Father', as the great Fella Kuti of Africa used to sing in his music. You see what's happening in Africa these days. In almost every corner of the street you must find at least one church," Koso said, smiling.

"Listen, Charlie, whether you serve God or not, is never my problem but don't try to blaspheme against God's anointed. It's an unforgiveable sin" Hyman warned Koso pulling off his jacket.

He had just come back to their cell and overheard Koso talking with Marcus.

"Look, according to my Bible Luke 19:40 . . .

'I tell if these remained silent, the stones would cry out'

Hyman quoted looking Koso directly in the eyes.

"So, you see boy! God doesn't care if you . . ."

"Omo, as I was saying before O.C Nico came" Koso said impatiently overlooking Hyman with his warnings.

He stood up and stretched his arms towards the far corner of the room while depositing some cigarette ashes on the *Aschenbecher* on top of a tiny table.

"*The wizard*, I think all these things, I mean your dreams are only what your frustrated and tired brains is telling you, which essentially has something to do with the rise in the tempo of our being crammingly held in this solitary incarceration, restriction of our individual freedom and social activities. It also has to do with the increase in 'volume' of their (the prison authority's) vulgarity and vehemence of applying this hard-bitten and mischievous 'law' against immigrants . . . consequently resulting in the escalation in the volume of intensity of our psychological and mental conditions" Koso said.

He sipped his fruit tea and cram down a bit from his bread and said mouth-full of bread.

"The fact that these dreams of yours happen daily . . . doesn't make them assume a mystical value or leaning. I don't subscribe to such belief, period" he concluded unpleasantly.

"Look, my friend," Hyman said politely, touching Koso on his shoulder. "Personally and from my Christian point of view, I don't either believe that this dream is special or will have any calamity attached to it. No, but don't misunderstand me. We never take our emotions for granted. Similarly we've to remember to pray to God for protection and guidance in every situation we may find ourselves. What I'm recommending is prayer. Prayer, as far as I'm concerned is supplication to God, a kind of pleading God to forgive us all our sins and to protect us in whatever conditions we found ourselves. Sometimes these dreams are from God. In the old testament theology, God is accustomed to communicating or giving warning to his people concerning impending dangers through dreams and visions."
He ruffled his badly grown hair backward and added contentedly.

"Some Christians believe that God can reveal our miserable lives to us in form of dreams and He requires us to correct it by means of prayers (devotion which must be holy and acceptable to God)."

"Listen, I'm not trying to be rude or arrogant," pleaded Koso contritely. "I only want Marcus to forget about these dreams and comeback to his normal self. Dreams for me are mere 'bagatelle and utopian'. It's an ordinary nightmare, Omo had awoken to" he maintained in his heavily Ghanaian accented English.

"As far as God is concerned, you're in a position to expostulate and remain a free-thinker you claim to be," said Hyman indignantly. "After all, we're in the Western world where they say everyone has his or her own freedom of expression and worship."

"Which is better than how things are done in Africa" Koso interrupted sharply. "You've seen why we Africans are still backward. The same Westerners that came to preach God to us in Africa are now preaching freedom of expression and so on to their people, yet Africa would not learn. Believe me, this is the key to the well being of the Westerners. People are not busy waiting for Jesus or Mohammed to come and help them like we're doing in Africa. They're busy working, and working for future generation. And having, progress and progress and progress."

"Who came to visit you?" Marcus asked Hyman, trying to control the situation. "Was she . . . I mean your blonde babe?"

Hyman Otta smiled and shook his head.

"No", he said.

Rather he explained that after his brief meeting with the reference officer where he was just speaking all the bla bla bla that full his mouth, he was then taken to the visitor's room where he met his friend Ahamed, who came with his Black girlfriend.

"They extended their greetings to both of you. He said he's trying his best to get a lawyer for me."

"Really, he must have been a good friend," Marcus commended.

"And, of course, I saw comrade Volvaskov at the office of the reference officer. I told him you're worried and he promised to see you at the *Spazieren*-ground."

"Good of him, he is such a nice guy," Marcus smiled.

"And, so, Omo, in conclusion to what we've been saying," Hyman said curiously trying to avoid Koso's eyes which constantly directed at him. "Believe me, Jesus Christ is the way, the truth and the life. The Bible said in 1 Thessalonians 4:14.

'For if our faith is that Jesus died and rose again, so, too, those who have fallen asleep (in death) through Jesus, God will bring with him.'

Hyman recited.

"So, you see, when we die knowing Jesus . . . we're going to live again. God has promised us everything through him . . . . even good health, freedom, prosperity, long life . . . . etc.," he said and added. "If we can put our faith and hope in God and worship him in spirit and truth, our conditions here will somehow come to an end and we'll enjoy freedom again. The Bible is true and God is real, my brothers . . . I pray always that God in his infinite mercy will listen to our entreaties and help us to prevail over our problems and to use his dominant hand and deliver us from this bondage . . . even to eternity in Jesus name . . ."

"Amen and amen!" shouted Marcus devotedly.

"Amen" uttered Koso, his voice a little more than a murmur.

CHAPTER THREE

The King fell at the old man's feet and began to weep and plead, saying 'I beg you, Sir, to spare, me, for I do not know I have sinned against you, that you should wish to kill me"

===(Seder Ha Doros, Jerusalem ed. (pp. 174=176).

They were eating silently, dugging into their plates of white rice and fried fish with relish, because as Africans, rice has continued to be the best food in the prison which gives them satisfaction. Other foods to them are too Europeanized. Yet Marcus has not regained his appetite fully since his recent predicament. For, whilst Hyman and Koso had almost finished theirs, Marcus has not even begun eating his. He had only finished the appetizing soup. Suddenly, there were hubbubs of keys outside the door. Instantaneously the door opened and two prison warders were standing there, one with a paper at his hand. He glanced through it, adjusted his reading glasses and perused out.

"Marcus Omofuma . . . *Bitte?*"

Marcus looked at his roommates, his eyes grown expressionless. He glanced back at the officers nervously and answered suspiciously.

"I'm the one," he said as he raised his hand upward.

"*Zusammenpacken, Du gehst nach Hause*" the officer announced insincerely, his beard puffy and haggard. "*Du hast fünf Minuten zum Einpacken!*"

"Pardon, sir, I don't understand you?" Marcus implored courteously. "Please sir, can you explain it in English?"

"Yes, you've to pack your things under five minutes. You're going out. I mean, you've been released from prison" the warder lied. "You must pack quickly, we'll be back in . . . Pretty damn quick, you understand now? So start packing" the officer ordered, shutting the iron door, as he walked off in a huff with his colleague.

"Praise the Lord. Praise the living God!" Hyman shouted almost immediately the warders closed the door back. "Boy! I told you that our God never sleeps. He has answered our prayers. I thought as much that everyone of us will be freed sooner. Glory to God Almighty for his mercies towards his people," Hyman was saying, shouting and praising.

Meanwhile Koso, who had earlier entered the 'cloakroom' to answer the call of nature, came out quickly, his face brightened up greatly.

"Omo, I knew it was coming. I told you not to have 'Angst', now you've seen it. Everything has come to an end. But . . . anyway, I believe you shouldn't forget that you still have some 'hip-hop homies' here in prison just like other Niggers always do. Please, remember to mention me to Phara'oh. Will you promise?"

Marcus's eyes were riveted on Koso.

"How do you suppose, Charlie, that I would forget even if I were mad, the suffering we have undergone together here? Hey! I would never forget. But, I'm still pessimistic about this whole set up." He said enigmatically.

He stood up and faced Koso and Hyman, who were by now helping him to pack few of his belongings, his face scrunched up startlingly and he broke down and sobbed like a child.

"As a matter of fact, I'm still . . . being haunted by this dream of mine" he whimpered bitterly.

"God damn you, Omo! You're kind of irritating us," said Koso firmly. "Shake it off man! You don't assume negativity in everything. Do you tend to blame yourself for being free? Fuck you, man!"

"I don't know why you're so chicken-hearted Omoba?" Hyman asked. "You ought to be grateful to God and be happy you're eventually going home, my main man."

He embraced Marcus and ran his hand through his tousled punky hair.

"Try to be a man, my friend . . ."

"I was even thinking of how you're going to visit us here, let's say by next week for 'us' to start work on that book we discussed the other day in the *Spazieren*. I mean 'OUR AUSTRIAN PRISON LIVES'" Koso said meaningfully. "Boy! I meant what I said, don't fail to visit. I want us started immediately, who knows if that book would be our stepping stone. You know Europe is a land of opportunity."

"And, opportunity they say, come but once," Hyman added jokingly. "Omoba has gotten his own freedom opportunity this day."

Soon after, Marcus finally recovered. As his roommates advised he has shaken off his fears, encouraged, he dried his tearful eyes with the back of his hand.

"I'm very appreciative of your support" he murmured to Koso and Hyman. "Both of you have been very good friends to me, I don't think I would ever forget our conditions together. You must not argue blindly . . ." he said to Koso, smiling incredulously, as he embraced them together.

A prison warder opened the door of their cell room and called out. "Omofuma Marcus, '*Gemma*', let's go."

"Hey take care guys" Marcus shouted back to his friends, following the warders. "Greet our other comrades for me if everything goes well, I'll come to . . ."

His voice trails off.

++

The idea of being able to move about freely, it seems, must be the height of happiness to one, who had been a prisoner. Marcus Omofuma could not even contemplate about the future. For instance, where he would go or where he would pass the night, if truly he is released. For him, it was a critical moment in a critical condition. 'How can, for the five months and almost three weeks' he thought . . . 'He had been a victim of this callous subjugation. Even now that they have told him that he is going home, he felt that his problems had increased tremendously. How can he trust everything they are telling him when they have been trying by all means to deport him, irrespective of his vehement refusal.' 'The only Whiteman, a friend once told him you will have to trust, is the dead one', Omofuma remembered and he had come to believe his friend's words more and more with the recent happenings. He believed he was one of those victims of circumstances of the Austrian government's harsh, intimidating, discriminative and xenophobic policies that are being perpetrated directly against foreigners. He also believed that this particular law that was promulgated by the government which gives the police the power to put him and many others in prison was an absolute disregard to their basic human rights. The intentions of the law are only against the trouble ridden immigrants like him and others. He was quite sure, as it is been alleged that Austria and few other countries implement this law of imprisoning immigrants. He recalled one day, a man approached him while they were *spazieren* in the prison yard; the man had painfully narrated to him how he has been living in Vienna with his wife, an Austrian, for the past twelve years. Now the *Fremdenpolizei* is threatening to deport him back to his country Ethiopia, because of a problem that resulted in him being divorced by his wife, regardless of the fact, that he's been an Austrian citizen since eight years. Not only this, a lot of other accounts by other people he came across here in the *Schubhaft* (the deportation camp), attested to the fact that no foreigner, be you an Austrian naturalised citizen or not, is free from this unlawful law of intimidation. After all said and done, Marcus Omofuma could only identify himself as another innocent and honest victim of this law of 'illegal entry' the police normally uses against immigrants.

All the while, he was locked in an empty room near the office of the reference officer. He has been there for almost thirty minutes, meditating on what would be his fate in the next hour or two . . . when the door suddenly unlocked and standing opposite him were three tall, broad shouldered and corpulent police officers, all in plain cloth. One of them proceeded towards him unceremoniously.

"I supposed you're Omofuma Marcus?" begins Lieutenant Rudolph Pirker, who was designated as the leader of the three officers deporting him, scowl darkened face as he spoke.

This sudden intrusion and the manner of approach with which the officer approached him, frightened Marcus as he answered in a more grave voice.

"Ya . . . , I'm the . . . it's me" he uttered, his small dark eyes staring piercingly at the three men standing in front of him.

"Pick up your baggages and follow us" the Lieutenant commanded in his shrill, harsh voice.

"But, please sir, where am I going to . . ." Marcus asked without any enthusiasm in his voice.

He refused to move and began to protest, insisting that he would never consent to go back to Nigeria under any circumstance.

"Not even under the threat of a gun . . . I'll never move an inch . . . you must not deport me, I've . . . my life is in danger in Nigeria . . ." he cried bitterly.

"Hey! Look here and listen very carefully you Nigger" interrupted the second officer Renner. "We haven't got time to waste with you bastard monkey. Try to behave good or . . ." he shouted, glancing at his gold coated 'corum watch'.

29

"We're taking you out. You've been 'provisionally released'" retorted the lieutenant, trying his best to be diplomatic this time around. "You've nothing to fear for . . ."

"No, no, no! I want to know what's happening" objected Marcus, trembling all over. "I'll never go back to Nigeria, after all the dangers awaiting me there. It is better I die here, than going back to still face the same situation. Please, don't force me to . . . ." Marcus affirmed, his face crumpled and he started to cry more and more, pleading to the officers.

Unable to hide his already boiling hot anger, the second officer Renner moved toward Omofuma, grabbed his arms, and swung him around with the help of the other officers in attempt to handcuff him.

"You f-u-c-king Nigger should not delay us any longer", he yelled at him, shouting deeply into his right ear which he squeezed with his huge hand. "Any attempt to be more rude might be very regretting . . . understood? . . . We're not here for your stupid Nigger acts . . . you better shut up that dirty mouth of yours and move or be forced to do so," officer Renner ordered.

He pushed him outside, while the other officers took away his baggages.

The lieutenant deliberately averting his eyes, ordered him to be taken inside the *Polizei* quarters with coloured bus taking position outside. On the way to the airport, Omofuma was subjected to more kicks, punches and beatings by the subordinate officers, while still on handcuffs and shackled to the seat of the bus. Meanwhile, he screamed, cried and protested vehemently against the non-stop beating and ill-treatment and forceful deportation they are undertaking . . . shouting that his basic rights were being infringed against his will. The more he protested, the more the officers hit him, trying to make him to keep quite. The two subordinate officers had been sitting side by side with him in the middle, while the lieutenant sat in the front seat with the driver.

"Hey!, black monkey, you better keep quiet and face the journey maturely or you might not live to regret after all" officer Weiss, the second subordinate officer cautioned, using so many other racist languages and threatened to beat the living daylight out from him if he continued to shout. "In Africa, have you ever spoken a word or protested as you're doing in front of the police. You *unehelicher* son of a bitch, I couldn't blame you, I only blame politics and some foolish liberal politicians and their liberal stances that made it possible for you Africans to come over here. If Hitler had seen someone like you, he would've cooked your dick for breakfast." he cursed unpleasantly, as he lit up a cigarette, dragged from it and directed the hard core of the smoke at Omofuma's face.

++

In the *Schwechat Airport* Vienna, Marcus Omofuma was taken immediately on arrival to a detention post at the back of the airport police station. He was hauled inside the cellroom forcefully, while he resisted and cried.

"I'll not consent to your threatening. I'm not going back to Nigeria you better take me back to the prison. I'm going no where . . . I'll enter no plane . . . I know my rights and must be . . ." he shouted on top of his voice with a gleam of hope appearing in his weary eyes.

While he was being dragged into the detention room, he had seen three men and four ladies, who dressed in pilots and air hostess's uniform and had hoped that their attention would help to force the officers relent from their effort to deport him by all means. A similar trick had helped him the last time he was brought to the airport. But today was different. The crew members did not look his way, nor did the officers relented from their actions.

"It can't be easy to take this 'Bimbo' inside the plane without problems, to do that is to draw the attention of other passengers" suggested Renner to the other officers with monstrous bitterness. "Listen, sir, I knew and have dealt with these Niggers many times to know them well. This *Arschloch* will prove too stubborn to us, if we couldn't handle him as supposed" he asserted.

He peeped through the tiny window of the cell to see if Marcus's continuous screams and roars have drawn any unwanted guest, but no, he only sighted some airport guards minding their duties.

"Once again sir, I suggest that we devise a possible way of tackling this issue, if not, I bet, it would turn out a disastrous experience for us, that I can assure you. But, I believe with my experience, this '*Schweine* Nigger' should not be a stress to us." Officer Renner said, facing the lieutenant.

"Let's bind him up then," proposed the third officer Mario Weiss contemptuously, "if that's the case, because there's no going back on this mission."

"Still, that wouldn't be enough. He will continue this shouting which could possibly upset the other passengers and even the Airline crew."

"We need not to worry about the crew, the station manager is already aware. They all know about the forceful system. Our problem is how to avoid the passengers in, ushering him into the flight. How do we take him inside?" asked the lieutenant.

He stared at Marcus, who was helplessly sitting at the extreme corner of the hode.

"You know what I mean? All eyes would turn against us, and I doubt it would not be for our good or good of the authorities."

"Then, we'll tie him up and tape his mouth from shouting. I and two other officers tried it the last time we accompanied one of these 'Niggers' home and it really worked for us" Renner opined bravely and added in quick succession. "That means, lieutenant sir, you have to notify the crew once again about our latest intention."

"You mean we have to gag him?" asked the lieutenant authoratively, looking directly at officer Renner.

"That's exactly what I meant, sir" answered Renner respectfully.

"And that is our only option now, sir" concurred officer Weiss supportively.

"That I would do immediately, but, gentlemen, let's hope this will not turn out to be catastrophic at last," Lieutenant Pirker said contemplatingly.
He left the room for consultation with the Balkan Airline station manager and the pilots.

"No! No!! I don't think it'll result to that, besides, it had been used before and has the blessing of the people at the top. What's more, 'if the hard way is the only way, so be it'. After all, he would be gag for few hours only," sighed officer Mario Weiss, who himself boasted of having being involved in almost twenty deportation trips to both Eastern Europe and African countries.

"These black Africans in particular are very strong and some of them always prove to be nothing but nuts," he called after the lieutenant.

In less than twenty minutes, the lieutenant had gone and came back. As he breezed into the detention room, he announced happily.

"Well, gentlemen let's say the crew are not in anyway our problem now. It's been taken care of. The manager, the pilots and the chief stewardess all agreed to our proposal, but we will approach this with greatest caution. You know I don't want to retire young or resign if it comes to that. My children are still young for me to go on forced retirement without pay," he smiled freakishly.

"Then, the die is cast" officer Weiss restored. "That's why I trust this Bulgarians. I mean, the Balkan management, they're worthy to be doing business with."

"Coming to that," Renner cuts in, "as far as this deportation business is concerned, they're number one in the whole world, followed by Swiss air."

"You missed it, buddy! After Balkan comes Aerofloat . . . our Russian friends, do you forget? For these airlines it is always business as usual no matter how you want it," officer Wiss corrected.

"You're absolutely right, my guy. I think after our Russian friends comes our Swiss."

"Listen, gentlemen, we don't have much time left. You can add up the fourth, fifth and the sixth inside the flight," the lieutenant jokingly said.

"Lieutenant Sir! These Niggers are like as the Africans say, 'oil in the palm kernel'," quoted Renner a bit gloatingly, kicking Marcus with his hard leather shoe, as he tried to drag him up. "Unless you chew it, fry it or ground it, the oil will never come out. Take it or leave it, all Niggers are irritating and this one here is not different. I know them like back of my palm."

"And if I may ask, how do you come about African sayings?" the lieutenant demanded interestedly, knowing fully well that officer Renner always professed that he hates Africans more than the devil itself.

"Well, that's a long story, sir, but the summary of it. My younger sister crazily fell in love with one of these monkeys because of his dirty dreadlocks, I mean crazy rastahair. You know these girls with their tastes. However, the marriage didn't last a long time, trust me, and the bastard is in Nigeria now, maybe, planning to come back. Yes, they all came back" officer Renner assured his colleagues. "Deport them today and the next week you find them in the streets again running around."

The story of his sister falling in love to a blackman prompted eruption of laughter within them, after which the lieutenant bade them to bound Omofuma's arms and legs and to gag him with adhesive tapes which he produced from inside his suitcase. Not even Omofuma's passionate entreaties for them to have mercy on him could discourage the officers from carrying out their acts, which they were enjoying with all alacrity. He started to struggle with them, but was overpowered by the two burly subordinate officers while the lieutenant stood against him.

Later, after much more beatings and kicking, Omofuma became too weak to resist. The two officers Renner and Weiss restrained, and bound his entire upper bodies, with more adhesive tapes like a condemned criminal facing public execution. As a matter of fact, he was treated practically as a man who has lost all his rights to live.

In between the detention room and on the plane itself, when eventually they were signalled by a Balkan Airline air hostess to carry him through the back exit door, with one of his shoes missing; Marcus was still screeching out in pain and was crying to be untied. The continuous squawking impelled the lieutenant, who was thinking what might be the consequences if their act is uncovered to give the order that his mouth be taped accordingly, before he was finally taken into the Balkan Air flight Twin Engined Tupolev heading to Lagos (Nigeria) via Sofia (Bulgaria).

The back exit door of the plane, they later found out was perfectly constructed to fit the wheel chair, with which the officers and the crew members managed to haul him through. Once inside, they applied more adhesive tapes up to his chin and by means of a plastic belt, he was strapped to the seat of the plane. Simultaneously, Marcus Omofuma was losing consciousness and was suffocating, sweating gravely.

Finally, with all the passengers boarded and everybody advised through the P A to put on the seat belt, and greeting and announcement by the chief pilot, who introduced himself; the flight slowly headed toward the runway . . . ready to take off.

"Gentlemen well done . . . I'd appreciated your courage in pulling this through," Lieutenant Rudolph Pirker commended, as he shook hands with Officers Renner and Weiss.

"But, buddy, now I know for sure why you hate these Niggers more than dead . . . You're f-u-c-king annoyed one of them screwed your sister," officer Weiss said to Renner innocently.

Officer Renner leaned his head backward and whispered.

"And they're still fucking her. Unfortunately, she married another Rastaman from Gambia . . . just last month."

"What do you intend to do this time around?"

"I've sworn by Hitler's blood, he would be in Gambia before Christmas," Renner promised bitterly, drinking from the plastic cup of red wine that was served by the air hostess.

"And, if she happens to follow another Nigger?" asked officer Weiss curiously.

"Then, that Bimbo would make his *last journey* from Vienna in the same way as the others," Renner retorted and smiled, stoking his Hitler styled moustache.

"Wishing you the best, buddy," snapped officer Weiss at Renner, sipping from his own cup of beer. "Good luck, boy."

CHAPTER FOUR

"From the grip of iron teeth I beseeched my God, my salvation. Feet sunk deep in Mire I screamed to Him aloud. The end of my exile He has shown me when, in my land, will the dove of freedom trill aloud? Even from those who know the depths of His books. He has hidden the knowledge of the end, so that my seers do not know the chosen time to call. Please, look down and see how I am crushed in suffering. No one knows me . . . To whom shall I cry."

===From the Pijut Anusa Pezra (Anguished cry for help)
Mussaf of the secound day of Rosh Hashanah.
By Yosei ben Yosei.

Having been silenced with the adhesive tapes, Marcus Omofuma remained mute. He had lost all his fighting spirit. He had no option left than to remain at the mercy of his three accompanying officers, who themselves had no mercy to show. He had been sitting in the last row at the left window with Renner beside him, while Lieutenant Pirker and officer Weiss sat behind them. His whole body had been wrapped including his mouth and a little up his nose . . . his arms were taped to his body. In the meantime, officers Renner and Weiss continued to joke about Africans.

About thirty-five minutes of the flight, Jelena Litov, a stewardess with the airline was serving tea, coffee and drinks to the passengers when she first saw Omofuma. Because she was a junior stewardess, she had not been formally notified before-hand by the chief stewardess, when she addressed other crew members. A young pretty girl of about 18 years herself, she instantly felt disgusted by the condition she saw Omofuma. She was often involved in deportations and sometimes deportees were handcuffed or in chains, but she had never seen someone with a taped mouth before. She had been involved most frequently in deportation from Germany and Austria to Africa, yet this trip had been something different. 'Maybe the way the man she was looking at had been treated as a nonentity' Jeleana thought. 'Not even an animal on board had to be subjected to such condition.' Jelena out of sympathy immediately approached Renner who was more relaxed on his seat next to Marcus, and asked.

"Excuse me sir, but why should this fellow be gagged while on board?" she demanded furiously.

"Because I think it's not any of your business, young lady," the lieutenant snapped at her, in a very low voice from behind.

"But, sir, I'm the stewardess here, it's my duty to know about the welfare of every passenger on board and beside . . ."

"Then, you must perform your duty well by . . . you must go and take orders from your chief stewardess Miss . . . Miss stewardess, okay?" lieutenant Pirker interjected angrily.

Jelena, felt ashamed and disgusted that the management was aware of this ungodly act. She left and went straight to the chief stewardess.

"Oh! Yes, I'm sorry you weren't around when others were informed about the man . . . Yeah yeah, ma'ma . . . I know it was disgusting, but as you well know and I know, deportation of any kind is a normal part of our job . . . for you and me to remain on this aviation business, most of these disgusting sights must be overlooked Miss Jelena Litov," the chief stewardess, Melina Bokov frankly asserted to her, when she confronted her at the storage cabin, as she was arranging some food items.

"Pardon me ma . . . but, what I saw there wasn't a pretty picture," Jelena snarled. "I don't think that was a good image for our airline . . . especially if anything went wrong."

"For Christ's sake, hey, damm it, Miss . . . whatever you said your name was, I've told you these things are necessary and have to be done for our survival, what more, we always have to trust the police to avoid complications on our flight and I trust the Viennesse police" the stewardess maintained decisively. "Let's say the station manager and myself . . . and even the pilots themselves have already weighed the benefit against the risk before giving the go ahead for this deportation to take place. Who are you to question our decision? And what do you think you're trying to prove?"

"Ma, I don't want to prove anything, but . . ."

Melina Bokov stared furiously at her.

"But what," Bokov shouted in a snappy mood, "nothing, but to show your continuous insubordination. Can't you take out your eyes on something that doesn't concern you . . . of which you've no authority against? Miss 'good samaritan'. Listen, the man was 'very angry' and it had been difficult to get him on board . . . Got it, Miss Jelena?"

"So, the authority knew already and still allowed this type of in-human treatment to go on on 'our' flight without taken into consideration the psychological effects their decision would have on those children choir group on board?" Jelena said brusquely. "Imagine what we're trying to teach them . . . ?"

"That had been taken care of, Miss . . . I mean, I personally had already ordered the Amsterdam children choir and their guardian's seats to be swapped . . . and that, I had been assured by Pitov . . . has been done," the chief stewardess asserted and in a logical conclusion.

She commanded, weaving her hand dismissively as Jelena wanted to open her mouth to speak.

"Miss Jelena, I truly think the insults are enough. And be assured that your attitudes and conducts must be reported and the appropriate actions must be taken. Now you can go back to your duty . . . you god-damm fool, who doesn't know from where her breads come. Remember, time was important and this flight was precisely planned. Any more delay would cause your instant redundancy, understood?"

Without uttering any atom of word, Jelena turned and left. She was scornfully ashamed of herself and the Balkan Airline which employed such heartless and stony people like the station manager and the chief stewardess. When she reached the back row seat where Marcus was still breathing heavily, she purposefully did not want to look in his eyes, because she thought it might be more provoking and disgusting. Instead, she plastered a stony stare at Lieutenant Pirker and his colleagues before she rolled the trolley laden with snacks and drinks away.

"I strongly believe your sins would eventually find you out, you . . . you nasty cops, you and your collaborators . . ."

Jelena prayed her voice a little more than a murmur and her face looked absolutely petrified.

+++

Dr. Natasha Tikov, a Bulgarian national, who at 40 years old, and with a wiry 1.90 meters, a pointed nose, blond and thick shoulder lengthy hair, and chocolate-coloured eyes, looked more like a Basketball professional player with her athletic physic and sporting outfits than what she was in real life. Dressed in Bulgarian national team green-white-red soccer track suits, a sleeveless red jersey and a pair of red adidas sport shoes to match. She was looking half her age. She was accompanied by her husband, Dr. Sokov Tikov, who in partnership with her, owned a private clinic, 'sonat clinic' on the outskirts of Sofia and their two children, a boy Inna, 12 and his younger sister Nija 8 years old. Natasha was in a very happy mood and was looking forward for a gorgeous return to her lovely city Sofia and to going back to her work once more. The work she was professionally trained for was caring and helping 'poor' and psychotic patients to overcome their grievances as a psychotherapist.

They were returning from the US, where they had been on holidays for the past three weeks. In the States, she and her family had visited many cities including Miami where they visited the famous beaches, Hollywood in California and finally the World Trade Centre-Twin Towers in New York, which her husband always cherished and describes as the most magnificent building he had ever seen. And they mandated to be their last port of call every year. They had taken a lot of photographs, which she was busy enjoying looking at over and over with her children and their father. The pictures had been one of her source of joy, because she was already thinking of how she would proudly present them to her friends and co-workers, and how she would explain to them where each of the photographs was snapped—especially the ones they had taken on top of the World Trade Centre and the Empire State Building.

The family had occupied the fourth row seats in the economy class of the twin-engined Tupolev Balkan flight heading back to Sofia, after spending a few hours transit at the Vienna International Airport. The same flight Marcus Omofuma had been boarded.

Halfway on the air, barely an hour after the plane took off Natasha had a stomach upset and was heading for the cloakroom towards the back of the plane. As she freakly weaved her way inbetween the compacted seats with many passengers already out of their seats, probably to straighten out, there was a slight manoeuvre of the plane while the twin-engined was on the autopilot. The resultant retraction sequence slightly shoved Natasha as she fell side ways at the extreme seats, holding her hand on the headrest of the seat where Officer Renner sat for support. When the plane was under control and the vibration had stopped, she was too petrified to open her eyes. But when she eventually did, what she saw made her shiver and even added to her anxiety. At first, she thought, she might have been under illusion or a kind of watching a Hollywood movie, but of course, she was not. What she saw was in real life; her instincts told her as she wiped her eyes with the back of her hand. The scene was unbearable . . . 'Something must be done' she concluded in her mind, as she raced back towards her seat, with her hand wrapped over her mouth. She had totally forgotten about her stomach upset.

+++

At the beginning of the flight, two male passengers—a forty-something year old man and his business partner that looks the same age—were sitting in front of Marcus Omofuma and officer Renner but after they complained they were moved to the seat row behind Natasha and her family, while two employees of the Balkan Airline were put in their place. Of the over hundred-and-fifty passengers on board the aeroplane, the two men, who were dressed in complete black Gucci business suits were the only passengers to have directly noticed the gagged blackman, and had formally called the attention of the airline crew member.

They had politely asked the attendant if the gagged man was a criminal, and the male attendant had stubbornly replied that he didn't want to know what he had done . . . , but that he thought that the man might have been trying to escape or refuse to board voluntarily.

"Anyway, the policemen accompanying him were responsible for him and should know what they were doing. We do not interfere in the deportation procedure even if someone is tied up," the attendant had concluded before asking if they would prefer to change seats, which they had agreed to without any alternative.

Yet, their eyes had not failed to look back at Omofuma and his escorters since they left Vienna. Sympathetically one of them was narrating to the other about an article he read recently in one of the European leading English news magazine called 'The Truth' (African Today)—which alleged that there has been a 'deportation alliance' made up from European's leading governments and airlines. And that this alliance were committed to enforce the inhuman asylum policies of the Western European (EU) countries by flying refugees back to the place where they fled from and where they often face death, torture or imprisonment. He also told his friend that the magazine further alleged as he quoted:

'By combing the extensive range of destination of its member airlines, the deportation alliance is able to offer the governments of the European countries an unrivalled service, flying refugees back to even most remote, war-torn regions—by using motorcycle helmets, sedatives, handcuffs and often plain force against those who are forced to fly deportation class; although these systems had led to several fatalities over the years', the man asserted to his friend. "The member airlines of the deportation-alliance which I know for sure that Balkan Air is a partner to . . . continue to tolerate the use of force on their plane. And that is too outrageous."

"How I wish, we could somehow help the course of that poor fellow over there?" his equally sympathetic listener friend asked, when his friend finished his narration.

"But, I don't think we could do anything other than what we've done, which was an official protestation to the Balkan and you'd hear their official response," was what his partner could only surmise, before he was cut short by a rather trembling voice of Dr. Natasha Tikov as she approached her husband and children.

"Hubby" called Natasha lousily to her man, "there're some shady deals going on at the back row of this flight. An ugly scene! I saw a man . . . maybe a boy, I'm not really sure . . . plastered all over with what looks like adhesive tapes, yet, he was strapped to his seat. It seems he's an African . . . Black man . . . It's like he's floundering for air . . . but, instead the man sitting beside him was sort of covering when he saw me staring at the man" she described, primarily concerned, considering her professional ethics. "Tell me why a man will be so inhuman to his fellow being? No, matter what. He was like someone on a round-body P-O-P? Like a would-be 'slaughtered' animal with his hands and feet bound."

Sokov, trying to get at whatever his wife meant, stood up, following her eyes which were still glancing nervously towards the back row seats; stared for a moment. He couldn't believe what his eyes saw. He turned to look at his wife and then at his children, who by now also were peeping at the back.

"What, for heaven's sake is happening over there?" Sokovo snorted derisively. "What pushed these nasty souls to put a human being in such condition?"

Naked hatred suddenly covered his face, as he stared at the back again and again, the situation dreaded him more.

"Damm it, look at how they wrapped him like a 'mummy' stucked to the seat."

"Oh! My good Lord, see see . . . Hubby, he's thrashing around again . . . wildly and trying over and over to get air," Natasha shook her head negatively for emphasis. She choked back her tears. "We must help this man. We can notify the crewmen or any . . ."

"Granted," Sokov replied. "But, do you think the crew members weren't aware of this . . . or rather how did they smuggled him inside. They must've known of this sick act. Well, for the benefit of doubt, let me try to find one of them and make a complaint against this officially . . . I mean, it's too barbaric to permit these dear-devilled monsters to carry this out in our own national Airline."

"Daddy, please, you'd better hurry or he may die," pleaded his son Inna as tears ran down from his cheeks, down to the immaculate white polo shirt he was wearing. His mother approached him, cuddled and kissed his forehead. "Inna, that's okay that's alright!"

"Please, help him, daddy, I don't like to see a human being been subjected to this sort of maltreatment," added his daughter Nija in a quavering voice, trying to hold back her tears.
These innocent emotions prompted Sokov to move hurriedly towards one of the crewmen standing near the compact-door that partitioned the economy class and the first class.He wrinkled his forehead in thought, as he straightened out of his seat, looking morose.

"Hello, please can I see one of the captains of this flight?" he made an exasperated face. "It's an urgent matter that needs his or her personal attention, if you understand what I mean?"

"Pardon?" the steward said, cupping a hand to his left ear and bent his head to Sokov, who was almost one foot shorter than him.

"I mean, I want to speak with the co-pilot or who-so-ever is in charge of this flight," Sokov shouted at the top of his voice angrily, standing on his toes.

"Excuse . . . me sir, please could you come again, I can't hear . . . the engine is so noisy" the steward pretended further, as he bent furthermore.

Sokov keenly and at the same time angrily explained his mission, using local Bulgarish dialect.

"Why, sir, what's the problem with the . . ." the tall, slim built steward asked, pinching the bridge of his nose.

"Bullshit, goddamn bullshit!!! Damn you man," Sokovo uttered impaitiently. "Don't pretend you don't know about it, you pompous and heartless Judas."

He thrusted his way in the direction of the first class lounge, but he was restrained by another crewman, a burly young man that looked more like Sylvester Stallone than someone working with an airline. He looked resplendent in his Balkan air uniform and cap.

"Yeah sir easy does it! What can we do for you?" the burly crewman demanded nonchalantly, blocking him with his huge body.

"Give way you monster! I must speak with the captain of this . . ."

"I'm the co-pilot" the Sylvester Stallone look-alike lied not minding his odd uniform, as he gently held Sokov by his hand, somehow pushing him backwards. "We can talk over there," he murmured, pointing towards the storage cabin, afraid that someone might suddenly stroll out from the first class lounge.

Sokov held back for a moment and struggle his hand free.

"Listen, someone is . . . one of 'your' passengers is sweltering down there . . . at the back," he stuttered, stretching out his hand and points down where Omofuma was struggling with his life.

He wanted to control his anger as he once again looked over at the back. The picture flashing off and on in his mind, the passionate pleading of his children to him to try and do something for the man continuously rang in his ear.

"If you fools couldn't allow me to talk with the pilot, I want you to be warned that I, Dr. Sokov Tikov would by all means report in details everything that occurred on this flight . . . during and after . . . to the appropriate authorities . . . together against your ungentlemanly behaviours."

Dr. Sokov angrily turned and followed his wife, who had been entreating . . .

"Please, Hubby . . . let go off your anger, forget these Arch-fiends. Cool it, Simmy" she implored him, calling him the abbreviated version of his second name 'Simonokov' which she always employed whenever he felt too angry. "Simmy, don't be upset because of these madmen. They're all pretending they didn't know what was happening, but I'm quite convinced now that all of them . . . including the Balkan directors knew about it. It's an open conspiracy. Yes, certainly, they knew before hand . . . they were all ordered to be blind."

She gulped back her tears with a red handkerchief and paused momentarily, then added phlegmatically. "Ergo, they'll all get their karmic rewards one day."

"Except me Madam . . . I'm totally against it right from the beginning and now been threatened with my job" Jelena Litov reasoned silently from where she stood watching the scene. "I hope the ravages of God will visit those responsible before Armageddon comes."

Dr. Sokov approached his children, who were so distressed that they were sobbing and could not take their eyes away from the three Austrian police officers and the entangled Marcus Omofuma. He caresses their backs and hairs, while their mother stood watching, aghast at the policemen's cruelty and man's inhumanity to man.

"It's just terrible, we can't do anything to help the man," expressed Dr. Sokov compassionately. "But, Inna . . . Nija, I want you to trust your daddy, I'm going to report this cruelty . . . they'll be punished . . . they would all burn in the hell fire."

+++

Only towards the end of the two hours flight from Vienna to Sofia was Marcus Omofuma said to have calmed down. And he was in that state until the plane touched down at Sofia Airport.

Earlier on, when food was served to the passengers, Jelena had wanted to serve Omofuma his own ration, but the police officers had denied her access to him. She once again did what was required of her which was to report to the chief stewardess. As expected, the chief stewardess promptly told her.

"Abide by the rules Miss Jelena. No foods for dangerous black Africans. For others, yes, but for Africans: capital 'NO'. Got it?

Unfortunately, Jelena had gotten no more will otherwise she would have tried to argue the chief stewardess out of her racist stance. She was afraid of being placed on instant redundancy. She didn't want to lose her precious job. She had silently bowed to the threatening of her chief and left unceremoniously.

And Marcus Omofuma had been refused food while the other passengers were having theirs—including Lieutenant Pirker and his colleagues. Jelena had gone back to the back row and in annoyance rolled the food trolley straight to the storage cabin. Out of personal curiosity and human sympathy, she had frequently gone to the back of the plane. Once she noticed that the police man next to Omofuma officer Renner was holding the end of the adhesive tape which went round Omofuma's head. And the other policemen (Lieutenant Pirker and officer Weiss) behind them each held the end of a rope or tape which fastened his head from behind. When the policemen noticed her coming this time around, officer Renner had move out of his seat in an attempt to block her from seeing what was going on. She had somehow peeped through a little gap inbetween the armrest and saw that Omofuma was as quiet as cold breeze. And Jelena had taken it that Marcus had finally accepted his fate after much struggles. She always heard her father saying that 'the bravest among men is he who embraces his fate and accepts his destiny without grudges even if it's an infamous act'. Still feeling disgusted, she had straight away gone to the tiny waste room of the plane to weep away the tears that grubbed down her cheeks. She had blamed herself for not having the will power and authority to intervene for this helpless Black man, whom she hadn't known before and might not be seeing again—but had come to 'love' because of the way he had accepted his torments and his tormentors . . . 'Just like Jesus of Nazareth' who didn't care either during his own ordeal. She was fully convinced that like Jesus Christ the man must have with his eyes beckoned her for food (wine) but those Roman soldiers—the Austrian police officers—and the monster chief stewardess—had overruled her from doing so. She considered all the atrocities meted out to him so far to be unjust and inhuman. Having convinced herself that she could not do anything to help his cause, she dejectedly went back to her duty and did not see him again till the twin-engined Tupolev taxied its way inside the Sofia Airport.

++

After the landing and after all the passengers had almost left the plane—with the exception of Dr. Sokov Tikov and his family—Jelena saw that the three police officers were still on borad and it was then she believed that the Black man must have been dead even before the doctors arrived. She stared as the policemen full of trepidation that more people—airport workers—may catch sight of their wicked deed, immediately unfastened the plastic belt (with which he was later strapped to the seat) and furled back the mouth tape. But the deed had been done.

At that very minute, they realized that Omofuma had lost consciousness. There was no serious effort to resuscitate him neither by the Balkan Airline first-aid team, nor the three police officers accompanying him.

By the time a doctor arrived—after so many minutes had been wasted—Marcus Omofuma was dead. Jelena had overheard as Doctor Simon Stovasjev, after applying his medical expertise, confirmed and pronounced him clinically dead. And he had openly blamed the police officers and the airline management for having caused his death. Dr. Stovasjev had also professionally questioned why there was no Balkan Airline emergency medical practitioner attached to the flight, in accordance with the international flight regulations regarding health and safety of passengers while on board, and whether these officers who were customarily ordered to escort (Omofuma) had not been trained in first-aid, in the first instance.

Jelena had been sorrowfully eager as she scrutinized the scowled faces of the Austrian policemen and the Balkan officials—especially the face of the chief stewardess Melina Bokov—as Dr. Stovasjev spoke.

And briefing the airport press corps later, Jelena had interestedly heard Dr. Stovasjev saying that the man (Omofuma) died of suffocation. He could not get enough air to support his critical condition in the flight and he had added emphatically. "He was asphyxiated by the adhesive tapes."

Jelena had also seen when Dr. Sokov Tikov and his family were being interviewed by the pressmen, explaining their experience with bitterness.

That very night Jelena cried like she had never done in her whole life. Later, around 2 am she had woken from a nightmare. In her dream, she was ordered to be locked up in the forward restroom of the flight, by the chief stewardess, for her arrogance when she threatened to cause commotion inside the flight if Omofuma was not immediately unbound from the adhesive tapes. While inside the restroom crying, she was surprised to see the emergency hatch of the flight unfastened and what seemed like an angel but with Omofuma's wrapped face appeared and stood by her. She wanted to scream, but the angel told her not to be afraid. 'He' meant to cause no harm to her . . . she was told by the angel that he only came to give her courage to fight and deliver the helpless black African, Marcus Omofuma, from his enemies. After she found her courage back, she had followed the white angel with black face as the door of the restroom automatically unlocked. They went through the aisle way until they stood opposite Omofuma and the cops, who wore the Austrian light-grey police summer uniforms. The angel had pointed at the overhead compartment and brought out a .44 automatic gun. With the gun in her hand, she had commanded the three police officers to untie Omofuma.

Look, you idiots, I've been given the authority by an angel of the Lord to free this man . . . so you don't have to disobey God's order or I'll shoot the hell out of you . . . release him or you're dead, she had ordered, levelling the gun at the officers.

The three officers simultaneously began to utter some unreasonable words, disregarding the threat, and Jelena had wasted no time as she pulled the trigger of the .44 and blasted the heads of the three policemen. Quickly, she had with a trembling hand, managed to cut the tapes and released Omofuma from his bondage. But all of a sudden, she heard a firm voice from behind commanding . . .

DO NOT MAKE A MOVE. DROP YOUR GUN
NOW. TURN AROUND AND HOLD OUT
YOUR HANDS!!!MISS JELENA YOU ARE UNDER
ARREST!!!!!!!!BE STILL AND CO-OPERATE!!!!!!

She was arrested by the airport security guards and was later charged
with brutal first degree murder of three police officers. On the day of
the judgement, she was sentenced to life imprisonment without parol.
However, Jelena had remained resolute even after the sentence was handed
over to her, when she proudly told the judge.

I Miss Jelena only carried out an assignment ordered by an angel of God.
I freed a dying man. I had no regret, no grudge and no more remorse for
what I've done . . . she was unrepentantly shouting as she'd been dragged
out from the courtroom to the prison by two wardresses.
The following morning, Jelena woke up with acute headache. She could
not understand the meaning of her nightmare. Omofuma's episode
remained a constant nagging ache in her heart.

"Maybe, the three police officers and their accomplices would be the ones
that will finally end up in prison without parol" Jelena Litov eventually
murmured soothingly.

CHAPTER FIVE

"Truly for Thy sake we are slain all day long; we are accounted as sheep for slaughter. Awake! Why sleepest Thou, O Lord? Arise cast us not off for ever! Why dost Thou hide Thy face? Why dost Thou forget our affliction and oppression?

===Psalms 44:22-24.

During the winter of 1999, around early February, Useni Mustapha, a young African of Senegalese origin, left his one-room-apartment in the 12th district of Vienna near *Philadelphia Brücke* very early in the morning. A normal everyday odyssey of entering the busses, the *U-Bahn* and *Strassenbahn* en route to *Kagran* where he always went every morning to register himself, before being apportioned his work for the day. He works with a company at *Kagran* that distributes advertisement papers and items to Viennese household every working-day, and sometimes the work will take him and others to the outskirts of Vienna. This is the only work an asylum seeker is partially allowed to do in Austria—often with strict police control.

Because of the fact that asylum seekers are not entitled to have any other job and are of course as any other people living in Austria expected to have a *Meldeadresse*, which if one could not be able to produce when being controlled by the police—would warrant an immediate six compulsory months imprisonment—Mustapha had been always serious and punctual to his work or else he would find himself in deportation prison again.
He had been imprisoned before for this same offence by the *Fremdenpolizei*, when he was initially sacked from the *Traiskirchen Bundesasyl* Camp.

51

Because there is no social and financial help from the government for the asylum seekers like Mustapha, he must abide by this *Reklame*-work even in the hazardous winter conditions and sometimes with the racist behaviours surrounding the company, just to sustain himself and save money to pay for his apartment monthly rent thereby avoiding police further harassment.

Somedays, he would arrive at the company—a bit late, because of some unforeseen circumstances beyond his control. In that case, the whole day work would be over for him.

Some other days, he might be earlier at the company before anybody, but the Turkish and Yugoslavish truck drivers, who were on contract with the company and had the power to choose which workers they wanted would overlook him for being black. In that same case, Mustapha would once again go without work. Nevertheless, he always strived to be among the first arrivals at the company and leave the day's fate for God to decide.

On this very fateful day however, at about five-thirty in the morning, as he waited for the underground train (*U6*) which would take him straight to the *U-Bahn* station *Floridsdorf*, from where he would connect his way to *Kagran*, Mustapha was approached by five bulky uniformed police officers.

"Stop where you are, and don't move!" one of the officers said in a commanding manner *"Ausweis bitte?"*

"Pardon," Mustapha pleaded.

"Can we see your identity papers?" the officer shouted at him.

As a law abiding citizen, Useni Mustapha without protest brought out his 'legal card' (a refugee identity card issued to him by the *Bundesministerium*) together with his *Meldezettel* and handed them over to the officers, who had all surrounded him. Instantaneously, before he knew what was going on, they seized and pushed him forcefully into one of the control rooms of the *U-Bahn* station. He resisted and was explaining to them on demand that he was only trying to board the *U6* to *Floridsdorf* on to *Kagran* to go to the company he works for. He was able to get his company's registered card from his pocket, showing that he worked for the *Kagran Reklame* Company. Yet, all these efforts could not convince the policemen.

"Shut up your silly Nigger mouth, will yee?!" snapped one officer. "We saw you selling drugs to some junkies," the officer allegedly accused.

"But, sir, I didn't stand with anybody . . . who said I sold . . ." Useni started to protest.

But before he could add any more, the police officers were all over him, hitting, kicking and beating him with rubber truncheons as two of them grabbed him by the throat, pressing it harder.

"Look here, you timid son-of-a-bitch!" one of them shouted at him. "If you try to show you have power . . . or that you're strong . . . we'll f-u-c-k your ass . . ." he threatened, hitting him on the back of his head.

As the beating took place, there was a short, fat, blond hair lady, who was standing some few meters away from Mustapha as he was waiting for the underground train before the cops had accosted him. As she stood watching, she was moved by the type of beating and assaults the officers were meting out to the black African.
She wanted to avoid any confrontation with the police and was about to find her way up the escalator but as headbutt from one of the cops at Mustapha and another dangerous kick that landed at his private part automatically made the lady to change her mind. She went directly to one of the officers to solicit on his behalf and to assure him that she had being standing for almost five minutes at the station even before the Black man came, that he hadn't spoken with anyone nor transacted anything with anybody and that no one even stood near him.

"How can this innocent man be subjected to such beating without restraint?" she questioned emotionally, and asserted strongly, "this is not only inhuman but uncalled for . . . as far as I'm concerned, this man has done nothing than being black, which unfortunately wasn't his making nor his fault and that shouldn't have in anyway been a crime."

"*Wie ist das so mit einem Neger?*" (What is it with a Negro)?," the officer demanded, speaking in German as he returned her glance with full hatred and bitterness, looking eyes with her and noting the hollow look on her face, while the other officers were still rough handling Mustapha without minding her being present. He went on "*Er ist ein Negerschwein* (he is a black Pig) *und alle Neger sind Drogenhändler* (and all blacks are drug dealers). *Neger gehören zuerst geschlagen, und dann nach dem Namen befragt* (Blacks deserve to be hit first, before asking their names)" the officer uttered without remorse.

"But, this man I still maintained did nothing to deserve these beatings, he is a human being like any other person, he has his own life to live like others and must be respected. White or Black, we're all the same" the lady insisted. "Don't kill anybody because he is black."

One of the officers commanded as he motioned her to move out of the area, shouting mockingly at her.

"Miss Nigger Lover, you have to mind your own business, understood? Now you can go. If you really want to protect these Africans, better advise them to return back to their countries and stop coming here. Austria should not be a country for them and we can't tolerate them anymore. You better go and live with them in Africa if you love them . . . Ma'ma."

Later, the cops noticed that Mustapha was gradually running out of steam and that his breathing began to ebb—he had already lost consciousness. And having being sure nobody else was watching, they made their way out and left him there to his fate.

The following day, it was reported in the Austrian *Zeitungen* that a Black man died at *Philadelphia Brücke* while trying to 'gulp down drugs' in his mouth which resulted in him being choked to dead.

This allegation later turned out to be a 'sweep under the carpet' because the autopsy report had contradicted the drug allegations.

Mustapha's sudden death and subsequent reports which contradict police's false allegation that he died while trying to swallow drugs, made him another victim of the ubiquitous police act of brutalities and callous disregard for the rights of others—especially the black African immigrants—later gave rise to the first demonstration carried out by the African community in Austria and so many White sympathizers. It was organized by the Association for democracy in Africa (ADA), the SOS-Mitmensch and many other human rights groups against racism, xenophobia, intimidation and brutality of foreigners. This demonstration resulted in mass turn-outs of people of all races, and became the first big manifestation by an immigrant community against the Austrian police.

However, contrary to expectation, the police malfeasance instead of minimizing, increased tremendously thereafter with Black men and women still being subjected daily in the streets of Vienna and other cities as nobody and as the only drug dealers in Austria and as the sole cause of the Austria's worsening drug situation which was more or less a global phenomenon.

++

The deaths of many Africans in Europe especially, that of Marcus Omofuma had revealed a considerable degree of ambiguity regarding the type of physical restraints which may permissibly be used during expulsion of deportee. The autopsy which was conducted in Bulgaria (shortly after Omofuma's death was confirmed by Dr. Vassil Stovasjev) by a team of expert led by Professor Radanov strongly pointed to death by asphyxia. However, another autopsy which was done in Austria (many days after the death) by Professor Reither, suggested that an undetected heart defect meant that it could not be said with the required certainty that there was causative link between the gagging of Marcus Omofuma and his untimely death meaning he might have died as a result of heart attack. But the questions were, 'does Omofuma proved to be having any kind of sickness prior to this forceful deportation? Does his medical files—which according to the law, was mandatory for every asylum seeker to have—detected the symptoms of any known internal illness? Or did Omofuma suddenly contact the travel sickness or airsickness as a result of the inhuman treatment meted out to him? And the questions could go on and on . . . If truly he died as a result of a heart attack as ascertained by the experts from Vienna, what was the immediate cause of the so-called undetected heart defects? And why was it that the expert report submitted by Professor Radanov, who was the first expert after Marcus Omofuma's death to assert that the cause of death was suffocation had been buried under bureaucratic furrows? Did the argument by some Vienna's leading Advocates, which stated that

55

testimony from officers of the court—including that of an independent and fully qualified Professor—in countries such as Bulgaria did not carry as much weight as those from Austria, has anything to do with the above counter autopsy report? On the other hand, was there some sort of political strings attached to all these scandals? Did the Austrian democratic authorities intend to play politics over the death of an ordinary honest, innocent and helpless asylum seeker whose only crime as a matter of fact was that he came to Austria to seek asylum.

Later, after two years of allegation and counter allegations among the public-spirited citizens concerning the reports of the Bulgarian experts and their Austrian counterparts and subsequent to the continuous pressure from the international human rights groups (among them Amnesty International) and the Africa community in Austria, on the 2nd of May, 2001, incidentally on the second commemoration of the death of Marcus Omofuma, an independent and another qualified expert from Münster (Germany) Professor Brinkmann, who was finally assigned to ascertain the actual cause of his death (because of his neutrality) was able to release his findings. In his report, Prof. Brinkmann maintained that Marcus Omofuma's death was a result the gagging of the mouth with adhesive tapes which brought about suffocation. This report therefore corroborated with what the Bulgarian expert stated initially.
And the reports also led to the question of the credibility and integrity of these unethical doctors for their conflicting reports, ignoring how this defenceless vagrant was physically ill-treated, intimidated and manhandled before and during the forcible deportation; while the expert that originally saw the corpse confirmed that he died as a consequence of the direct torture, cruel and degrading treatment meted to him by the police accompanying him on his cataclysmic sojourn in Austria.

The atmosphere was hardly permissive for Marcus Omofuma. It must be emphasized that to beat, torture or gag a human being was a highly hazardous measure. The 'gagged technique' which allows the police departments responsible for the deportation of individuals to gag and use adhesive tapes to silence people's mouth in order to forbid them from protesting must be abolished. So to say, according to sociologist, 'people with any hostility, aggression or intents to hurt mainly through the expression of actions may be deleterious to other people.'

That means that these officers assigned the task of dealing with helpless and unarmed individual—who may only be protesting for their basic human rights—must pass through psychiatric training and their standards of humanity, care, and dignity should be priorities for the selection procedure.

Marcus Omofuma and Useni Mustapha's deaths were never accidents, nor were they the only isolated incidents that happened across Europe. They are only two out of handful of other asylum-seekers, who had died in recent years in the hands of the European police during forcible deportation from European airports.

In August 1994, another Nigerian national, Kola Bankole, died of heart failure on board a plane from Frankfurt (Germany). He had been restrained, sedated and gagged with a device made from socks and a belt by one of the federal Border police officer during yet another forcible deportation.

In September 1998, Semira Adamu, a Nigerian died of asphyxia within hours of an attempt to forcibly deportation from Brussel's National Airport (Belgium). A statement by the ministry of Interior later revealed that she had been handcuffed and hackled by the Gendarmes during the deportation operation. It also confirmed that one of the Gendarmes officers had pushed a 'Cushion' against her face, causing instant suffocation.

Yet, in March 1999, Khaled Abu Zarifa, a Palestinian, died of suffocation at *Zürich-Kloten Airport* in Switzerland during deportation after an adhesive tape was placed over his mouth and was strapped into the chair against his will with a hard rubber cord.

In view of the above ill-treatments and the subsequent deaths of these individuals and many other deaths that had not been made public by the European authorities (because of the circumstances that might surrounded those deaths and which always helped them to bury such death without public knowledge), it's high time the world body must speak out. The world at large will not be sitting quiet while such atrocities happen around her. People must express concern about 'insufficient measures' of protection in cases of individuals under an order of deportation. It must be recommended that provisions concerning the protection of asylum seekers should fully conform within the relevant international standards. Clear instructions must be given to the police by the competent authorities to avoid any incidence of maltreatment by police agents and it must be emphasized that ill-treatment by law enforcement officials shall not be tolerated and shall be promptly investigated and punished in case of violation according to law. European authorities must examine the safetness of the use of methods of restraint and ensure that they do not endanger the health and safety of any deportee.

CHAPTER SIX

"Blackmen, you were once great; you shall be great again. Lose not courage, lose not faith, go forward"

===Marcus Garvey.

On Sunday, the 2nd of May 1999, the very day Marcus Omofuma supposed to have arrived Lagos, at about four o'clock in the morning, Hyman Otta, suddenly woke from his sleep. He sat up and blinked in darkness. Something had awakened him. He felt tickled in his throat, which made him to cough. 'What was happening to me?' he seemed to ask himself. He shook his head to and fro to assure himself he was fully awake. 'Which type of dream had I had, for the first time in my life to cause me to be terribly upset like this?' he murmured silently to nobody, but to himself. He went straight to his cupboard, his hands trembling and took his Bible. With the Bible in his hand, he tried to still this sudden tremor of his hand. He went toward the tiny window, where there was little twinkling of light from the electric bulb outside their cell room (because the switch of the electric bulb inside their cell room has been positioned out of their control). 'For one to be in prison, means that almost everything, including his right to control the electricity in his cell room remains out of his reach' he sighed thoughtfully. But he was not a criminal prisoner. He was a proud and righteous prisoner of an 'illegal entry'. An extreme right policy being practised in Austria, and other right-wing controlled countries of Europe, basically against foreign immigrants.

59

Hyman opened his Bible and read Psalms 6, 35, 51, 55, 91, 140 and finally 142. After which he knelt down and started praying intensively, asking God to cast aside and declare preventable whatsoever his dream might have meant. This aberrant time of prayers, prompted Koso Osei to wake up. Irritated, he stared fixedly at Hyman.

"Charlie . . . man, what did you mean by this early morning nuisance?" Koso whispered from top of his double-decker bunk, and gave a heavy sigh. "It's too early, my man to pray to this your God . . . Even this God of yours might be annoyed at you for disturbing him while sleeping . . ." he senselessly declared, as he drew his blanket over his head and continued his sleeping.

When Hyman finished his prayers—it took two hours—and, till the time the electric bulb inside their cell was on, it was around 6 am. From where he was kneeling, he was shocked to see Koso staring mischievously at him.

"Man listen, I would never be an obstacle between you and your God, but please don't try to be one between me and my precious sleeps. Spare me that shit ok! These abnormal prayers will never be an excuse to inconvenience me in my sleep. Even as a prisoner, sleep remains the only thing that has not been restricted from me . . . Not even by Austrian laws where everything a Black man did is declared illegal" Koso chuckled, changing the tone of his voice. "Or, has the Austrian Parliament implemented a new law against normal early morning sleep, Mr. Preacher?"

"I'm very sorry, if I've been disturbing you," Hyman pleaded in a low but firm voice, trying all his best not to laugh at Koso's joke. "You know it wasn't often I prayed in the middle of the night. I had a very bad dream concerning us . . . we two and Omofuma."

Hyman shifted in the direction of Koso, who on hearing, that the dream also concerned him quickly rose from his bed and pulled himself together.

"It was so terrifying that my blood pressure must have risen to 250 and above."

"I believe you guys are not trying to surpass Dr. Martin Luther King Jr. and his dreams these days" Koso said amussingly, "last time it was Omofuma, now you've taken over the mantle from him."

"Charlie, please could you drop these jokes for a few minutes and listen," Hyman seriously asked. "I thought you claimed to be dream 'guru' . . . Genius, help describe my dream and tell me what it means"

"Alright, what's about the dream? In a situation like this, I mean, like the one we found ourselves in . . . one cannot blame himself if he joined the league of dreamers. It's been said that almost every prisoner became a dreamer before they left prison. And it is not a peculiar thing for a man's thinking to constantly reflect in his head even as a dream or vision especially when the man is under captivity, where he always thinks round the clock on how he would become a free man again," Koso asserted in his usual nonchalant attitude, his juting chin raised, his thin lips fixed in a contemptuous smirk, small eyes glinting. "So, buddy what is your message this time around? As a Dudu, my ears are always yours."

"Can't you for once know when someone is serious or not?"

"Just, go on and unfold your dream, boy, as they say, 'experience breeds confidence' . . . I also believe that 'hard conditions in prison or any where else breeds irksome dreams' . . . after all, you've already disrupted my 'Zizz' . . . so I've no alternative than to remain your loyal hacker."

Well, I knew you to be always funny, but, look Charlie, I had a dream where we, that is, Marcus, you and me, happen to be with many other people—Whites, Chinese, Arabs and other black brothers. We were all grooving in what seems like a get-together, a kind of partying if you know what I mean. Everybody was having fun. There were lots of eating and drinking . . . assorted types of foods and beverages.

"With some beautiful 'senoritas' also, or you forgot?" Koso interrupted interestedly.

"Oh! No, there were no girls. I mean I did not see even one. It was all men party, you know."

"Buddy, I was not among, you must count me out . . . that was automatically a gay party . . . It was not me you saw, maybe you saw somebody that looked like me. I only go to parties that men and *okpeke'* are fully represented," Koso jokingly declared. "You can continue, but I'm not the one you saw, mind you?"

"Okay, you were not the one," Hyman agreed, knowing Koso better, he could never complete this story if he insisted.

Hyman smiled at Koso, using his hand to wipe out the sweat that had drenched his face and continued.

As everybody seemed to be enjoying himself, with Rock n' roll music all over the place, hammering out from the speakers, a real rollicking party indeed. Just as we were about to dance the person that resembled you and myself, because Marcus declined, not quite two minutes or so later, I couldn't remember all that happened, but all the same, I saw three men from where I was, they looked like giant monsters as I only saw their backs. They were dragging Marcus forcefully outside the big hall, while he was kind of demurring to draw our attention, waving his hands frantically towards us. As I thought, he was like gesturing at us to come to his rescue as he started to scream. However, because of noise inside the hall, I couldn't hear a single word from all he was saying, before I could move a step forward, one of the men had already stretched out his hand, using something that resembles a ribbon with red-white-red Austrian flag and a Nazi logo, and muffled it around Omofuma's mouth. At once he was hoisted up and hugged out. I dashed out virtually in pursuit of them . . . with you or the person that looked like you following me

Hyman corrected himself quickly just to keep the story going, as Koso wanted to protest again.

I heard the stamping hill of the person behind me, but to my utter bewilderment, Omofuma had being squeezed into a waiting white Volkswagen van and driven away. I pursued the van, and Marcus was like signalling and shouting, this time around I perceived the sound of his voice echoing in my ear Hyman!!!!!!!!Koso!!!!!!!! I missed you two . . . We're going to see no more. Bye! Bye!! Bye!!! Maybe this sound I heard was my own imagination, maybe it was real, that, I couldn't ascertain for sure, and then I think that was exactly when I woke up.

Hyman sadly, raised his little dark-brown eyes like those of a pig conscious of the slaughter room.

"Charlie, what can you make out of this dream?"

Koso laughed at him uncontrollably.

"Hark! My man, let's say this dream of yours might precipitate fear, especially to dream 'Bhakta' like you" Koso grinned. "Yet one's belief remains one's belief no matter what. There's an adage that said, 'even if everything in this world faded away, one's belief doesn't fade'. One who believes in a particular thing always dies with his or her belief. 'What do I make out of this you asked? Well for me, I knew and believed that Omofuma is as safe as air, inside the city by now. Maybe he is having a good time with that his 'Big Ikebe Miniature' right now and you're here dreaming of his extinction, man! You must arise to the truth of life, since you're no 'yahoo'-be a smart guy, okay."

"But, you have not answered my question. You do not take me to be your senseless brother Akota, do you?" Hyman insisted. "What can the bye . . . bye . . . bye mean?"

Koso jumped down from his double-decker bed.

"The only thing I can say, boy, is . . . as you rightly suggested all these dreams are nothing but pure imaginations. That's all your thoughts or what you over-carried from where Omofuma left."

He went to his cupboard, took his packet of Marlboro, took a stick of cigarette and lit it. He glanced at Hyman, dragging from his cigarette.

"Nowadays you people normally wake up . . . with 'story, story, story, ooo like my friend Fela Kuti sang in one of his album, making me to smoke, smoke, smoke ooo" Koso chanted and took a chair and sat beside Hyman. "Always remember that 'a thinking mind is a working mind, the more the mind thinks about a particular thing, the more the chance that mind would never be at rest until that particular thing is gone and forgotten.' This is exactly my own humble opinion on these dreams."

"You Thomas, I'm not preaching nor trying to coax you into believing. Nonetheless, what you have to know is, these dreams do not only show the fact that they were coincident with each other, they were collateral to coming evils. I forgot to add that as I was pushing the van, shouting in return back at Omofuma . . . at least to create awareness, I was tripped from behind and returned back to the hall by some muscular men, who masked their face like the Cobra Polizei. They were able to gather all of us together and pushed us deeper, down the extreme corner of the hall and shut the big middle gate behind us. All of a sudden, the music automatically stopped. Every food and drink immediately turned and became solid rocks. I heard people screaming and crying like we're being tormented in hell fire if you know the Bible story . . . could you imagine that? In a twinkle of an eye, what seems at first like a happy gathering changed and became a place of doom and gloom. Mark my words I foresee the aura of gloom around us. By and by, we'll soon know what's going on. But, as a man of God I denounce devil and all the workers of iniquity, and continue to pray God to give us the power to prevail over whatever evil satan is planning against us . . . for no weapon fashioned against us shall prosper . . . And we shall overcome someday, in Jesus precious name, amen" he prayed courageously.

+++

That same morning, at around nine o'clock, they tuned their Radio to Radio Orange 94.0, an FM station, which traditionally broadcast music and news about Africans living in Africa, Europe and across the world. The station air on Saturday and Tuesday between 9am and 10am and from Wednesdays, Thursdays and Fridays around 5 to 5:30 in the evening. They always look forward to these programs because that was the only opportunity as prisoners of conscience in a strange land to come in contact with Africa and its various cultural music, and arts that made the continent rich and thick. They've discovered the station recently after someone told Omofuma about it during the *Spazieren*.

At present, there was the rhythm of the South African Reggae Star, Lucky Dube's lyrics. 'God created man in His own image . . . The Bible did not tell us whether He was a Whiteman, or a Black man, or an Indian man . . . when I see a white man I see the image of God I see a Black man I see the image of God, I see an Indian man I see the image of God . . . coloured or whites . . . we're all images of God . . . God is one . . . 'thumping relentlessly from the portable medium-sized radio with an inbuilt alarm clock. Hyman and Koso had been dancing and enjoying the program, when suddenly the presenter of the program for the day, Amoa Owusu, who recently joined the African Radio International (part of Radio Orange) after he graduated from the Kumasi School of Journalism, and further studied at London School of Journalism—where he acquired his masters in mass communication—unabridgedly broke off, and as he used to say, 'doing what people say he does best' . . . he expressed rather tragically.

'Please, my listeners, I'm sorry to break off in this manner . . . but for breaking news . . . according to the report reaching my desk . . . a Nigerian (name withheld for special reason) has been reported to have died on board a Balkan airline flight . . . while being repatriated back to his country . . . This day is a very dark, sad, and bad day for all Africans and we at the Radio Africa Orange 94.0 offer our sincere condolence to the family and friends of this great African" DJ Amoa Owusu commiserated. As he repeated, "once again, according . . . '

"What?" shouted Koso, awkwardly, trying to absorb the breaking news.

"Charlie, what . . . what did he just say?"

"It looked like there was a big problem . . . a tragedy, of course . . . he was saying something about the death of a Nigerian" Koso was saying dragging heavily from his cigarette.

"Oh my God," Hyman Otta cried out in a loud voice. "No, no, no God why have you forsaken your people? They've killed Marcus. They've eventually forced him to his untimely death . . . I saw it coming" he said and broke down and started crying uncontrollably, sobbing like a baby, "God, why, why, why?"

"You're right. You're right . . . God dammit, man. You were fucking right about that dream of yours. From now on, I'll never argue with you. I hereby apologize and retracted all my allegations. I'm only a fool and a doubting Thomas . . . These people are crazy murderers, boy!" Koso declared, as he patted Hyman at the back. "Of course, they've murdered an innocent soul."

"He was begging us to come and help him" Hyman sobbed. "How I wish I was fast enough to pursue those monsters . . . who knew I might have saved him . . . oh . . . oh . . . oh!!!"

Koso nodded his head in agreement.

"Maybe, you would've saved him actually . . . you only dreamed this morning, and he was supposed to have been . . ."

"I don't mean saving him in the dream . . . you see I've been fasting for all of us, before the day he was tricked that he will be released . . . but, the devil deceived me that very day. I just stopped for no cause . . . hoping to continue afterwards now you see what my stupidity had led to . . ." Hyman was lamenting sorrowfully, blaming himself bitterly. "These fasting and prayers would've made them to at least, send him back here as they've done on two previous occasions . . . That would've been better . . . that would've been . . ."

"Nevertheless, even that would not have prevented it . . ." Koso consoled and added rather philosophically, "let's not begin accusing ourselves for what we've done or what we failed to do, instead, let us direct our anger and point to the whole truth of the matter . . . that the Austrian police had succeeded in assassinating Marcus Omofuma. And Mother Africa will always fight for her son . . . SHE MUST FIGHT THE KILLERS ALL THE DAYS OF THEIR LIVES."

+++

They were still in this painful mood, contemplating on what would be the actual meaning of the later part of Hyman's dream, where he said they were locked up and the sudden change that occurred, when the door of their dungeon unlocked. O.C. Nico was standing in the doorway without his usual smiles. A man that's passable as a woman, his face an androgynous rubber mask, his nose a bit of a honker, with his henna-brown hair feathered and counterpart. Because of his homosexual tendency it's been openly said among his fellow officers that he loved to associate with foreigners . . . mostly black Africans, (that he found them too easy to coax for his own sexual chimera. But that had absolutely not been the case.) According to O.C Nico himself, his grandfather was a fervent supporter and one of the pioneer leaders of Adolf Hitler's hitmen (The SS officers) who had committed one of the worst human atrocities in history during the Second World War when millions of Jews and other immigrants were massacred. The worst genocide in history and as a child, he had seen pictures and heard his *Opa* boasting about his personal involvement. His immediate family and other relatives were all members of the extreme right party, with an anti-foreigner and somehow Nazi ideologies enacted in its manifestos.

This past and present family extreme political stances had always been a worry for officer Nicole (O. C. Nico) as he's known to some of the prisoners—and he was constantly having problems with his family members over his liberal views on certain issues especially where foreigners were concerned. A good and reasonable man, officer Nico had bitterly and fully paid for his liberal stance, when his family rejected and disowned him at his early youthful age. And since then, all his friends, both, men and women have been mostly foreigners.

In the deportation prison camp where he had been working for the past six years, he had made a couple of friends, and was equally helpful to all immigrant prisoners who happened to come his way. Because, as he proudly told a prisoner friend one day. 'I want to contribute back, even in a little way for all my family's atrocities towards foreigners.' Sometimes he would be on duty and the other officers would single out the Black prisoners and order that little or no food be served them. In that case, O. C. Nico would from behind supply them leftovers. He always spent most of his salary on many Black prisoners, buying provisions for them to supplement their food. None of the African immigrant who spent time in the camp since officer Nico started working there had ever said anything bad against him.

Having known Marcus Omofuma for more than five months and even discussed with him on man to man basis—unlike his colleagues who treated Blacks as animals—O. C. Nico had heard the tragic news of his death the previous day the very day it happened. He had cried over his tragic demise and now appeared to be looking for a way to console his roommates and fellow African brothers.

"Hi Guys! Why were you shouting?" O. C. Nico asked curiously, trying to put on a cheerful face. "You're not used to making noise, are you?"

"We're very sorry, sir," Hyman and Koso respectfully replied simultaneously, when they saw he was the one interrupting their thoughts.

"Hah, I don't mean to . . . I'm only joking," he smiled his usual, I-don't-care-smile.

"Thanks . . . sir, but we just heard over the radio . . . a bad news about a Nigerian," they hurriedly said, staring directly at officer Nico for his reaction, "we immediately presume that . . . was he the one, sir?"

"When was Omofuma released?" the good *Beamte* asked, still feeling indecisive as to how he would break or comfirm the sorrowful news to these helpless Africans.

"Presumably on Friday . . . just after mid-day" Hyman assured.

He felt edgy, dreading the sudden sad mood the officer's face appeared to have taken.

"Then, I think he was the one" affirmed O. C. Nico.

He spoke at length, comforting them to take it easy and bear with the situation.

"Look guys, my advise to you is to be calm, and let's see what's going to come out of this, maybe it may even lead to the extinction of this prison camp and many others alike" said O. C. Nico presciently, and tapped Hyman and Koso on their shoulder as he turned to lock the door.

"Thank you sir, we're very appreciative of all your efforts and concern" they called after him and went back to their contemplative mood.

CHAPTER SEVEN

"It is idle, a hollow mockery, for us to pray to God to break the oppressor's power, while we neglect the means of knowledge which will give us the ability to break this power. God will help us when we help ourselves."

===Frederick Douglass (1817-1895).

That afternoon Koso and Hyman felt too weak to go out when it was announced from the prison public address system that it was time for *Spazierengehen*. Yet, they had to go. Firstly, they got only one hour in the whole day to be outside their cell room and secondly, to know if the other prisoners had heard about the news.

It was an atmosphere of tension and suspicion when they eventually emerged from their cell. Many other inmates were staring at them with sorrowful eyes—thinking whether they had heard the news also—for it had been circulating through the prison premises. Everybody that heard about the news was completely dismayed by the sudden death. Nobody knew who would be the next victim. The whole prison camp was undergoing a period of mourning like a big family that suddenly received the news of the death of one important member (bread-winner).

For the fact that Marcus Omofuma had spent over five months there, made it possible for almost every prisoner to recognize or remember his face when they heard the news at first. He was always a convivial man and would easily and amicably converse with other detainees, no matter who you are, whether White (from Eastern European countries), or his fellow African brothers, or Chinese who are always in majority. Even newcomers in the deportation camp adored him, mostly for his vast knowledge of history, politics and current affairs—including what currently happening in the prison quarters.

Occasionally, most of the inmates—mainly the Whites—used to be astounded about his intelligence. Just a day before he was taken away, many of them had gathered around him as he elucidated on the recent 'asylum laws' code named 'Operation Roundup' (OR) which had been promulgated by the government to apprehend more immigrant—citing an increase in crime amongst the immigrant communities and rise in unemployment—as the main reasons.

He was also well known to the prison officials and had charmed many of them with his good manners—including O. C. Nico, who was his confidant and source of survival and most importantly his unofficial source of news. For example, Officer Nicole was the source that tipped him about the Operation Roundup.

Now, this *history wizard* as some of his close friends (both in the deportation prison camp and at the *Traiskirchen Bundesasyl* camp from where he had been arrested and brought to the prison) used to call him, was dead. No more to be seen again. There would be no other person that would replace him as the prison minister of information. 'When the Iroko plant fell down, the birds disperse.' Koso had quoted to Hyman when they first heard the news. And Hyman had accolade, 'like a high-profile prison inmate, he often used his great brilliance to acquire friendship.'

And that had been the sad mood Hyman and Koso found themselves in, as they approached to join other inmates—when one of their good friends, Andrea Volvaskov, from Ukraine, who for the past three months had been awaiting deportation after his final application for asylum had been rejected by the authority—extended his hands in greetings to them as he broached the matter and asked.

"Did you people happen to hear any news?"

"What news?" replied Koso, trying to put on a false front, bluffing that they had not heard anything. "Which news, there're many nowadays?"

Volvaskov held Hyman on the hand.

"I thought you bought a radio the other day, Hyman? Or is it for mere decoration?" Volvaskov joked and added rather seriously, his face changed automatically. "Anyway, it doesn't really matter now . . . the news is every where . . . every radio, TV stations and newspapers. Your friend is dead! Especially it is all over the radios in the past hours."

"Which one of our friends?" inquired Hyman, his eyes widened in pretence and astonishment, "as you know almost four of them had left in the last one week or so?"

"Including Omofuma? I mean *the history wizard*" inquired Volvaskov.

"Yes, of course, he was released last two days or so . . . he was the last to regain his freedom."

"Incredible, I believe what I heard is true . . . but . . ." murmured Volvaskov furiously, nodding in agreement.

He adjusted his biconvex contact glasses and straightened his dark-blue suit, and then added in a very quiet voice.

"It's obvious now, for mere speaking with him the other day . . . even looking at him on Friday . . . it seems he had premonition of death. He was telling me about a terrible dream he had the previous night before the *Beamten* called for the end of the walkaround . . . he didn't finish . . ." Volvaskov was trying to remember. "It was a pity . . ."

"How did they . . . broadcast the news, was it in English or German?" Koso asked.

"Well, I heard it first in German and later it was repeated in English," assured Volvaskov.

"Did the radio mention his name?" Hyman inquired, just for talking sake.

"Not as you would think, you know. These types of news always are . . ."

"He was a very nice fellow to associate with . . . he didn't bear grudges. You never found fault in him," Hyman was saying emotionally, tears spilling down his face. "Believe me Mr. Volvaskov, he was one of the types you can live with your whole life without problems . . . oh! Why did he have to die in such a painful way? Do you know his fare well words to us? I could remember exactly what he said . . . 'I'm still pessimistic about this . . . whole set up . . . I'm still being haunted by this . . . dream of mine', you see, he saw what was coming his way and he wanted to avoid it by all means, but these heartless people . . . oh! oh!!"

"It is okay, that's alright," Volvaskov consoled, as he held Hyman by the shoulder. "Our crying and prayers will never bring him back, but our actions might help to soothe his soul in the spiritual world."

"Oh poor Marcus, I believe his soul would rest in perfect peace," echoed Koso, hissing and all the same, patting at Hyman. "Charlie, be a man! You got to control yourself or we can go back to the cell."

Correspondingly, some other inmates, both those who had heard the news and few who maybe were hearing it for the first time in the *Spazieren*-ground, joined up with them from where they stood at the corner, to commiserate with them for the awful news. The fear of the news seemed to overcome and overwhelm all the inmates. They all felt like cows that are being driven to the same abattoir. No one could help them at these troubling times in their lives, except God. (That is to those who believe in him.)

As they gathered, Andrea Volvaskov looked up at every one of them, cleared his throat and began in a very firm and forceful tone.

"I want every comrade to listen and listen for good. To sit down and cry for the dead will never in anyway help to solve the problems facing us today.

According to 'my' much adored hero and the greatest freedom fighter of all time, Dr. Martin Luther King Jr., 'Our nettleson task is to discover how to organize our strength into compelling power so that government cannot elude our demands. We must develop, from strength, a situation in which the government finds it wise and prudent to collaborate with us. It would be the height of naivety to wait passively until the administration had somehow been infused with such blessing of good nature realism; the other is childish fantasy" he quoted.

He glanced round their faces, his hands inside his trouser pockets, his voice at a very low setting, his eyes blinking, as he went on.

"To cry is to be discouraged, comrades! We'll never fold our arms and expect the gods to come for our rescue. Neither will we allow this atrocity to pass without articulating our grievances. We must rise up to the challenges ahead" suggested Volvaskov, who was a former labour union leader in his country Ukraine.

An outspoken critic of his home governments dictatorial policies against the masses before his recent arrest and imprisonment, after which he fled from his country when the government resumed its clam-down on activists; and he continued in a steady and strong voice.

"Something must be done about this injustice. Comrades, we must react now, because, the consequences of not reacting is greater than the price we may pay in the future or in subsequent events. This attitude of the authorities, I believe will proliferate, and if we all feel apathetic and demoralized, we will all lose the fight individually and collectively. Remember the saying, 'if some Danes are under siege, then all Danes are under siege'" comrade Volvaskov declared in an authoritative voice, staring at the faces of his fellow inmates one after the other, like a politician elaborating on important issues to the electorates in order to win over their votes, while his inmate friends stood silently listening attentively to his address.

The atmosphere was as quiet as a grave yard, as he paused momentarily. He was confident that his address is having an impact in the mind of his co-inmates. He seemed satisfied with his look and went on.

"The powerful should not be allowed to destroy the individual. Death in such a way is not only unnatural and callous, but also unfortunate and painful when it occurs to somebody so young and so fit, like Marcus Omofuma . . . *The history wizard* as many of us have known and called him . . . It was also unbearable especially when he was so closed to you" comrade Volvaskov opined, as he bent and lowered his head in sorrow, trying to let his speech digest on their minds. And like a Shakespearian orator, he added emotionally, "friends, comrades and fellow prisoners of conscience, we come to bury Omofuma and not to praise him . . . so let every comrade start thinking on how this burial will benefit our collective souls" he concluded unflinchingly and lifted his clenched hand in comradeship gesture and shouted. "Esprit de corps"

The atmosphere remained quiet for a while as all the inmates were nodding their heads in a contemplative mood, tears rolling down the cheeks of many, especially the black Africans.

"But, how could we . . . or rather, what could we do to put up a common front?" politely asked Andrew Peters, who had just joined the gathering, sad and very much interested in Volvaskov's incitemental speech.

"What comrade Volvaskov proposed is that we must device feasible and effective means to protest against this wicked and undue behaviour of the Austrian police" Hyman expounded thoughtfully. "We must vehemently raise our voices in unity against racism and nepotism, and strongly condemn this ungodly act."

For the first time that day, he felt he'd gotten back posture and courage because of the spirited speech Volvaskov had just given. He had been contemplating on the same idea all along, but he wasn't sure how the other inmates would react to it. Now that his comrade friend had helped to set up the stage, he thought, there was no going back. He has got to seize the opportunity, as he continued.

"As the saying goes, 'when another man's corpse is being conveyed to Golgotha, the foolish offen took it as bunch of wood', and 'when push suddenly came to shove, then it was no more a joking matter'. The authorities are no more playing. They plan to kill all of us. They've started with Omofuma and they will continue if we all keep our mouth shut. Could we wait until another casualty, then another, and another and . . . before we begin to defend ourselves?" Hyman demanded passionately, pausing for a moment.

"Nai, No, No, No," echoed the whole inmates, murmuring and nodding in disagreement.

"Then, gentlemen! I think it's high time . . . we must demonstrate against this remorseless killing, let us say 'No' to more causalities, let us say 'No' to this policy of forced deportations, let us say 'No' to this illegal entry law" Hyman was saying in a strong, but compassionate tone.

He glanced at comrade Volvaskov, who gestured him with his eyes to continue. He grinned with his eyes and went on.

"Gentlemen, today history would be made in this prison if we would all stand up to our rights. It's now or never."

"But, what do we have to do . . . how can we protest Hyman? I mean, you can suggest one way to start immediately. There isn't much time to waste you know?" interrupted Peters inquisitively.

Being a Nigerian himself and one who was recently taken to the Nigerian Embassy by the 'Fremdenpolizei' to procure his travelling certificate (TC) which would have been used for his deportation—if not the fact that their request had been declined—he was under pressure to support whatever action that would be proposed.

"You must not forget that we're still in confinement, and that our rights to perform many actions are limited. There're limits to whatever we might decide on" Peters suggested and added quickly, because of the way most of the inmates stared despondently at him, "however, I'd be the foolish one to cause discouragement among my fellow comrades. Of course, I'd be the first to endorse anything that we might finally agree on. So the question is what's next?"

"Possibly" said Volvaskov committedly, seeking everybody's attention, "I believe, the first and the only viable action we can undertake for the meantime to fully register our feeling is to adhere to a collective hunger strike."

"For how long?" enquired one of the inmates hurriedly.

A tall, huge man from Kosovo, he had known Omofuma for just two days before his death. Yet he came to like him for his extreme views, mostly his utterly condemnation of the ethnic cleaning of Kosovo Albanians during the recent Kosovo war.

"Well," comrade Volvaskov replied, using a handkerchief to clean his glasses, "well for as long as the authorities will accept and change their stance, as long as these brutal killings and hostilities cease, as long as our freedom is achieved, comrades. Until these demands were accomplished, we'll never stop. We were going to protest with the strongest possible terms . . . other actions might even follow as time goes on . . . nonetheless comrades, I think we were embarking on the right way to our freedom."

There was registered prudent look at the face of many as Volvaskov added his last statements. A good number of the inmates had never before tried to observe even an hour fasting, much more, 'as long as' proposal that the comrade was suggesting, which seemed to most of them like the Bible saying 'Thy kingdom come'. What if the authority would decide to overlook, that means that majority of them might even die of starvation before 'the Messiah comes'. However, they had all felt sad on hearing the news of Marcus death and as one of them had earlier suggested, 'it would better to search for the black goat before night came, because when it became dark it may be too late'. So no one knew who would be the next target. Eventually, none of the inmates said anything discouraging.

"We hope that our goals would be achieved!" Mascovic, the guy from Kosovo uttered at long last. "May the Almighty Allah see us through . . . Insha Allah"

"Insha Allah" echoed all of the inmates.

"What's more, when do we start off" seriously enquired Wakil Muhamet, an Afghanistan man, who was facing deportation with his family of four—his wife and their two little children-, and had spent four months already in the prison camp. "I agree and would like every one of us to kindly accede to this planned action."

"I think, we will all try and comply with this action if we are to tell ourselves the truth" Koso Osei contributed for the first time.

He had earlier on dismissed the plan when Hyman brought up the idea in their cell room, citing the fact that most of the inmates would never like the ploy, in which case, he feared the authority would overlook few of them that may have decided on it. Now he had been proven wrong and Hyman had been right for the second time that day. The consensus among the prisoners was encouraging and overwhelming.

"Of course, we've no other option than to follow this route, owing to the fact that the melody song has suddenly turned to a war song" Koso asserted.

"Comrades" Volvaskov called out in the same mild tone of voice, somehow happy that his plan was taking a positive shape. "Do we've any opposition? Except those of us who may have been on patient list . . . like Diabetic patients or people that are placed on a special diet. Apart from those individuals who fell into these categories, do we all agree to embark on this journey?"

"Yee . . . Yao . . . Yee . . . Yao" murmured the prisoners of conscience simultaneously.

"Let every comrade be warned that this journey may never be so easy!" comrade Volvaskov shouted over their murmurings.

"Whatever be the outcome, we would abide . . . we . . . would . . . abide . . ." they all seem to be chanting . . . "We would abide . . . we . . . would abide . . ."

"Then, we must begin at once, let the action start immediately from this *Spazieren*-ground . . . comrades, the action from this afternoon's meal! We all agreed?" he asked.

"Agreed, agreed," all the prison inmates echoed, few of them in a voice that put doubt in their ability that they would fully liaise with other, while many of them believed that the hunger strike action would eventually help speed their course to freedom.

Few minutes later, the *Spazieren* was over, and the inmates silently went back to their various prison cells, with the first course of action already on board.

++

By 3 pm, that same day, even before evening food of boiled potatoes with vegetable was served to them, the hunger strike action had already taken full effect. Up from the third Stock, down to the first floor of the prison, the story was the same.

'*Danke*' (Thanks). I'm sorry; I'm okay!'

Almost all the detainees declined to be served, with the exception of very few—and others that were on diets (mainly sick ones). At first, the prison warders, who were escorting the workers that share the foods, thought the prisoners were joking. But after they approached many cell rooms and received the same response, they began to assimilate the shock of the action. Many of the *Beamten* questioned the inspiration and possibility of what the inmates thought this their selfish action would lead to.

However, having done that and having received no concrete answer from any of the prisoners, they came to the conclusion that as a matter of fact, it was not a joking matter. Rather, it was an urgent and serious issue that needed to be reported at the top.

++

Eventually, two subordinate officers were sent to report this rare phenomenon (for in the history of the camp, there had never been any collective hunger strike. Hunger strike issues had always been an individual affair). The officers went and reported to the chief-*Beamte*. The chief was at first a bit surprised and refused to intervene. 'That should be their individual problem. I think one has the right to say yes or no to free food. You do not force one when he declines a gift, do you?' he had told the officers that came to report to him. But, after much protests from the two *Beamten* that the situation was rather a serious one, the chief-*Beamte* consented to go around with them to see if he would be able to use his rank to persuade the prison inmates to rethink and abandon their threat.

Basically none of the warders would have been concerned in what was going on among the prisoners, if not for what happened to Omofuma. The negative effects the news bore already and the unanimousness and complete unison with which the inmates confronted their task.

"So, what's your opinion on these prisoners and their actions" the chief *Beamte* vaguely inquired from his subordinate officers.

They were descending down the stairs way towards the corridor.

"Do you think they were right or not?"

"These *Schweine* had no right whatsoever to perpetrate this, sir!" callously remarked one of the warder, Rudi, who had been questioning his colleagues on why they should be so worried about the inmates refusing to accept their food. "Whatever might have happened, sir, I believe they must be stupid to reject food. These prisoners do not have any right to refuse food."

"Listen Rudi, it takes one thing to be a criminal prisoner and another thing altogether to be a lawful prisoner. Let it be in your mind, that these people are not in anyway criminals and they should never be treated as such" O. C. Nico snapped at officer Rudi defensively. "Let's not forget that most of these fellows had been forced out from their various countries due to life threatening circumstances. For instance, some fled as a result of war in their countries; many absconded due to intimidations and direct torture from their home government. I personally spoke with many of them and . . ."

"You forgot to add that many of them . . . in fact, almost everyone of them according to recent statistics, nearly seventy percent were just economic refugees . . . Mr. Psychologist or Mr. Sympathizer, I don't know which to refer you as . . ." officer Rudi said impatiently. "Yeah, of course, they had to concoct different sympathetic stories about themselves and their families and their countries, or else no one would believe them . . . countless stories . . . 'Oh, I lost all my family members in a war' . . . 'The government had declared me wanted because of my involvement in this and that . . . 'I broke down the prison wall and escaped . . .'" officer Rudi mockingly recounted, his face in grimace. "Or, when you simply ask how they managed to come over here . . . 'Yeah, a Catholic Priest helped me out . . . ' 'I flew without passport' . . . 'I was smuggled out through the ship' . . . 'I walked all the way from Africa to Europe' . . . and uncountable other stories . . . ?" Rudi stated scornfully, describing every one of the inmates as being untruthful about their asylum stories . . . "Sir, I swear these crooks were all economic migrants who found their ways here in the name of wars and persecutions and yet, bringing along with them every sort of criminal activities."

"I agree and still disagree with some of your opinions," O. C. Nico maintained. "I believe few of them may fabricate their stories because of one reason or the other, nevertheless the majority of them have more acute, genuine and intractable problems. There's no doubt about that. You've to look at . . . or listen to what?"

"BINGO" called out officer Rudi at O. C. Nico, a note mockery in his voice. "Did you forget, my friend that the look in man's eyes was not evident, they will continue to deceive liberal-minded folks like you, and not my very self . . . NEVER!!!NEVER!!!" he shook his head in disagreement, his voice a bit higher and insulting.

"Gentlemen that's enough, that's ok," interrupted the chief *Beamte* jokingly.

A good and patient listener, he always knew when a joke had turned to an insult. He put on his friendly smile as he motioned his officers to cool it off.

"I didn't intend my question to be personal . . . I only asked your opinion about this action. Besides, I presume the inmates staged this protest against what happened to their former fellow inmate. Personally, I denounced the action but that did not mean they were totally wrong. In fairness, they were right in what they were doing . . . I mean, I think they've every right . . ."

Officer Rudi stared at the chief disappointedly.

"Chief Hum . . . Oh! *Nein*! *Nein*! Even you, sir?" Rudi cried out bitterly. "You sounded as though you were supportive of this mess, when did you join the liberal ranks, sir?"

The chief-*Beamte* smiled at Rudi.

"My son, one doesn't have to belong to the Liberal Forum or the Green party before he would say the truth. Well, that is not a matter of joining ranks. We're now living in a world that's dying to ascertain the truth, while the truth is being suppressed everyday" the chief argued with a great solemnity. "However, the fact of this matter is, it was terribly upset and devilishly bad for a man to die in the same way Mr. O. died. It was a mortal sin that was committed," the chief maintained, lowering his voice as they stopped in front of the first cell room.

+++

Apparently, the chief-*Beamte* and his subordinate officers seemed to agree and disagree in principle on various opinions. But, one thing that was absolutely clear to everyone of them was the fact that the inmates had avowed and persevered in spite of threats from the junior ranking warders. When in the long run, the chief and his men arrived at the A/B stock cell 1, which fortuitously was the cellroom Marcus Omofuma had stayed in all his days in the prison camp before his death; and of which the only occupants now were Hyman and Koso, the chief became aghast at how they remained adamant, unconcerned and very busy playing their poker cards . . . when the iron-door was silently unlocked. They did not even care to look up from the corner where they sat around a tiny table.

After watching them momentarily, the chief called out to Koso and Hyman.

"Hey! Meine Jungen, . . . grüssen . . . Guten Tag" the chief greeted politely.

Immediately, Koso and Hyman jilted the cards in their hands and stood up, stared at the officers who had by now covered the door way. If there was any surprise on why the chief *Beamte* himself would appear so quickly to intervene, it did not show on the face of the Africans who scowled at them defiantly. Instead, they were a bit reluctant to return the greeting.

"Good evening, sir," both of them replied, trying to appear nonchalant about the sudden interference.

"Wie geht es Euch?"

"Gut, aber nicht sehr gut!" Hyman replied in his adulterated German.

"Für mich ist alles ganz schlecht!" Koso added.

"Warum so schlecht?" the chief asked.

"Because we lost a very close and trusted African brother" Koso answered in English, unable to continue in German.

The chief asked why they refused to accept their food, and candidly told them that it was a right thing for them to mourn their dead friend. Nonetheless, it didn't sound right to do it in this manner. He also condemned the inmate's niggardliness about the action.

"This hunger strike may eventually turn out to be a disastrous decision for you," moaned the chief indistinctly. "Did you put your health into consideration before advancing on this selfish resolution?" he barked at them, losing his temper.

"Sir, I thought this is the only way for me to show my grief over the death of Omofuma. Chief, how could I eat? What appetite do I have, when my friend and roommate was out there dead" said Hyman mournfully, tears treading down his cheeks. "Chief, how do I convince myself I wouldn't be the next target?"

"And beside, in Africa, we were not keen on eating . . . when a young man of this age dies" Koso lied. "Especially, when that person dies in such mysterious manner Omofuma died. As Africans, we were expected to go through periods of intensive miseries. Until we're able to find out the mystery surrounding such death . . . we don't eat and we don't bathe."

"You see my point" officer Rudi whispered to his colleagues. "These Bimbos were . . . ever-ready in telling stories . . . believe me, they can swing you around at any given time. You can't even hear a single truth from anyone of them. Even when they greet you, 'Good morning' . . . you can still detect an atom of untruthfulness from it."

"But, he may be correct about what he just said. That's African tradition" O. C. Nico interjected. "He'd said it's the African way. And not European way or the global way or are you from Africa?"

"BINGO!" Rudi grinned, still in a low voice. "There you go again . . . You might still believe him if he told you they would never eat again until Africa became a super-power."

All the officers, including O. C. Nico and others who had joined them, laughed over Rudi's jokes, after which the chief *Beamte* advised.

"Listen children, it's possible for you to mourn your friend without placing your health in a dangerous position . . . You must retreat over your plan. Ok my good friends. And lets wait for the decision of the authority."

"Sir, I don't mean to sound unruly, yet, I can't and will not" Koso stated thoughtfully. "Even the hunger strike is the beginning. More actions would follow as time goes on. There's an African adage . . . 'A Bird (the black Kite) said that hence men have learnt how to shoot without missing, it had learned how to fly without perching . . . Got it?"

"Meaning what?" the chief asked interestedly.

He felt himself caught unaware not only by the rudeness of Koso and Hyman, but also by their astute remarks. He had never had the opportunity to really speak intensively with any African inmate as he had been doing at that very hour. For him it was a kind of an eye-opener as he stared at the Africans open-mouthed, as if they came down from the space.

"Meaning what!?" he repeated.

"Meaning 'we' are not going to turn back from 'our' plan . . . Period" Koso replied authentically, frowning, his face. "No, we will not back down . . . under no pressure. We rather go down with the ship."

"I said it before hand" murmured officer Rudi teasely to his chief.

He glanced round at his colleagues and back at the Africans, looking irked and hard-nosed.

"There's no need talking with these hard-bitten prisoners. They've already made up their minds, and nothing would change their witless stances, unless drastic measures were taken in return or we could even disregard them entirely. Sir, could you imagine their lofty utterances?"

The chief *Beamte* was nodding thoughtfully all this while. He had detected some meaningful remarks from Koso's last statement. 'We' and 'Our' 'He may've been underrating how coordinated the action had been' he thought. Instantly he started to calculate in his mind, the shape the wordings of his immediate report to the prison commandant would take. Now he had been assured as to the collectiveness of the action, the report already had priority.

Meanwhile, officer Rudi and O. C. Nico continued their heated argument, for or against the immigrants and the position they had taken, with the other subordinate officers taking sides or just been neutral.
At the end, the chief and his men having said all they had to say, and done all they could, agreed that their mission had failed, at least for now. He infuriatingly ordered their cell door be locked and they left for other cell rooms. Their stories of defiance were echoed by other prisoners.

++

The next morning, being Monday the 3rd of May, after glancing through the report drafted and signed by Martin Baur, the chief-*Beamte* who parenthetically was also the second-in command in the prison hierarchy, and who incidentally had tried all his possible best to persuade the inmates to end the hunger strike yesterday evening; Commandant Christian Gospel furiously asked his secretary to arrange an emergency meeting of all the high ranking officers in the prison. The main agenda to be discussed according to the circular his personal assistant was directed to distribute is 'the most startling dilemma that befell this prison since its inception'. He bossily ordered her to stop all she had for the day and to make the meeting her primary concern.

"Look, the tension is very high and this problem must be resolved immediately or else, all the press will devour us" he had told his PA.

++

"This hunger strike action is a complex problem which required a complex solution," the commandant began solemnly, after he had greeted the audience.

They were all sitting quietly around the round mahogony table inside the mini-conference hall within the prison office block. He stared round at them to make sure everyone of them was listening attentively.

"Some of you might have heard about the recent happenings in our prison, since yesterday evening . . . but for the benefit of those of you, who are not aware . . . there was a collective hunger strike going on among the whole prison inmates."

He paused, momentrily to acknowledge shock reactions of his executive board members who were hearing the news for the first time. Instantaneously few of the officers bent their heads against each other and whispered together. He glanced at their faces and saw how what he had just said changed the atmosphere as they all seemed to be listening with all alacrity. Many of them had not heard about it and equally could not believe it, as such a thing had not been heard of before. There had never been a collective hunger strike in the prison. It had always been an indiviual thing. The shock showed in their eyes.

"Of course, as you might have known, this was already having a deleterious effect in our prison premises. I must inform you that it horrified me personally that these incidents were transpiring in one of the darkest periods in the history of this prison. These reports right here on my desk written by Martin Baur, the chief-*Beamte*. And I would love if he could please elaborate on it before we proceed. So, gentlemen and ladies let's listen to him attentively."

"*Guten Morgen* . . . ladies and gentlemen" greeted Martin Baur contritely, bowing his head with courtesy, like a catholic Priest officiating, a mass. His face puffy and haggard, yet, in full control of himself. "As you've heard from the commandant, I personally witnessed and supervised this uproar yesterday. In fact, what I saw and heard from these inmates . . . I meant, how determined and in unity with which they expressed their grievances baffled me. I was in my office at about 15:45 pm yesterday, when my subordinates came to report that almost all the prisoners they had so far confronted, had declined to accept their food. The officers complained about the seriousness of the inmate's stance. I became furious and finally I decided to go along with them, hoping that my presence would persuade them to change their minds. But, I was totally wrong. Individually and collectively, they maintained, that 'it had been observed in honour of their dead friend Marcus Omofuma'. Not even my argument that the action would endanger their health and that it could not help their course could convinced them. Yet, what perplexed me most was how loyal they all seem to their deceased friend, and how awful serious they take the issue."

The chief paused, as he straightened his dark-green *Beamten* uniformed suit, his shoulder sloping, ashamed that all his efforts to stop the inmates from carrying out their actions did not work.

"And obviously I was struck anew at the mysterious way human beings communicate with each other and how quickly these prisoners were able to spread their actions, bearing in mind that they did not do *Spazieren* together. Permit me to say this, because it wasn't included in my report (out of commission or omission). 'The officers on night duty yesterday reported the continuous chanting and disruption the inmates created throughout the night and the fear that this will continue today. These prisoners are resolute and united absolutely in carrying out this action, with some of them openly threatening to do something ugly in due course. In that case, I would like each of us to please use his or her good humour and prudence when contributing to the solutions of this sensitive plight. Thank you all."

He made a bow once more and doffed his officer's cap.

Following his somehow long emotional speech, the audience applauded heavily for his vivid account and how he had attempted to halt the insurgent act at the onset. Later, when the ovation had died down, the commandant stood up and thanked the chief *Beamte* for his efforts; and he also used the opportunity to remind (the officers, with few civilians around) that the Interior Minister directed that the situation should be handled with care and the problems be resolved amicably as soon as possible, noting that the eye of the world were focused on Austria, and the entire ministry of Internal Affaires to see how these situations should be controlled.

"You've heard from *Herrn* Baur himself," said the commandant promptly, his bald head and smooth face with thick black 'Hitler moustache' glittered together with some colourful ribbons attached to upper side of the breast pocket of his officer's uniform. At sixty years, he still looked strong and very fit for his post. Lifting his voice a bit higher, he went on. "It's all about using our individual human senses to arrive at a genuine and amiable panacea for this problem."

He used his white handkerchief to brush his sweaty forehead, sat down.

"I'd like to know if there were any given directives from the ministry," asked Michael Schuller solicitously. "I suppose they would've known how to deal with such situations better?"

"Yeah, I forgot, no, there was no directive. I reported about the action to the ministry only a few hours ago as soon as I saw the report" answered the commandant modestly. "But, it was obvious they were paralysed now considering the load in their heads already."

"Well, I'm of the opinion that this cannot cause us any headache nor would we just sit tight here dissipating our precious time on what's basically trivial," uttered Michael Schuller negligently, confirming his extremist and anti-immigrant beliefs.

He had been a high class representative of the extreme right party in the prison establishment . . . for that had been the Austrian culture. All the top political parties have high ranking officers that are affiliated to, who represent their various interests in many governmental establishments, including the police, army, labour union etc.; and for Michael Schuller, who had had a heated argument with his wife that same morning before coming to work . . . concerning her passionate stance on Omofuma case, this time was the exact opportunity to make his extreme views known.

"It baffles me as to why anybody should be disconcerted on whether these fugitives stopped eating their 'gratis' food? . . . They did not work for this food. Nobody gives a damn if they eat or don't eat" he stated bluntedly. "Look, I think we better discuss other things . . . these bloody prisoners will eventually come back to their senses if we forget thinking about them."

"We can always learn from the mistakes of our enemies as well as our friends," interjected chief Baur courteously, signalling 'no, no, no' with his finger.

He stared at officer Schuller in mockery disbelief, and continued in the same solemn voice.

"I must warn you ladies and gentlemen, that if we suddenly take offence and leave this issue to fester without due considerations . . . we will all live to regret our decision. I implore everybody to cool his or her temper and set aside biased views. Let us be rational in our deliberations. We can make history when we handle this with care or the contrary history would be made if this minor problem turned cataclysmic."

"A novelist wrote in one of his books that 'once power is out of hand, or the situation produced by power is out of hand, there is nothing anyone can do. The problem everywhere is how to control power,'" quoted Dr. Cinthya Rabl.

A woman in her fifties, and the chief medical attaché to the deportation prison camp; who had worked with the prison authorities for almost twenty years, including her services in different prison—both criminal and non-criminal prisons. Ashen in complexion, ashen hair, about 5ft2 in height, she wore a glint light-brown rimmed reading glasses to match her well tailored light-brown suit. She always had a sunny disposition with herself.

She stood up from her seat as chief Baur stared at her and saw who had interrupted him and sat down quietly.

"I would suggest, with my position as the chief medical officer to be entrusted along with the chief psychologist"
She briefly starred at the psychologist, who nodded his head that she was on track as they had discussed earlier.

"To deal with this matter, we would be glad if asked to examine and see what we could come up with concerning this problem. For the meantime, I think it's more a psychological problem that these inmates had than what some of us were forced to believe."

She glanced at the commandant, then at Michael Schuller, controlling her anger against his comments, as she adjusted her glasses.

"I strongly believe that with the assistance of our chief psychologist, whom I had trusted for over fifteen good years as a working colleague and his team, together with my own team, we might be able to change the present situation . . . to at least a better standing."

"When your team with that of the psychologist tried and the situation remained unchanged?" enquired the commandant anxiously. "What, then could be done . . . what would the next step be? You've heard everything *Herr* Baur said regarding these prisoners that they had already made up their."

Dr. Rabl smiled at him.

"There would always be alternative ways, Mr. Commandant. We have to count one before counting two."

"Men need order, Commandant," shouted Michael Schuller with a grinding emphasis of hatred and bitterness. "I'd be the last person to believe in the school of thought that said persuasion should be the only way this issue would be tackled."

"Nobody said that, *Herr* Schuller, we're only trying to look at the mirror from the front side and not from the back side as you've suggested" Dr. Rabl snapped.

Michael Schuller was annoyed for her abrupt manner, but he did not care to look her way as he continued in his narrow-minded stand.

"There must be other forceful methods to resolve this so called problem. And let me say this once and for all. 'Any softly-softly precedent that we will apply now would surely have a very bad portent for this prison in the future. I foresee no reason why these fugitive criminals should be threatening an establishment that had been in existence for ages."

"Point of correction, *Herr* Schuller" protested the commandant hastily, interrupting and at the same time flagging his hand in disagreement, being indignant at Michael Schuller. "There was no record that said these people were here because of any criminal offence, so stigmatizing them as criminals is unacceptable, and moreover, I would never permit the abusive remarks in this meeting anymore, enough of that. To the best of my knowledge, this would not be a personal issue. Nor should some of us use it as an advantage to bear grudges. The pride of this prison is at stake, gentlemen and ladies, but I assure you, in shortest possible time we would all overcome this uncomfortable circumstance . . . As the saying goes: Slow and steady always wins the race."

It was later endorsed by many at the meeting that the best option so far was to allow the doctors and psychologists to carry out their scheme and to report back to the executive board of the prison by the same time the next day on what they would be able to achieve.

CHAPTER EIGHT

"But when they bring you in before public assemblies and government official and authorities, do not become anxious about how or what you will speak in defence or what you will say; for the holy spirit will teach you in that very hour the things you ought to say."

===Luke 12:11-12.

Immediately the officers had left, the team of doctors and psychologists decided to invite the prison imates one after the other, rather than counselling them on a communal basis. The idea for the individual approach was suggested by the chief psychologist who determined that it would be an easier and more effective method to confront this problem. He also advised his colleagues not to use any harsh words on the prisoners regardless of how obstinate or naughty some of them might appear to be.

"You should all remember that the ethics matters most before anything in our profession. The 'Beamten', I presume, would remain in an ambience of frenzied expectancy yet, I think we all simply have to acknowledge that it would never be an easy task. Nevertheless, I still believe that it's not an impossible mission" the chief psychologist had advised his colleagues enthusiastically, as silly smile popped up his face. "I'm optimistic that all things being equal, and with my confidence in your abilities, we would settle this whole matter quietly. Always bear in mind that when you deal with snakes, you learn to be a snake charmer."

Hyman Otta quietly followed a *Beamte* while the other offficer came behind him with a baton in hand like they were escorting a dangerous criminal. He limped weakly over a side walk. It was all he could do to climb the stairs to the oblong room which Dr. Rabl used as her personal office. The *Beamte* knocked at the dark-green painted wrought iron door. The door widely opened and he was ordered in. Hyman entered, stared around the room, and recognized the doctor at once. (He frequently met with her because of his leg ulcer problem, which he got when he was beaten and imprisoned by the Sudanese rebel leaders). The interior of the office was painted milk-coloured, and sparsely furnished. The walls were ornamented with posters like a typical hospital waiting-room. Some affiche display many chronic diseases affiliated with human lives. One portrait directly behind the doctor's desk being that of a young woman diagnosed as having HIV symptoms breastfeeding her child. Another portrait was that of two teenage junkies sharing needles together.

One of the female nurses scooped out some books and files out of a big bookshelf adjacent to where the chief psychologist were sitting and deposited it on the table in front of the doctor, as she whispered something to the chief psychologist stooping her neck, and in a quick movement, Dr. Rabl straightened up towards Hyman, her face shining and glistening with much powder, rouge and eye-make up, all in the same light-brown colour of her suit, with a soft shade of lipstick that made her look hard and artificial.

Dr Rabl smiled lightly at Hyman and greeted, glancing at the dossier on her desk.

"Good morning Mr . . . Hmm Mr. Otta. You can take your seat and have a little chat with us."

"Good morning doctor, morning, sirs."

Hyman stared pleasantly at the doctor and the two men sitting beside her, gazing bleakly at the floor, still standing nervously.

"*Morgen, junger Mann*" answered the chief psychologist. "Why don't you sit down" he asked, as he stretched out his hand in greeting, and at the same time pointing at a vacant armchair opposite the doctor. "You'd speak German? Mr. Otta."

"Thanks" Hyman replied as he sat down facing the doctor. "Oh! No frankly I would like to learn the German language, but had not got the opportunity. I was attending the language course before my arrest" he said forthrightly unable to conceal his amazement of how politely they seemed to be to him so far. He thought, they would have been shouting at him as he stubbornly entered the room.

"Do you smoke Mr. Otta?" the chief psychologist asked, as he lit a stick of cigarette, offering him the opened cigarette packet.

"No, thank you sir" Hyman declined politely. "I haven't tasted cigarette since I was born" he lied.

"Coffee?,"

"*Nein* . . . , *danke*, it makes me to vomit every time I perceive the odour."

"I'm Mag. Robert Rupp, the chief psychologist, as you might know and here is Dr. Rabl, and Mag. Fredmund Koch my assistant" introduced the chief psychologist, his custom-made dark suit and signature hairstyle, with his bushy moustache and goatee, and oversized horn-rimmed glasses glinting. "We would like to put forward some questions to you and would expect to get very straight answers from you . . . you got me?"

"Yeah" Hyman murmured.

"First, who organized this action?" the chief psychologist asked concretely.

"I don't understand what you mean, sir?"

"He meant how was this action organized and spread in such a short time without notice," explained the assistant psychologist.

"Oh! Is that what you mean, I don't know sir."

"You said, you don't know, then, how did you hear about it and how come you're involved?" inquired the chief psychologist calmly.

"I don't know that either; is it obligatory that I must know?" Hyman asked impatiently. "Has Austria also laws that say one must know everything."

"Listen, Mr. Otta, I believe you could help yourself by co-operating with us and being unambiguous, not being snobbish" advised the chief psychologist couteously in a very soft and mild tone, "Who knows, you may even receive an 'impromptu liberty' . . . Did this sound important to you? That is, do you believe it could happen right now, right from this office . . . Mr. Otta?"

He raised his eyebrow in assurance and gave out wistful smile, dragging from his cigarette, sending the sequence smoke upwards.

"Yet, it's only one thing that would guarantee the feasibility of it happening, *junger Mann*, your maximum fraternization. I don't know if you understand what I mean?"

Hyman could not believe his ears. The same type of tricky words they used for Marcus Omofuma that had sent him to his *last journey*. He tried to remember the word Omofuma had said the reference officer used. 'Yes, that he had been released on provisional release order' Hyman remembered and laughed in his mind, 'I would never be a fool to accept your bogus freedom assurance' he uttered silently. He was not a fool nor was he a betrayer and beside how could he implicate himself. He shook his head, remembering the warning one of the inmates had shouted to him while being brought here by the warders. The man had told him that the officials were promising heaven and earth to get to the root of what was now known as 'hunger strike scandal.

"Sir, I understood you very well, but the fact is under no context would I be broken. I'm involved because I am supposed to be involved. So, I would certainly not be a traitor or Judas as you might be proposing to me. You better advise your government and police to abolish this law of illegal entry and to stop these unjust killings, than wasting your time trying to find faults where there's no fault."

"*Junger Mann*, were you not afraid to speak to us like that?" asked Rupp.

"No sirs. No ma, because, I had the spirit of the 'living One' with me and He had directed me to say the truth, no matter what. You asked me to tell you the organizer of this action. Well God is and was the sole organizer. However, I would like you to know that 'he who prepares the pounded yam of stones in the mortar of atrocity must eat the food with the soup of dust in the plate of agony. This is an adage in my native land."

"Mr. Otta, what could this adage of yours and your rudeness meant?" demanded the assistant psychologist.

"Sir, our friend did not die a natural death (hence, the hunger strike action pivoted on it). I still believe he was strangled," Hyman said, his lips trembling and he was tearful. "I was with him in the same cell room for almost . . . for one he did not grouch about a single pain in the head, sirs, madam not even once. Now he was a dead man, Uhu . . . Uhu . . ."

"That's ok, that's . . . ." comforted the chief psychologist.

He touched him lightly on the shoulder.

"Pay attention to me just for a little while, I knew you were concerned about your friend. But, I'm sorry I am not here to discuss that with you. I'm worried that you and your friends don't know what you are getting yourselves into. Young man, be reminded that refusing to eat your food can be hazardous. Didn't you realize malnutrition could cause havoc to your system . . . Mr. Otta?"

"Yes, of course, it could even damage your health and might render . . ." reiterated the doctor a bit grumpily.

She had earlier admonished using only a soft approach, but now seem to be losing patience after speaking with more than ten of the inmates without any progress.

"This stance of yours is absolutely wrong, I've to warn you."

"I concurre doctor, but my stance is my stand."

"You did not think this stand is a selfish one?"

She said this in a grave voice, angry chill swept over her, angry that Herr Michael Schuller would laugh over their failure to convince these hardened set of prisoners.

"Do you know the rule of hunger strike in this prison?"

"No, ma, I don't know."

"Then, listen carefully, you have to lose ten to fifteen kilos of weight before you would be considered eligible for release, and secondly you must be moved from your present cell room and taken to a more restricted cell from where you would be coming for doctor's control till you completed your fifteen kilos task. Anything less than ten kilos would not help, and even with that, when you were released . . . remember, the police could still re-arrest you again because you were still illegal person in Austria."

She meant what she had said for it had been the law that if anyone undergoes a hunger strike in the prison for illegal entry, the police still had the right to arrest that person until he or she completed six months term, in which case he or she would not be arrested again for two years. After a period of two years had past, he or she would be entitled to be arrested for another six months.

She glanced directly at Hyman's frowned face as she explained this to him, bitterly aware she had spoken the truth, but in rude manner.

"And afterwards it may turn out a dreadful experience for you . . . Mr. Otta . . . you see why you must co-operate with us to save yourself the agony of being everlasting prisoner in Austria?"

Hyman Otta stared upward for a moment, being human, he was very afraid of this latest threat from the doctor. Someone had told him about this six month in two years laws, but he had not believed him, yet, now, the chief doctor had confirmed it. 'Did he really want to be a prisoner forever because he came to Austria as a result of threatening from the rebels at home? Would he agree with them and may be released actually or should he remain adamant after all he was not the only one in this. All these he thought for a while and then declared respectively.

"One thing is certain, I was convinced this was one and the best way I could mourn my friend and regain my freedom. I don't give a damn . . . about dreadful experience or whatever that will come out of it . . . in whatever way you look at it, it will only result to death" he said with a scowl on his face. "Yeah, I would rather have to die a righteous death here in the prison than going through such humiliation that Omofuma went through . . ."

"That would not be necessary, my dear young man. Indeed, not," interrupted Mag. Fredmund Koch decisively, "you should not die mourning your friend, would you? Was it your custom in Africa? I don't think it is wise."

"No, sir, but in as much as African police are known as being corrupt, inefficient and disrespecters of human rights, my common sense told me that they wouldn't have done such a thing in such a judgemental manner. How could they?" he asked and gave deep sigh. "This is a very bad time for the police. Its departments are full of intriguers who are really willing to intimidate and maltreat immigrants. Yes, most of them are malicious traitors."

"Malicious traitors" shouted the doctor back at him furiously. "Do you know what you're saying or have you lost your senses."

"I haven't doctor" spurtered Hyman, "I'm only speaking the truth. My Bible told me that it's only truth that will set us free."

The chief psychologist gave a wistful smile, somehow awkwardly.

"I did not mean to pry into your affairs, Mr. Otta. Or could I say 'Bible Guru.' Not withstanding, I supposed it's my duty to advise you against your precarious moves. 'Better safe than sorry' this action would do you no good. It's a good thing for one to mourn or to remember a dead friend, but, that doesn't warrant extreme sadness and suicidal mourning as you had been doing" he asserted. "Too much of everything, they say, is too bad."

"Admitted, sir . . . still and all, he was a very brilliant young man. Had it been you knew him or had got in contact with him, sir, you would have liked him and probably became sad yourself. Could you imagine what it looked like, for such brain to escape and flee from his country because of life threatening problems and coming over here for protection, instead he got killed."

"Okay, lets say, you had to shoulder a lot of pain. He was your friend, and you've been with him to know him better" the doctor said, ranting. "The fact is, he's dead now and I did not think anything could change the situation . . . listen, you could keep your friend in your heart and memory, but organizing this silly act of defiance cannot help. Did you think your friend would've loved what you were doing now? I bet he would rather have advised you not to . . ."

"He would've done the same and even more . . . yet, that's not the issue now. The thing is I cannot see that as tragedy, madam."

"Mr. Otta, if I may ask, how far did you go in your education and what did you study?" queried Mag. Robert Rupp, pondering over, how bold Hyman had been with his well spoken orthodox English.

Hyman recounted depairingly.

"Gracefully, sir . . . I was a student of St John's Theological Seminary in my native Dinka land, Southern Sudan; and ought to have graduated next year, if not my predicaments. All my aspiration then was to become a priest of God. Perchance, I would've been ordained in two years time, but all my hopes were now in disarray . . ."

"No wonder, the fault lay entirely with your African-Christian-Anglo-Saxon Puritanism" Mag. Rupp remarked.

"Mr. Otta, you're a very intelligent young man who would aspire to excel in life. Why not take my advice and help yourself? Why can't you be careful with your health" Dr. Rabl asked. "Don't be a . . ."

Hyman sounded anxiously.

"One cannot be too careful in difficult times."

He glanced at the doctor and the two men that sat beside, anticipating that one of them will utter another word, but, there was only the sound of his breathing. He swallowed and said in a tiny voice.

"Well I will try to think over your proposal. It had been a great relief in a way for me to be given the opportunity to air my views" he said pleasantly. "I'd appreciate all your advice and concern about my well-being. Thanks and God bless you."

The chief psychologist stared directly at Hyman's small dark-brown eyes.

"Not yet, could I say your main reason for not co-operating with us, was because of your connivance in co-ordinating this act . . . Mr. Otta!" the chief psychologist insinuated bluntly. "Indeed I'd have the suspicion that you were the masterminder of this action. With the level of your thinking and attitudes so far, one can easily see it . . . Is that not true, Mr. Otta?"

"I'm flattered, sir, yet, I don't think it matters now anyway!" Hyman said a bit modestly. "Or are we going back to square one? Believe me it doesn't, for one cannot question God's authority, can one?"

"Oh yeah, it mattered a lot because I believe one of you would eventually confess as to . . . you got me? By then it might be too late for you. Remember, you could only trust yourself, but could not always trust others. I'm not trying to threaten you, Mr. Otta, however, it would turn out severe and traumatic experience if we later found out that you had a hand in this. Better look for a way to disorganize this now, Mr. Otta. Better be safe than sorry" warned the chief psychologist committedly. "Better be safe than sorry."

"Then, you could look for your informant and please allow me to go back to my cell."

Mag. Rupp charged accusingly.

"Mr. Otta, I put it to you, that it's only you among these inmates have the brain or whatever it will take to stop this action."

"You were only flattering me more and more, I'm nobody."

"Of course, you were our man, someone had already confessed to that," the doctor bluntly said, as she dropped the handset of the intercom extension on her desk. "One of the inmates had just told my colleague in the other office . . ."

"Really" asked Hyman nonchalantly.

"It's so, that's what he phoned and reported" Dr. Rabl assured.

"Then, I think it's a matter of confidentiality to my own person, if that is the case," Hyman answered a bit annoyed, losing his temper for the first time. "This was a question of depriving ones liberty and basic rights. In a society where there was justice and respect for human rights, I believe one should had the guts to stand up for his rights and take non-violent actions if he felt his rights had been infringed or at least stand against such tyranny."

"Mr. Otta, speaking of infringement of rights, I did not think any of your rights had been infringed by anyone, or did you think otherwise?" Mag. Koch curiously asked, afraid that Hyman discerned the phone trick.

"Hum so many times. No single day that passed on which we were not ill-treated here and many of us were been subjected to excessive verbal and physical pressure by the authorities, sir, I swear by God."

The chief psychologist found himself speculating for some seconds, looking at the doctor, and at his colleague.

"As a matter of fact, I did not actually know this, though, of course, I'm not trying to defend anybody. I think this conversation had finally come to an end, Mr. Otta. We could call it a day."

"Thanks, once again," said Hyman excitedly.

He felt a sure of happiness that he had not had for so long.

"You've been a great help for me."

"At the very least, young man," Mag. Rupp said, seeing the excitement in Hyman's eyes and noticing that his colouring had improved after such a short time. "I don't know what's ahead of you, but I wish you much luck!"

Hyman left them there and was met outside the door by the warders, who were still waiting. They escorted him back the corridor to the rear of the building, back to his cubby. He was contemplating what their next move might be. Full of determination that nothing would make him change his mind.

CHAPTER NINE

"If there is no struggle, there is no progress. Those who profess to favour freedom and yet deprecate agitation are men who want crops without plowing up the ground. They want rain without thundering and lighting. They want the oceans without the awful roar of its many waters. This struggle may be a moral one, or it may be a physical one, or it may be both moral and physical, but it must be a struggle. Power concedes nothing without a demand. It never did and it will . . . Men may not get all the pay for in this world, but they must certainly pay for all they get."

===Frederick Douglas

It was around 1 pm when Hyman finally came back to his cell. He didn't see his fellow roommate Koso Osei. 'Where would he be now? It might be that they had come and taken him as soon as he finished with them. Did they invite him before he came back? Or was it a coincidence. Could it be that immediately he left to meet them, that Koso was also called . . . but by whom?' he seems to be thinking. 'Had it been he had seen him before he was summoned, he would've urged him not to betray their plans or any of them. He could not doubt that some of the things he had just heard from the doctor and psychologists was basically truth. That threaten of trust to a great degree was what he had feared most. It was true that men are sometimes untrustworthy creatures yet his inborn tendency told him that their agreement before embarking on this hunger strike had been a man to man agreement, in other words, a gentlemen agreement. But, how was he sure that others will behave and respect their 'gentlemanly accord' which they had all sworn themselves into. It would be provocative for some of them, who are particularly sensitive especially comrade Andrea Volvaskov and his friend Ognyan Stoyanov who regardless of the fact that he wasn't present that day (he was not feeling well and so remained inside) enthusiastically supported the action. If there could be any cowardly act of betrayal from any of them, no matter whom it may turn out to be, it would be catastrophic for all of the inmates.

'Whatever happens,' Hyman said out aloud, talking to himself. 'I would never be the spoiler. Why could I, after all, what the psychologist had said might be true . . . that I'm the master minder, so I couldn't implicate myself or could I? . . . No, No, No I couldn't. I'm constant as a northern star" he asserted, as smiles creped up his face. "If there was no irritation, there would be no reaction.'

Another thing that he remembered and laughed to himself was how upset everybody who was concerned in the prison seemed to be these days. Now he came to believe the old English proverb that 'when poverty enters the door, love flies out of the window'. Of course, that was true, if with just little pressure from them ordinary asylum seekers could unsettle the authority like this, what would happen when these journalists would hear about it and start their opprobrium, they could never endure it. The pressure would be much more unbearable, when and if the human rights groups became involved. And other concerned citizens stuck by the actions and would openly censure the authorities for dragging the already hated name of their country (Austria) through the mud. In addition, Hyman thought every God-fearing person should tackle the issues and condemn them, mainly, when they heard about the recently proposed law, prohibiting any prisoner who was on hunger strike to be released until he or she lost a certain amount of weight.

Hyman Otta was still contemplating and memorizing all the prospects about these issues confronting the prison inmates, when he suddenly fell into a trance.
In his half conscious state, Marcus Omofuma was still wearing the dark-blue jacket on top of black jeans and black T-Shirt (just the same clothes he wore on the day he went on his fateful voyage *the last journey*). He entered into their cell room and sat down on the same position where he was sitting

in the morning he had the dream. He called Hyman and asked him to sit opposite him. 'Do not be shocked to see me Hyman' he said. 'I want you to listen very well and don't forget anything I tell you. It was not my fault. They were demanding something from me Oh! yes, I did not recall what they asked, but, their demands are highly contemptible and the height of arrogance . . . Before I could tell them that I didn't understand . . . I had already moved . . . yes they moved me forcifully, believe me. In principle, I didn't believe this question could give rise to misunderstanding, yet, that was what it turned out to be. Bear this in mind always, Hyman, as you might not hear from me again. Never in this world, not even in the other ones you've not known yet 'Can the wronger became the wronged, the wronged the wronger?' They wronged me, I was not the wronger. One couldn't blame a man for taking precaution with his murderers. Man, they were three, yes three though one of them wasn't too wicked at all. The other two were bloodthirsty racist murderers. They may think they win today, but, I assured you that I had never surrender to them. Not now and probably not forever. We were still wrestling, no one had won yet. One more thing before I finally go. These murderers and torturers would never, under no circumstances be freed from punishment, and I want you to hold them responsible for violation of international law, because I told them before it happened. Don't forget, under no circumstances would any of them go free; and believe it, that life is about the journey, not about arriving. The end of one's life is a vaguely sad thing. The matter of life and death are not always there for man to decide for another man . . . but just like destiny far more immediate than its owner knew . . . mine was extinguished and enacted by these men. Please promise me you would eventually write a book about my journey just to expose the Austrian asylum system for the whole world to read and eventually watch it as a movie. Only this would make me rest in perfect peace where I'm going. It was said that there are many different ways to liquidate human blood . . . three of them rather chose this way like vampires which they truly seemed to be . . . I had searched extensively amidst all bosom 'buddies' to take reprisals for me, prior to my choice, and remain strong-willed that you will never fail me. But, be warned . . . Be warned . . . that he, who sets out on revenge, always digs two graves. Yet, I know and just believe you must prevail, but it will not be easy at first. It will take more, more, more . . ."

++

"Hyman Hyman!! What's happening, what's the matter with you? Are you okay? Are you okay?" shouted Koso, who had returned to their cell for the past ten minutes or thereabout, thinking that Otta had dozed off; for actually they didn't sleep at all yesterday night. When Koso came in he had decided to wake him up, but changed his mind to allow him get some sleep. Until he started hollering, 'No not me, no not me . . . okay, okay, okay!!!"

Hyman stood up from his bed. He felt a kind of vibration all over his body, shivering from his legs through his thighs, up his wrist to his forearms, his shoulders, his neck and right to the top of his skull. He became so thunderstruck that he couldn't hear or answer anything Koso was saying. The thought streaked through him that he might have fallen asleep.

But, no, he was just speaking with Marcus Omofuma. Yes, he told him to sit down and started telling him everything. Or was it only that maybe he had fallen to imaginary state of the issue at hand. The more he thought the more he was feeling sick and shivery.

"Oh my God, why did you allow your servant to be in this state?" he exclaimed eventually, seeing Koso standing near his bed for the first time that afternoon.

"What's the problem? I suppose you were sleeping when I came back and intended not to interrupt you . . ."

"Did I? No I wasn't sleeping at all" Hyman confusedly replied.

"Maybe you were a bit fatigued, it seemed as if you had drifted off . . . but, then why didn't you notice when I came in?" Koso said. "I meant, even a dead man would've woken up considering the manner of the warders that brought me back, the way they jammed the door behind me."

"What did you mean? You were just coming in now, weren't you?"

"Actually, I had been inside for almost six or seven minutes before you shouted."

"I shouted? Really, did you hear what I was saying or you said shouting?" he furiously asked.

"Yes, of course, I heard you shouting, 'No, not me, not me and then later you're like agreeing okay, okay' . . . that was exactly the time I woke you up" Koso assured.

"You meant you were the one that woke me?" he asked, using the back of his clenched hand to wipe off some sweats that had started emerging across his face. "Then, I must have fallen into a 'wee' sleep or could I say, sort of being in a hypnotic state . . . I wanted to ask you one thing Koso, did you believe in metamorphosis?"

"What's this metamorphosis, I don't understand, I've never heard . . ."

"I meant the transfiguration of soul . . . that a dead person would somehow appear in physical body and be seen again; in Hinduism or Buddhism religions they call it 'samsara'. I once read a book about Hindus when I was at school which attested to the fact that such things existed. And, also it confirmed the Christian beliefs of life after death or rather resurrection, which was basic of Jesus Christ coming and teachings," Hyman was trying to composed himself.

"Well, as you would've known my position in these things, I don't believe in life after death either, but why did you ask?"

"I saw Marcus this afternoon inside this very room! I was . . ."

"You've started again, Charlie, I could believe your dreams, and not this metamorphosis of yours, forget that," Koso interjected.

"I saw Marcus, this afternoon, inside this very room," Hyman bluntly repeated. "Look, when I came back from their summons I was just meditating on what I had discussed with the doctor and the psychologists, when he came in and started speaking with me."

"Come on, Hyman, did you know what you had just said, that you saw a dead man . . . somebody that had being dead for some days now. No way my friend, is either you were joking or maybe you had became deranged, man!"

"Boy! I swear, I'm not joking, it's never a joke."

"Listen, Charlie, there was nothing like seeing a dead man. I really knew that this hunger strike of a thing would eventually cause another thing . . . Now you were seeing a dead man. Maybe before tomorrow, you might even see your dead great-grand fathers. Charlie lets consider and cut this off before . . ."

"Since I knew you, you were always like this, but eventually you would still 'd'accord'?"

"The dead doesn't exist, my man, if you wanted to argue on that, I could only tell you that if the dead still lived on the surface of this earth, then it was only in the minds of those who constantly remembered them," Koso argued further. "I strongly believe it was what you're thinking in your mind when you came back and couldn't meet me to talk with you. Or perhaps, you might have succumbed to a very powerful reverie merely because of your too much thinking of these problems or simply weariness."

"Charlie, you missed the point, you must not doubt the spirits," Hyman cuts in.

"Nonetheless, just as I did not want to be sceptical anymore or rather, that I had promised to believe your views. What did he tell you when he came in?" Koso asked, losing some composure.

"You might be right about me becoming crazy, yet the fact still remains . . . whether it was in daydream or real, I could literally tell you all that happened before he entered, but not all he said. Anterior to his appearance, I became cognizant of allured aroma, just like irk of scent one perceived when visiting the Mortuary. He was dressed in the same attire he worn on that day."

Hyman told Koso everything he could remember Omofuma said, but became nervous and was short of words towards the end.

His incoherencies made Koso to ask.

"But, what did you answer him, when he suggested that you avenge his death?"

"To tell you the truth, I did not understand myself saying anything, it was like he was talking and I was listening and listening . . ."

"It was possible that was when you commenced shouting, 'No not me, okay okay!!'"

"Possibly, what could I say, if you insisted I shouted so," Hyman said shuddering. "Does it mean I disagreed with him, Koso, do you think so?"

"I don't believe you disagreed. You later changed to okay okay! And beside he said, he trusts that you can do it, but then, how could you take revenge for him . . . this was one thing I couldn't make out, or when you said he told you that 'In principle, he didn't know that the question would've given rise to misunderstanding' what can this mean. Could it be he was arguing something with the police officers before . . ." Koso reasoned.

"My brother that was another thing I couldn't comprehend. Or was it as you suggested that all these might be what had being ruminating in my mind. In fact, I think I'm sick of all these. Why me, God, after all my adversities in Africa? Why can't I've peace of mind in my life?" Hyman emotionally asked. "Since my childhood I've never known peace, it was either war, or I lost my father and younger ones, or I was imprisoned by these disgruntled people, who called themselves, the Southern People's Liberation Army led by that monster John Garange."

"Man, that's alright, things would soon come to be good" Koso asserted.

"Now see the kind of state I found myself again in Austria prison. God why can't you answer me and let me have peace for once in life" he asked sobbing seriously. "Charlie, does bad luck, mean bad person?"

"I don't think so. It's not true, bad luck does not make a bad person, not when that person did not create his own destiny. Yet, one thing I know for sure is that freedom has a price and some people must pay for that or else it's not worth to be called freedom. Right from ages, many people have been shedding their blood for freedom. For instance, in America, Martin Luther King Jr., died for freedom; Malcolm X was assassinated for his roll in championing the rights of Blacks and for his fight for recognition of them (the Blacks) as free humans in the majority White society; the last but not the least, Nelson Mandela of all people was incarcerated for good twenty seven years by White folks in his own native South Africa for crying out against Apartheid . . . Or wasn't it your christian belief that Jesus died for world's freedom?"

"Yeah, of course, you're right, even Jesus . . . my lord was killed for the sins of the world."

"Boy! Spear me that. Allow me to finish before you start your preaching. I know immediately I mentioned Jesus you must come out from slumber. As I was saying, so, man! In our own case, I strongly believe Marcus Omofuma had to pour forth his blood for amelioration of Blacks in this land (Austria)" Koso said with nostalgic smile. "What remains now is for you and me . . . not to let him down . . . just as you said he told you. They say, everything man does in this earth, he does out of longing for better life or out of a sense of moral protest. However I ascertained this, our action as a way to our freedom and betterment, period. Virtue is always rewarded. And believe me, I'm not someone that believes in prophecy . . . yet, I can't help this. There's a kind of hope that our action and campaign of some concerned people outside this prison will help to get us out and with more clamourings the government will be forced to erect a monument as a mark of honor to Omofuma."

"Do you really mean these things you're saying?" Hyman excitedly asked.

"Guy listen, the government must be forced to do it as a sign against forgetting and suppressing one of the darkest chapters of Austrian police history. But this I figure out might take some time" Koso predicted.

"How do you come about these predictions? Charlie, I know . . ."

"Man! I'm not joking anymore. I saw and heard good news today."

"So you're telling me not to loose hope . . . you're giving me hope that everything would be alright, Charlie" Hyman smiled.

"Hyman, 'mon' men, listen" said Koso desirously. "The first president of my country, the late Dr. Kwame Nkrumah, once said that if we have to change tomorrow, we are going to look back with some courage in order to look forward. We will have to look with some courage, warn hands on the revolutionary fires of those who came before us and understand that we have within ourselves, nationally and internationally, the ability to regain what we have lost to build; a new humanity for ourselves.' So my friend, what we were about to embark on is part of what will later be Marcus Omofuma's history in Austria . . . take it or leave it" Koso maintained.

"Yeah I forgot, he also told me that I must write a book about him and his last journey."

"Really, that's absolved. I hope the book would become a best-seller if you could do that. I mean, his story was a pitious story."

"Hm, hm" uttered Hyman. "Boy! You're really surprising me this afternoon. I didn't know you as such an eloquent speaker before. In fact, I swear, I'm a bit more emboldened by your words than I was earlier. You must be a very tough man perhaps one of those, whom people think they've known all about them, yet they knew nothing . . . before I forget, you said you heard something today, what's up?"

"Well, that was what actually spurred me before I even come to face with those scoundrels that call themselves psychologists. In the waiting room, I saw a 'Johnny' . . . a JJC (Johnny Just Come). He said he was just coming . . . they arrested and brought him in. So I asked him about the outside world . . . I mean how the news was received. 'Oh, you meant the scandal', he had quickly countered me, 'Oh, it's the talk of the town, the African community, the human rights organizations and many of the press people have all voiced their anger against the way the police and the ministry of Interior are handling the 'scandal' so far, the 'Johnny' told me" Koso happily recounted.

He held up his hand to stop Hyman interrupting him and added gaily.

"The greatest news was that one of the most respected government affiliated news magazine (The *Profil*) reported boldly in its front page that human error will solely be to blame in this destructive mission and it contemplatively cautioned that any attempt to manoeuvre or sweep the truth under the carpet by the authorities would be a deplorable mistake" Koso quoted delightedly, "Charlie, we're already winning."

"A deplorable mistake" mimicked Hyman, nodding, "which means that one day your prognosis about Marcus will be brought to fruition . . . who knows, he might then be officially recognized as the first Black martyr in Austria. Guy, who told you about it, I mean the article, I'd say your in-coming friend?"

"Nai, oh no, I didn't tell you, I met comrade Ognyan Stoyanov. Of course, he was the one that told me . . . he even showed the newsmagazine to me."

"Who did you speak with? Was Dr. Rabl among them?" Hyman inquired.

"No, they were three men in all . . . talking bullshit. I didn't give them any face at all, you know what I can do . . . all the while I sat dumb . . . not until one of them who said his name was Franz Boheim uttered effrontrily that I was the most confounded self-destructive fellow he had ever known."

"What did you reply him?" asked Hyman hastily. "You must have told him he was the most destructive murderer in the world today."

"I told them, that I've pleasure in what I'm doing . . . quoting from one Buddhist's saying, that 'if we could get what we want, when we think we need it life would present no problem, no mystery and no meaning' . . . but to my utter bewilderment, I discovered that they were staring at me over and over with a mixture of shock, and shame and disbelief."

"Why?"

"I supposed for the fact that I was able to recite such words . . . for one of them expeditiously asked whether I was a Buddhist. I said I'm not, but that I use to converse and read their books when I was in Ghana. He later professed to be a Buddhist himself . . . And said that although he ironically was not always interested in the opinion and affairs of most Black people he was fascinated by my knowledge of Buddhism, and that he had always had the belief that all Blacks that came to seek for asylum here are functionally illiterates. Do you know what?"

"What? I think the man speaks the mind of many Austrians . . . A lot of them think so?"

"The man automatically became very friendly. He encouraged me to seek and study more about Buddhism, that it was a religion every self-possessed person ought to believe in, and he also promised to send some 'books of Buddhism' to me."

"Did you accept his offer?" Hyman asked dispiritedly. "I believe that will be one of his strategies to get you over. You can't trust these psychologists and their cunning ways."

"Does one spurn open-handed gifts? I thanked him, and used the opportunity to tell him that his attitude is worthy of emulation; and that it's a manifestation of the fact that sometimes 'we are coming at a common problem and looking at a common solution that everyone should reason well and tackle the issues facing us together" Koso declared.

"What was the position of the other two men while you were discussing with him for so long and yet, on issues unrelated to why you were sent for in the first instance?"

"They were furious and I believe to an extent shocked at first, one of them was even exasperated by his behaviour that, he questioned him in German, but he answered him that that's the right way to do it . . ."

"Meaning what?" Hyman suspiciously inquired.

Since that very moment Dr. Rabl spoke in the Intercom . . . and said one of the inmates had confessed . . . his mind had not settled down, and beside it was generally known and said among Blacks, that most Ghanaians living in Europe could easily betray other, just to achieve 'peppers' as Ghanaians used to accentually pronounce papers (Passports or Visas). Could he trust this one Ghanaian friend he had come to known for over two months in prison, at this crucial period of their life. He wanted to openly ask him if he had already sold them but instead he said.

"Koso, don't you think that he tried every tricky means to get you to co-operate with them . . . ?"

"Well, that, I can't actually say, although, I perceived he was trying to entice me with his offers conceivably, his thoughts might be that I would be able to be wheedled into quisling with them."

"Do you think he will not get you through these Buddhistic connections?" Hyman asked frettingly.

"You must be stupid to ask me such a question, man!" he said, staring at him in angry consternation.

He still could not think of anything appropriate to say again without using foul and insulting comments (for naturally he was a stammerer, and anger always boils in him just like a boiling pot of soup, whenever he felt huffy with another fellow). To avoid getting into conflict, he chose to walk away from Hyman and end the conversation.

"Oh! Charlie, I didn't mean to offend you with this," Hyman pleaded, and cradled him with his hand. "Please forgive me for being too curious. It was this brink of disaster that caused my being cynical. These morons want to coerce many of us into renouncing our actions. They tried it on me also, and failed woefully. Charlie, please don't mind me . . ."

"Look, Hyman" he said, overwhelmed with laughter. "Although, I can tell you not to trust anybody, because most 'on lookers' are traitors, it doesn't make me a fool not to know that this was for a friend, a former roommate and for my own freedom. 'He who has privy to the incendiary stroke of thunder will never treat Sango the legendary god of thunder with levity" Koso said in proverb. "So you would have to understand that betrayal by any of us at this stage, will not only be an act of cowardice, but also aberrant and abhorrent to we all."

"I'd understand that, it's said, trust, but take care whom you trust. I don't for once distrust you rather I was concerned if others will wholly be loyal to this task. Do you think they can't get somebody who will renege on his pledge?"

"This is a very sensitive question I must tell you. Of course, we'll agree that the battle will never be all that easy . . . with the type of pestering and later cogent utterance they used, just for me to confide in them and unveiled the perpetrators of this act. To tell you the fact, I don't think many people will be able to prevail over these tricks without yielding to their demands" Koso said, little bit pompous. "I'd never know of other stocks but at least in our stock, I only fear one guy, Petar Panayotov, that Romanian guy, you remember his comments that very day. In fact, comrade Ognyan Stoyanov confided his fears to me this afternoon, that Petar is as deadly as a Cobra (Snake), and that he might be the only curb between us and liberty. I'm nevertheless became increasingly suspicious of him, when the comrade confirmed that he eavesdrop on his conversation with one *Beamte* this morning as they were serving tea and bread."

"Then our chances are slim, or you'd say otherwise? The doctor had already threatened me this morning that one of us had confessed" Hyman said. "You don't see it so?"

"As far as I know, he can change nothing. By mere looking at him, he comes across as a guy who's a little bit unhinged and little bit out there, a little bit timid . . . if you know what I mean?," Koso mocked and added. "To many people who know him well, he's nothing but a zombie Mr. Follow, Follow, who no dey move unless you tell am to move" Koso chanted in 'pidgin' English. "I don't see the reason why he will be so important in this whole deal, yet the fact is, he doesn't know much either . . . I mean how it was organized."

"But, he was present that day and he heard those speeches."

"Hold it, man . . . isn't it your Christian Bible that said, many have eyes but don't see, and ears, yet they don't hear. Believe me, Panayotov is like those people."

"Did they tell you that we will be stopped from going out for *Spazieren* as far as we continued the hunger strike?"

"No, they didn't . . . Why?"

"Well, they said as from tomorrow morning, if we don't change our mind that there will be no *Spazieren* . . . that it was against the prison law for anybody on hunger strike to move around" he asserted. "But the point here is, these undesirable elements are striving to make things even more onerous to us than we would've been expecting."

"Oh! My redeemer" Hyman groaned. "How could they make the same mistake again? How can they deny and violate our dearly earned rights? You should've known that they will try everything to dissuade us from carrying out action . . . One thing is, they are going to even apply more harsh conditions. We will witness more repressions and dismissals of individual rights from the prison authority especially, if there will be no much pressure from outside and within this prison. I must confess that I perceived this right from beginning. They might even start to inflame hostility among us, seeking to discredit most of us."

"Which means, this prison will soon turn out to be a more ghastly place for all of us, more like been in the wilderness."

"That's not a better comparison, it will be equivalent to one being on consuming fire . . . like you saw in your dream, remember. But, I believe we'll prevail, when the public, the human rights groups and the media who will make sure they do background reporting and not accepting anything at face value; will finally be involved . . . Until then, the authority will become conscious of the very fact that not only is Marcus Omofuma's cruel death on trial, the Austrian's way is also on trial." Koso answered in a low voice.

++

Otta and Koso were inside their cell playing poker card and finding solace from the rhythms of Bob Marley's 'Redemption song' vibrating out from their radio. The days used to be longer for them nowadays since the authority prohibits all inmates with the exclusion of few of them that are not observing the hunger strike from going out for *Spazieren*. It was one of those chilly spring evenings, all cloud and shadow. 'It was a strange thing', Hyman thought. For in the last two days they had been in isolation. Their cell's ironed-door had not been opened, unless on few occasions, when they would be summoned by the doctor or the psychologist or by the reference officers, who had joined in the effort to discourage them. 'All the officers', he sometime thought were all hardliners and unrepented sinners. 'If not, why would they have taken such hard stance against us' Just like the Egyptian Pharaoh who was obstinated and made his heart unresponsive when Moses and his bother Aaron asked him to allow the sons of Israel to go and worship their God . . . The authorities were also obstinate in their minds and remained apathetic. They don't give a damn. Nobody thinks about them. Nobody cares. No beliefs, no conviction and no enthusiasm. The type of discourtesy he received from Dr. Rabl just yesterday when she used some verbal words for him 'that he had been distasteful and an unrepentant dissenter' had been disturbing. But all the same, after all were said and done, as a Christian, he still believes that what was, was and was so decreed by fate. 'Who are we mortals to fight against destiny' if and when it's the Will of God everything will become normal again. He always seemed to get 'carried away' unless there was good music from the radio which was precisely what was happening now. To him nothing was more close to human emotion than music. He was still meditating with Bob Marley's Redemptional lyrics (not even paying much attention to their poker game) when he overheard a guttural, raucous voices from outside and some hubbub of keys. Instantaneously, the door opened a few inches.

The *Beamten* took a quick look around the (paltry triangular room which had been their abode for the past two days when the authorities determined to pressurize them more, decided to segregate the inmates apart from contact with each other). Inch by inch, the door finally flung open. Hyman immediately turned off the radio and stealthily looked the newcomers being shoved into their cellroom by six hefty prison warders, forcibly as the two young men bloodly fell down on the floor of the cell.

CHAPTER TEN

"God has counted your Kingship and terminated it; you were weighed in the scales of judgement and found wanting. Your Kingship is broken up and given to Media and Persia".

===Daniel 5:26-28.

As agreed on the last board meeting since the crisis started, the next day at ten o'clock in the morning precisely all of them were already in attendance, together with three new faces—two men and a lady—who had been ventilating their discontent on the handling of the hunger strike issue with the commandant prior the other's entrance.

"Good morning gentlemen and ladies," begins the commandant disquietedly. "Before we get down to business, I'll like to present formally to you all our guests."

He glanced at his left and right toward the three quests sitting with him at the conference table.

All eyes followed him and he continued with a broad smile on his lips.

"Sitting by my left, as some of you might have known is my good friend Dr. Paulus Lukas; from the ministry of Internal affairs" he introduced, as he outstretched his hand towards him.

Dr. Lukas, a very tall man, with big broad shoulders—like that of NBA-star, blue eyes and a well trimmed moustache, elegant with his dark-brown 'Tirolian' traditional suit; stood up and made a bow to the audience with his sunny smile.

"And on my right hand side," the commandant said, "is Dr. Inge Lugner, from the department of the prison controller's union."

She straightened up, dresses in modish black blouse on top of a well tailored shinning black gown, with black shoes to correspond; and genuflects, blinking her large eyes.

"And sitting beside her, is Magister Josef G. Berger from the External affairs, who takes the place of the director of the ministry."

Mag. Berger nodded from his seat. He seemed easy and relaxed, almost lethargic with the rather sad, natural intelligence of self thought. A man, that didn't smile so easily, and a soothing habitual person in sharp contrast to Dr. Lukas.

"I'll like to call upon Dr. Rabl to please, brief us on the sequels of their assignments" said the commandant chivalrously.

Dr. Rabl stood up from her seat, raised her eyebrows in the direction of the chief psychologist, who was sitting some seats away from her; the bones of her face long and delicate. She was wearing a blue-black suit with an expensive cherry-red shirt and flat black shoes, looking quite beautiful in them. She greeted the gathering and depicted how resentfully the team had tried all they could to persuade the inmates, but to no avail.

"I mean, the chief psychologist of the prison, Mag. Robert Rupp" she points her finger towards him. "We've undertaken everything humanly possible, I can assure you ladies and gentlemen that, initially I personally was disgusted by some of their hubric, however, we were able to convince some of the inmates and were trying to achieve some affirmative results . . . until the new order which restricted their movement and as a result confined them to their various cells, while most of them were even removed from their original confinements to a more restricted space. As if that was not enough, it became too much and too dangerous for these inmates and even us to operate when the latest order was given, putting them into more and more inhumane subjections—contrary to our originally agreed measures" Dr. Rabl declared.

Glutted by the whole problems and she went on in a disarming frankly tone.

"This particular issue, to tell you the fact, ladies and gentlemen, will paint all our efforts black in the eyes of the masses. Perhaps, these recent orders when disseminated are bound to transcend the news of the dead (Omofuma's death). I'm depressed the outlook of these dictum has certainly shown how inept we all have been in handling this predicament, and the outcome, I'm sorry to say, would not be good for any of us unless we quickly change and be lenient in some way . . . I thank you for the opportunity ladies and gentlemen. Thank you all."

Dr. Rabl concluded her face like that of a woman that suddenly received the news of the death of her one and only son. She sat down and searched for a tissue in her handbag to wipe her face.

The commandant felt personally uncomfortable, merely because the said orders had come from his office directly. Not withstanding that he was pushed by some of his intransigent officers to take these harder line. Yet, he at least was absolutely in no doubt that for her to point out undisguisedly that the orders were ineffective without conversing with him first was a big let down to his person. How could she bluntly speak out on this already heated atmosphere, she would've come to him privately and expressed her dismay, than being vociferous as she had chosen to be. He had been somehow humiliated for the first time in his entire career—and by a woman for that matter—career that had spanned for over thirty years, and had taken him to almost all the prison in the country, making him one of the most travelled officers in the prison department. This was where he finally received his first blow', he thought; nevertheless, he was able to hide his feelings.

"Have you anything more to divulge, Mag. Rupp?" the commandant asked uncommittedly.

The chief psychologist, upstanding, respectfully addressed the guests by their names, the commandant, and his subordinate officers, and then greeted the audience.

"Good-day, ladies and gentlemen," he said, as he used his left hand to align his bow tie. "I've been looking forward to this meeting and it turned out to be exactly the very people that matter."

He quickly glanced at the two men and the lady sitting side and side beside the commandant. His instincts told him, they were already feeling tense and irritable. He had seen Dr. Inge Lugner jotting down points in her notebook as Dr. Rabl was unleashing her critical report. He continued,

"Firstly, I'd like to report to this gathering that my team and that of the doctors have done all we can do in trying to persuade the prisoners to end the hunger strike. I personally talked with many of them and what I heard from most of them make me come to the conclusion that we have all underestimated this problem. Many of them were not stupid as we have surmised. They seem to know what they're doing. One of them, I'd like to quote, told us bluntly that 'freedom has price, and that some men must pay that price, or else there would be no peace. And again that true freedom doesn't come at once or so easily.' Yet another of the inmates was more polite. He said that, 'forgiveness overcomes fury, and mercy defeated malice.' One of them from Ukraine told me, he had been involved in labour activities all his life. He even went as far as narrating to me (off the record) about the 'labours of Hercules' for examples, about the slaying of the Nemean Lion, the capture of the Cretan Bull and the recovery of the Golden Apples of Hesperdes. What I'm trying to emphasize by this, is that the prisoners are well organized. They seem to have motivated themselves up to the extent that I fear nothing will make them to rethink. This situation to me is deteriorating considerably that I believe it must be very unsatisfactory to everyone sitting here today. We must avoid confrontations with the press. I think we all know the truth of the whole matter and the pivotal cause of these prisoner's actions. And I also believe that these inmates became, well, victims of circumstances and were just doing their best within the situation. The doctor just reported to me this morning how some of them had already lost very good amount of weight. 'Anger, they say displaces anxiety.' If I'm to advise, I'd suggest that few of them be released on a kind of . . . gradual arrangement. Ladies and Gentlemen, we all will agree that these problems erupted as a result of an entire life ruined over one indiscretion, one mistake."

"*Guten Morgen alle*" compliments Michael Schuller, showing great displeasure at the presence of the three VIP guests. "I really expected the situation to deteriorate. I'm not in any way impressed by the remarks of our liberal psychologist friends."

He glanced toward Dr. Rabl and Mag. Rupp, his face contorted with awful anger.

"Let us be very careful and not formulate a sort of precedent that will be calamitous for the establishment in future. I don't want to sound too despotic, but to capitulate to this threat of hunger strike, gentlemen and ladies, cannot serve as a good paradigm for the future . . . I repeat, cannot serve as a good paradigm for the future. Let us not betray our country. The reputation of this prison and its system would tarnish if we'll allow this to take place. I believe that with stronger arm tactics, they'll change their minds (even when they have stony hearts), terminating this gratuitous action" officer Michael Schuller propounded to the audience. "If people were such fools that they could not stand the truth, then you've to feed them with something else."

He glimpsed around, momentarily, uncertain on how the audience, specifically the three guests would assimilate his suggestion and then he added bitterly.

"Men can not be ruled by kindness, but rather by severity. Sometimes it takes extraordinary law and action to inject some sanity into them (inmates). When the authority is confronted with some extraordinary challenges, 'it must find strength and power to prevail against them'. Let us be realistic and legally defend of our country's rules and regulations. Let the world hear about our hard conditions of accepting asylum seekers so that people will understand and stop coming here to seek for asylum. 'THEY ARE NO MORE WELCOMED IN AUSTRIA" he uttered concludedly, and dropped a bow, before slumping back into his chair.

There were lots of murmurings mainly from the headtable. They spoke in muted tones and confiding with each other. Moments later about four other officers spoke, with two of them substantiating the first two speakers, while the remaining two had variant stances in scavenging for the solution of the dire straits facing the prison. One of the speakers, the chief *Beamte*, Martin Baur recommended the rescinding of the ban of *Spazieren* and, to split up the inmates and the perpetrators of the hunger strike punished as a matter of priority.

"In my opinion," *Herr* Baur said fervently, "in as much as we may exercise leniency for some of them, we shouldn't tolerate mischievous acts of organizing from the perpetrators. They seem to be callously wicked and wantonly cruel. It had been ascertained that there exist a little coterie of conspirators. They must be made to pay and a lesson must be learned from this foolishness."

"How do we know the perpetrators and how do we punish them?" asked Dr. Rabl.

"I don't know how, Frau Rabl" replied chief Baur. "Yet, I believe that when some of them are intensively interrogated, we would eventually come about their names, and as for the punishment they deserved, let me remind you that 'people who start fires always end up smouldering themselves.'"

"I take the position that everyone here knew about these practices and the consequences that usually follow," Michael Schuller cuts in infuriatedly, "we should not be putting an act or pretending to be *Karl Böhm* or saints. We're not in Ethiopia. This is Austria. Anyone intending to become a charity worker should resign and better look for social work."

The audience allowed themselves string of laughters for the first time.

He paused for a moment and then added.

"Let us cease from this pretence and stop thinking as if these are personal matters. I think what chief Baur just suggested should be taken into consideration."

"Gentlemen and ladies," called out Dr. Paulas Lukas, who was the spokesman for the ministry of Interior, "let me use this chance and make it categorically clear to you all, that the Minister himself is saddened about the whole affair and how it has been handled so far. I think we've heard an ample recommendation from various speakers. I can say I felt a surge of disappointment, especially about the decisions to 'quarantine' these prisoners. I'm not personally in support of this order which prevent the inmates from going out for their normal one hour walk around; as the law states and even the order of confining them to more isolation by taking them to small cells doesn't help the issue at hand."

He swallowed, adjusting his glasses he stared directly at the commandant, his eyes glittering with honest pleasure.

"Let it be clear to all here that this problem when allowed to escalate will aggravate even more than any of us could imagine. What concerns us now is how to make amends for the way 'we' have behaved so far, and be sure that this entire case is resolved peacefully before the world eats us like *Apfelstrudel.* I would've liked to hear from Mag. Berger of the External ministry . . . prior to my presentation of proposals from the ministry."

Mag. Berger stood and inclined his head in respect.

"I thank you, Dr. Lukas for granting me this window opportunity to air my views in this issue and that of my ministry. The commandant, sir, Dr. Lukas, Dr. Lugner, officers of the law, the superintendents of prison, warders and wardresses, distinguished ladies and gentlemen" he addressed, with a chilly sangfroid, and straightened his trademarked dark funeral suits, as he stared passionately at Susanne Mayer, who as the secretary of the *Rossauerlände Schubhaft* (the deportation camp) was called upon to jot down the minutes; a tall, slim, blond-hair, blue-eyed young woman of thirty, but still very much in contention. Mag. Berger looked up at her and smiled, and then professionally continued as a diplomat he was.

"Let me remind every Tom, Dick and Harry here, that as well as ratifying the UN convention against torture, our country has equally ratified the other international treaties prohibiting torture and cruel, inhuman or degrading treatment or punishment; including the international convention on civil and political rights (ICCPR) in 1978, and the European convention for the protection of human rights and fundamental freedom (European Convention) in 1989; and that we're members of many international human rights treaties which guarantee the right to liberty and security of persons. These specific ratifications have inevitably rendered these harsh proposals non-viable and besides, the external affairs ministry is primarily bothered on how these recent blunders would besmirch the image of our country in the eyes of the International communities furthermore."

He turned to face the commandant with frosty indignation.

"I believe, to command a crisis such as this at times is the most unfortunate thing that can befall a man. However, it was such circumstance that makes a man. Sometimes we risk so much and in turn lose all. It's better to voice the obvious frequently than facing the consequence of things going badly. This problem I think must be solved. There's no more room to procrastinate. The more we procrastinate the more damaging to our image both at home and abroad. A man they say is without exception stoned dead, by hands disparates to his own, commandant. But this I suppose will all be your decisions. It basically falls under your jurisdiction; whatever suggestions we might offer is only for you to be rational, compassionate and fair with these prisoners. On the contrary, any attempt to postpone the inevitable will be a major catastrophe to this country, mostly now that everyone believes the press people have not heard of it or any piece of gossip in connection with it. Anticipation of death, they say, is more dreadful than death itself . . . One more thing, ladies and gentlemen, I don't believe in the aphorism that cops are biologically incapable of keeping their mouths shut; but, in spite of that, I'd recommend everyone for the time being to please, stay away from these cliques of pressmen and women that were agog to uproot every atom of news. I caught sight of a large number of them this morning as I approached the prison premises on my way to this meeting. Only the commandant, if necessary, will talk about these deliberations and the happenings."

The meeting later ended around noon, after about two and half hours of consultations before Dr. Paulus Lukas announced the establishment of an ad-hoc committed on the crisis, as instructed by the Minister of Interior.

The eight member committee comprised the prison commandant, Christian Gospel, Susanne Mayer, as the secretary, the chief *Beamte*, Martin Baur, the chief doctor of the prison, Dr. Cinthya Rabl, Superintendent Michael Schuller, Mag. Josef Berger of the external affair's ministry, Dr. Inge Lugner, of the department of the prison controllers union (who during her own speech strongly supported the idea that all the prisoners would not go unpunished, referring to the likeness of such crisis, which she said that in the truth was not up to this present one, but as the head of the prison board then, she was able to control it not by absolute clemency, rather by being over-stricted), and finally, Dr. Paulus Lukas himself representing the internal ministry. He was also directed by the Minister to be presiding over the day to day deliberation of the committee, who were given only two weeks to report their findings and recommendations directly to the Minister.

CHAPTER ELEVEN

"How long?: The answer: As long as we permit it. I say that Negro actions can be decisive. I say that we ourselves have the power to end the terror and win for ourselves peace and security through the land."

===Paul Robeson

On leaving the conference hall, Dr. Lukas was heading for his official black 605 Peugeot limousine, where his driver and retinue were awaiting for him, for the next rendezvous of the day. John Nelson, a very reputable investigative journalist, who was reporting for a monthly newsmagazine (*Augustin* press) with the cunning of Clark Kent swooped in front of him, glancing quickly at his gold plated Omega leather wrist watch.

"*Guten Tag*, Dr. Lukas" Nelson called out to him, in the manner a store owner normally greets his steady clientele.

"Tag, Nelson" he answered, looking up at him with a beaming smile. "Yes, what can I do for?"

"Hm hm, please sir, if you can spare some minutes," he said dutifully, "I'd be appreciative of your views of the recent happening, and of course, why you are here so early today, sir," he put the questions to him simultaneously as they proceeded down towards his car.

Dr. Lukas stood, and motioned to his driver, who was already standing near the limosine in anticipation of unlatching the door.

"I've nothing to say, in any case" he replied the journalist brusquely. "I'm here on an errand. I don't think I've got any time to squander . . . if you can understand what I mean? I have to go back to my office at once. I must be with the Minister for more consultations . . . please my friend, I hope you can excuse me" he was saying, at the same time directing his steps towards the slightly ajar portal of the car.

"Just 'your' brief, on this issue, even in a nutshell, sir," Nelson demanded, bringing to a focus his wireless recorder, as he somehow blocked him, and obstructing him from moving into the limousine.

He gestures to the photo-journalist chaperone take a snapshot.

"Gentlemen, take it easy!" the driver snapped at them, his brown eyes dulling as he stretched out his hand in protection. "Will you move back a bit?" he asked in a voice slow and sluggish.

"Gipo," called Dr. Lukas to his driver, "it's okay, I don't think there's any cause for alarm" he smiled his sunny ever-ready smile, striding backward. "Now John, what's your question, could you please come again?" he asked, emotion thickened his speech. "But, let it be short and sweet."

"Oh sir, it would be as short and simple as the 1967 Israeli-Arab war and sweeter than Africa honey."

Dr Lukas smiled again.

"Go on."

"Honourable Doctor Sir, first and foremost we'd like to know what and how your ministry is reacting to this tragedy, I mean . . . about the death of the Nigerian asylum seeker . . . Marcus Omofuma. Lets say there're strong speculations going around that he was gagged with adhesives tape all over his body and mouth . . . and it has been rumoured that he died as a direct result of his treatment by the three police officers accompanying him on this ill-fated *last journey* . . . Sir, your personal views and that of the ministry?"

"As you might certainly know," answered Dr. Lukas with deep exhalation of repose, shrugging, "I can't comment on that issue and besides the case is still fresh. The ministry is treating this allegation and counter allegations with utmost seriousness. Not until we will have gathered all the facts accurately, will there be any official press release. All the same, I can personally reassure you, Nelson, if you will only trust me that, the ministry is not sleeping over this issue. The Minister has already ordered a high-powered advisory board that can conduct an inquiry into the case without fear or favour, and give recommendations to the ministry on how to confront the situation . . . till then I'd advise . . . I don't . . ."

"Granted sir, yet talking of high-powered investigation, can we trust the outcome . . . I've been aware that all the members of the panel will be single-handedly designated by the Minister. Why not a kind of broad based commission of enquiry which will be established by the government itself and not the Minister?"

"Well, what I've just told you is about the constitution of a body, I'm very optimistic that it'll be up to standard as you want."

"But, that doesn't answer my question, sir?"

"What's your question?"

"A broad based commission of inquiry which will . . ."

"Listen, my friend," Dr. Lukas interrupted, flagging down his hand, "you must understand there are normal procedures in any democratic government. This issue at hand falls within the jurisdiction of the Minister of Interior. Do I make it clear for you?" he asked, glancing at his watch. "But, I beg you to be brief, Nelson! I've other things to do . . . you equally know I didn't want to offend you" Dr. Lukas said, his eyes sparkling mischief. "One more question, Nelson, and I'm off."

The journalist ignored his threat of one more question.

"Sir, the answer wasn't so clear, but then, we want to know whether these policemen were informed of the risks of gagging and again whether gagging of deportees is permitted as a form of restraint; and if so, under what circumstance?"

"What, I'll tell you and please bear it in mind (off the record) is that" Dr. Lukas said, his voice for a moment seemed hard, with a frown, "gagging of the mouth . . . nay, gagging of anything . . . as far as . . . forced deportation of individuals out of Austria is concerned, is neither permitted nor prohibited. It was simply a failure in the system. Ha, oh, nai, gentlemen" he sighed. "I believe, I've spoken enough, I'm sorry, I'll not take any more question."

"Yes, sir, but, this last one. The head of Vienna's police branch, was reported to have banned the use of gagging in 1998 after the death of the Nigerian national Semira Adamu by asphyxia during her forced deportation from Belgium; he was alleged to have stated to his subordinates in the cause of their meetings then that deportees are to be returned to the police jail if expulsion is only possibly through gagging, what can you say about this, sir?" asked the reporter with grotesque peevishness as he quickly switched off the recorder and extracted the cassette, and simultaneously inserted a new cassette all in a professional manner.

"I don't think I've any remark to make on that. I think the best thing to do, is to look for the said officer and confirm from him. Personally, I've never heard or read about said comments. Nelson, please, I beg your pardon, I'm almost one hour late already" he lied. "I'll see you next time. You initially promised your questions to be as short as the six days Israeli-Arab '67 war, but they've turn-out to be longer than the Vietnam War. Next time I'll rather be more careful with you my friend" Dr. Lukas said jestingly and pushed his way into the black limo, whence the driver slowly drove away out the prison compound.

++

Inside the Limousine, Dr. Lukas felt extremely exhausted from the long meeting, and the interview, which even seemed longer to him. By and by, he was still very happy that the hunger strike issue, which was his primary concern, did not arise in the course of the interview. He believed that the press might not have gotten hold of the story. Everything seemed to be under control for the meantime.

"*Herr* Gipo" he called after his chauffeur through the car's intercom system, "I think you can drive straight away to the 'Café Royal', I've an appointment there by 12:30 . . . I need to be there in time."

"I believe we were some minutes late already, sir" replied Hans Gipo, as he made change of direction on the auto route to the 2nd district of Vienna were the Café Royal is situated.

++

John Nelson having finished his meeting with his most trusted source as far as the deportation prison camp gossips were concern—O. C. Nico—at a nearby bar Parlour, made his way back to the prison premises for his next engagement that afternoon. On his way, he hurriedly glanced at his watch hoping he wouldn't be too late. Officer Nicole had just fed more than enough secrets to him, even more than what a CIA agent would've been executed for, if caught by the authority. He happily looked at a postcard he had received from his mother for his thirty-fifth birthday from Australia where he was born and raised. Journalism was in his blood. His father had been the political correspondent for the *London Sunday Times* and *The Times* and later the editor of *Tasmanian Examiner*. Nelson's great grandfather and grandfather had also been hard newspaperman. At eighteen years of age John left Australia to attend the School of journalism in London and began the career that was to lead him to Vienna. It was while working as a reporter for the *LSJ's weekly journal* team that he embarked on an excursion to South Africa. He took his black girlfriend with him, a bit naively and never realised how experienced first hand the racism of Apartheid. He never realised how blatant it could be. Nelson himself was color blind in the humanistic sense of the word and so he suffered even more for the controversy his relationship causal while there. Since then, he vowed to fight racism wherever he encountered it. Years later, Nelson got a prize assignment from the Augustine Press to examine in a series of article the rise of the Far-Rights in Europe and that led him to Austria. John Nelson followed around a young charismatic politician from

Austrian's Kärnten whose metconic rise to power in his Far right party and their subsequent national success was to shake the pillars of democracy in the budding European Union—The piece created so much controversy and raised the readership of *Augustin* press, that the editors asked Nelson to cover the German-speaking countries for them.

Nelson discovered an Austria that had never undergone De-Nazification like Germany, and so was still troubled by its Nazi past. The leadership after the war often were the same people, who were part of the Third Reich. Austria never admitted to itself that it was as much responsible for the Holocaust as Germany.

There was no real suppression of the National Socialist sentiments and the demonization of its perpetrators was relatively minimal. Austria was able to hide under the fig leaf that it was Hitler's (Germany's) first victim. Austria liked to believe that Beethoven was Austrian and Hitler was German.

Nelson felt it was his responsibility to remind Austrians that *Opa* (grand-father) was often a monster. It was Nelson's personal viewpoint that only an open Immigration policy of Minorities to Austria is the best De-Nazification program possible (like in Germany) in this day and age. The Marcus-Omofuma-case made him fume. And he vowed to uncover all the scandals surrounding the whole atrocities.

+++

Reporter John Nelson and his compatriot paparazzo Peter Preiter edged their way cautiously through the throng of *Beamten* on the way to the receptionist Bureau. In his right hand was the letter of appointment which was faxed to him by the personal assistance to the prison commandant, *Fräulein* Lisa Egger; after he put in so much effort, trying to get in touch with the commandant.

On reaching the reception desk, he was questioned as to who he was and his mission by a lady *Beamte*, before she directed him and his colleague to speak with the receptionist *Fräulein* Sylvia Strobl, a hefty young woman of twenty-six, with candy-apple red-dyed hair that reached her shoulders. She had a very pretty rounded face without make-up and dressed in her decorous dark-green *Beamten*-jacket.

"Good afternoon, miss" greeted the two men simultaneously.

"Good afternoon gentlemen" she said in response, motioning with her left hand for them to give her some seconds.

She was on the telephone. After a split second she deposited the handset to its place, rather charily, turning to face them.

"Yes gentlemen, what can I do for you?"

"Oh! I'm John Nelson from the *Augustin* newspapers."

He was staring at her in astonishment, for the thought that the lady might have recognised him from the previous meeting with her. He placed the appointment letter on top of the counter for her comfirmation.

"We booked an interview with the commandant, I think, he would be . . . already waiting," John said, and looked fixedly at his chronometer, "we had a minor collision along the auto-way coming, and that had been the cause for our lateness; please, could we be able to see him straight away?, I believe we're very much behind schedule."

"Ok, Herr Nelson, but I must get authorization from his office first" she said, glowering at the reporter (who by now was engrossed in a little dialogue with his partner) "I think . . . Herr Nelson that, you know the rules" she derided him, while dialling the commandant's office with the oblong-shaped intercom on her bureau.

"Okay-dokey beauty, but please let it be quick," Nelson uttered pertinently, looking askance at her, "as I said, we're already late."

After placing her call to the office and being told by his PA that they were expecting some quests, she was then directed from the other end of the phone to usher the visitors to the office. She straightened up from her seat; flung her thick, frizzy hair backwards, regaining her poise; she stretched out her hand to Nelson and to Preiter, as she should've done originally. They found such a 'male' gesture quite comical after her previous exhibitions, but controlling their urge to laugh they took it and bowed conventionally, tapping along behind her towards the office. She tapped on the well fortified dark-green coloured floorboard door, and waited. In a second, the door flung open and they were baded in by the PA.

Commandant Christian Gospel stood up from the mahogany Grecian couch at the rear of the 'Bonheur du jour bureau' and extended his hand in greeting.

"*Guten Tag, Herr* Nelson, I've being expecting you" the commandant said ungrudgingly. "Why? You're a bit late today, just unlike you. What held you my good friend?" asked Gospel, staring blankly at him.

"We are sorry, sir!"

"Oh! Oh!! Don't mind please, you can get seated over there" he said consecutively, pointing at two empty chairs.

"I think, I must apologize for my lateness, before anything else, commandant sir, please, I'm sorry for being late" Nelson importuned to the prison commandant. "It was as a result of circumstance beyond our control. There was an accident on the motorway . . . 'en route' here, sir!"

"Oh! Hope you're alright . . . my good friend. You can go on and ask your questions" the commandant wasted no time.

"Thank you sir" Nelson replied professionally. "Firstly, Mr. Commandant, we'd like to know where and when exactly, did the officers start abusing the Nigerian, Marcus Omofuma, before they muzzled and took him to the airport for onward deportation."

"For once, Nelson, I can't understand your question," commandant Gospel acknowledged disturbingly, "I don't know what you're talking. I think, you could, please, state your question clearer" he suggested awkwardly.

John straightened from his chair and regarded the commandant with some surprise.

"I don't intend to be hard sir . . . I assume you've seen the dailies, it had been widely speculated in some of them . . . that the Nigeria national was first beaten, handcuffed and gagged somewhere before being taken inside the plane as the case may be . . . some even reported that many eye-witnesses saw this" Nelson clarified. "So, my question sir, is, whether you're aware of where it happened? Or do you confirm the sources that maintained that the abuse started from your prison?"

"No not at all. I wasn't apprised of this information," said the commandant Gospel, being distrustful. "I have not seen or read anything like that in the newspapers as you suggested."

"Rightly-ho, sir, but why was he forced, after it was already known that he had in the past resisted fiercely deportation on two previous occasions? Or did you think the policemen acted with decorum by smothering him?"

"Gentlemen, the truth of the matter is, the whole mess was all bureaucratic. For sure, he was not the only one applying for asylum that has lost his application or can I say, was rejected by the asylum department. Or was he the only prisoner who had been here, before being deported" commandant Gospel answered tactically. "My job . . . our job here is to keep our beady eyes on these inmates pending their deportation or release. We don't have any involvement in their decision or as per se, concerning their fate, what might become after they were brought here. I believe you're getting me" he said, mindful of his shrewdness. "All their fates are in hands of the Fremdenpolizei. Of course, sometimes you've the expulsion order in respect of a foreign national who is determined to stay on a state territory after their appeal for asylum has been turned down by the officialdom . . . Law enforcement officials may on such occasion have to use force in order to affect such removal."

Nelson reacted immediately and asked.

"But, what about the permissibility of the use of entire body gagging and mouth gags during forced deportation, who orders these techniques to be exerted in such situations, Mr. Commandant?"

"As a matter of fact, the use of adhesive tapes or similar materials against individuals for deportation . . . in a prior agreement has been prohibited by the Interior Minister without exception for a long time" replied the commandant sarcastically, glancing in the direction of the main door adjacent to where he was sitting, as it opened slightly and his secretary appeared, bringing three cups and saucers, and a flask of cappuccino and with a container of almond cakes.

She bowed and placed the cups and saucers in front of the three men, with the flask and a container of almond cake in their centre.

The commandant paused and continued.

"Gentlemen, as I was saying we can not ascertain the real fact of the case without hearing first from the officers involved. Human beings said one psychoanalyst," quoted the commandant, "sometimes saw themselves in the centre of controversies, involved in facing the limitation on their power and potential and in, deferring to what is forbidden and what is impossible."

Nelson drank from his coffee cup slowly.

"Sir, were these officers trained in first aid treatment in case of emergency?"

Gospel maintained, holding on his unwavering view.

"I can assure you that all our officers were well trained and are professional in their respective field of operation. Sometimes one can make mistakes in the course of discharging his or her duties."

He sips from his cappuccino and takes a bit out of the almond cake, and then he added as a matter of buttressing his points.

"These mistakes, actions, loses and sometimes there consequences are part of life; universal, unavoidable, inexorable; and are still, necessary because we grow by making mistakes, learning from our mistakes, losing, leaving and letting them go" the commandant lectured, "In the actual fact, it's said, that 'central to understanding our lives is to understand our mistakes and losses'. Don't forget, to err is human and to forgive is divine."

Nelson ignoring the long winded speech of the commandant asked fervently.

"What steps has the authorities taken so far in ascerting the facts and correcting the mistakes?"

The commandant responded defensively.

"A panel of investigation has been put in place on a fact finding mission to unveil the truth and then recommend to the appropriate body, that is, the Minister of Interior, who will sequentially take necessary actions."

Nelson asked, more or less being convinced as to what would be his answer.

"Sir, what was the state of health of Omofuma before embarking on his *last journey?*"

"Herr Nelson, I'm not a doctor. I'm only a baby sitter," he smiled wistfully. "I think you better ask the doctor about that . . ."

Nelson asked interestingly knowing full well that many doctors were attached to the deportation camp.

"Which of the doctors?."

"I don't know, or do you think it is also my bloody duty to have knowledge of the prisoner's physical state?" he said awkwardly.

"Not at all, sir," Nelson replied shrewdly, "but I would expect that in such a controversial issue, you would've his complete file at your disposal by now . . . ?"

The commandant lied back in his rocking chair, puffing on his Cuban cigar.

"I'll try to get you some information as to . . . concerning his health."

The journalist scrutinized his thoughts with contempt.

"Yes, of course sir, you have other problems I believe," he murmured. "It's been speculated that the inmates here (in this prison) have for the last three or four days since this incident happened . . . applied the game of truancy, reference to their food . . . I mean, there's a hunger strike going on in the prison, isn't that true?"

"That's correct," said the commandant, without hesitation.

He felt agitated that the hunger strike has in the end reached the news media, especially a journalist as powerful as Nelson.

"In fact, this is the main issue that I've to deal with at the moment. We tried to persuade them to abandon the action, but to no avail. The Interior Minister has given directives and temporary committee has been set up."

Nelson instantly interrupted.

"Can I have access to these prisoners that have been segregated and moved to smaller cells, sir, especially those prisoners that were in the same cell with Marcus Omofuma?"

With an overwhelming expression of shock on his face, the commandant stuttered.

"But, N . . . N . . . Nelson, where . . . did . . . you . . . get . . . all . . . these . . . informations?"

The journalist smiled.

"Why, sir, from my various trusted sources."

"Who and where?" the commandant questioned, somehow commanding, forgetting he was dealing with a reputable journalist, not his subordinate officer, and outwardly showing that this little piece of information hurt him deeply.

"Commander, sir, with all respect I've my sources, period! I don't think it's proper to reveal my sources . . . or to be asked to do so, sir. I believe it would be ethically wrong to do so. Can we have . . . ."

The commandant shook his head yes.

"Right, gentlemen, I believe, there's no skeleton in our cupboard. It is ok for me . . . you're free to visit and interview anybody you wish to . . . but, I'd personally like to accompany you on such visits."

"Thanks for the opportunity, sir!"

"My pleasure" commandant Gospel answered, frightened by what he had spontaneously agreed to, possibly with great regret.

Later it was scheduled that the journalist John Nelson together with his camera man Peter Preiter would be coming over to the prison the next morning around 9am before the meeting of the members of the ad-hoc panel which had been set for 11am precisely.

On his way out of the office, Nelson, who had gazed at the commandant's secretary with lust the moment she came in to serve them coffee, slipped his complimentary card on her desk, while thanking her.

Fräulein Lisa Egger looked up at him and smiled.

"You're highly welcome."

+++

Regina Frisch was sitting at table No. 10 in a dark corner of the Café Royal. She had been the girlfriend of Dr. Lukas for the past three months. Whereas he was divorced with two children, a boy and a girl she was a single mother of a daughter; recently she was able to secure a job of the assistant secretary in the ministry of the External affairs. As a staunch follower of the ruling party (the Social Democrats), it wasn't so hard for her. Her father, Hon. Dr. Gernot Frisch of the blessed memory had been one of the pioneers of the Socialist Party, which had been ruling Austria since the formation of governmental era following the end of the second world war, and the subsequent Allied government that ruled in 1955 and had also worked as an erstwhile ambassador to many countries which included, Australia, Venezuela, USA, South Africa, to name but a few. He left his mark as a reputable diplomat, who contributed much to the internal human rights and Third World development, and to the attempt to rehabilitate Austria's bad reputation as part of the Nazi war machine and the Holocaust. Most importantly for Dr. Frisch, was his contributions to the world's acceptance of Austria back to International Unions, which prompted the construction of a United Nation building (Vienna International Centre) in the 22nd district of Vienna and other important institutions.

At the age of twenty four, Regina had been cherishing the idea of becoming one of the Austria's top diplomats in future just like her father, whom she wanted to follow in his footsteps, and whom she adored much before he died in 1996 from brain-tumour. She believed that with the help of her father's political legacy, and his allies that were still in politics, she could achieve her goals. In addition, with her own contacts of which Dr. Lukas was the most important, she felt sure that her place in politics was secured.

Regina had just finished her first drink of mineral water and was slowly peeking at her diamantine wrist watch—a special birthday gift from Dr. Lukas—pondering in her mind as to what might haven been holding him up. 'Since three months they had been meeting frequently at this Café or the others (like the *Guten Tag* Chinese Restaurant at *Schwedenplatz* or the Bristol Hotel at *Karlsplatz*, where they usually spend their weekends together) he had never been late', she thought. She was thinking about this sudden change in attitude, when the waiter led him to where she was sitting.

"*Schatz, ich liebe dich* (Darling, I love you)!. I'm sorry for being late today" said Dr. Lukas devotedly in his apologetic voice, sitting himself down right beside her and slightly kissed her.

"Love, you do not need to worry yourself, it's only few minutes. You must know that I'm the mother of all unpunctuality. It's only today that you entered the league and you've not been promoted to the second division, much more, been in the premier division" Regina joked, in her usually humorist etiquettes. "Now tell me love, how was the meeting?"

Before he could open his mouth to speak, she drew him closer, and planted more kisses on him and patted at his cheeks just, to make him unwind.

Dr. Lukas hesitated somehow feeling more relaxed than when he came into the Café.

"I think there's a very big problem at hand, even bigger than the one we already had . . . Yes, the end of a human life was vaguely sad, but that shouldn't be the reason for these prisoners to take the law into their own hands . . ."

"What do you mean, taking the law into . . . ?" she asked. "You seem to be upset about that. I noticed it immediately you came inside, love . . . why? Don't tell me that it's about the hunger strike issue and the stance taken . . . taken so far by the prison commandant and his associates."

"My God, Schatz, from where did you get this information" he said, a bit disconcerted once more. "I do not suppose the media have got the Scandal by now . . . have they?"

"You can trust these Viennese's news moles, darling, I don't know where or how they ferret out some of their tittle-tattle" she was saying, and at the same time thrusting and drawing his attention (with the tip of her finger) to the *Profil Zeitung* column, on the second page, boldly printed and entitled:

THE BIGGEST SCANDAL OF THE YEAR

And subtitle in light letter—head under it:

Commander Christian Gospel The Prime Executor Of This
Brutal And Inhumane Act Set To Resign?

"You see, I was just perusing the article before you came in" she asserted and posed a question, full of abhorrence and; not really for him, "I mean, why should this 'brute' Gospel take such a hard stance at this point when our country's image is already tarnished out by the general public? It's like using gasoline to douse a house enshrouded by flames."

Dr. Lukas took the newsmagazine hurriedly, glanced through the column. He read rapidly down and then towards the attached article, but there were no sources quoted. Yet, the story was well tailored and all the facts ascertained by whom ever the reporter might be. He looked at the Lepidopteran-shaped ceramics arched ceiling of the Café Bar; figuring what Mag. Berger had just warned against was uncovered already. 'No, things are getting out of hand'. He shook his head. Something must be done quickly to end this scandalous affair and as the paper suggest, somebody is getting benefit over these issues if not how could the news spread out quickly. Faster than how HIV spread in Africa; or does this adage that, 'Cops are biologically incapable of keeping their mouth shut, true? 'Now', he thought, he must get in contact with the prison commandant and warn and at the same time, ask him to scrutinize his subordinates and find out which of them sold this piece of news to the press. He played with the idea, shook his head again disappointedly.

"No, some of these facts would've been a sort of classified informations," he said out aloud.

"Which facts are you talking about?"

"Whoever, that had betrayed his superiors must be seriously dealt with. It's not good to do business with these cops, they can easily kill someone's political career . . . or don't you think so, Schatz?"

He seemed surprised as to how she was staring at him while he was speaking, for she had not known him as a man of words, much more of being too conservative a man as he seems to be this afternoon. However, she was still learning to understand people's personalities and emotions, especially when they are under pressure. Regina felt she should be a good listener without being intrusive, but that, she should express her own opinion in every conversation, without being seen as a dogmatic person by her adversary.

She asked.

"But, who . . . or which people do you think are susceptible to leaking this news to the media?"

Dr. Lukas replied in frustration.

"Do I know? Can anything good come out of these Babylonians? One of the things I know that had been conceptually and empirically validate in this world are that 'cops are incapable of keeping their dirty mouths shut . . . A friend of mine once told me this, I doubted it, but I have now come to realize I was wrong all the while. You wouldn't believe the havoc this news will cause. To be frank, Schatz, I'm becoming more defeatist and scared stiff of the social disruption, which these recent predicament will help to egg on the electorate. It would never be good for many of us and the party in particular . . . bearing in mind that this is election year and besides the recent opinion polls was not all that ok for our party. But, for the record heads are going to roll because of these scandals, take it or leave it . . . my darling girl."

He leaned front-way with his elbows on the table, paused for a moment and furiously continued.

"I hardly predict things, but I perceived ugly situations coming especially for the party in the next election. It's only about four months away from now. You read this paper?"

Regina shook her head that she had read the paper.

"Of course, I forgot you gave it to me," Dr. Lukas acknowleged still in his firm and steady voice. "Tell me, how can the Minister claim that everything is under control, when in the real sense of it, everything is under fire . . . you saw it, didn't you?"

"Love, I've seen it, but, I didn't take that stuff seriously before. This was a dumb statement from a man of his rank. I don't suppose, he meant all those stupid things he said there. It was very unwise of him to make such provocative and indiscreet declarations. The ultimate example is this column . . ." she said, pointing to the phrase in one of the articles in the paper (which almost half of it covered the Omofuma stories and the consequences that followed) . . . where the Minister was quoted to have said:

'The officers who escorted Omofuma had carried out their duties without blemish'

"Or the most damaging . . . this place, where . . ."

She pointed again.

'He was directly quoted to have made that blatant lie, that there was nothing like a hunger strike going on in the deportation camp',

"That, fool of a Minister, forgetting that some of the journalists were already informed about the hunger strike before posing the question in the open press conference? But one question I want to ask and please, do not feel annoyed about this, love, for I'm not trying to be pomous or overcritical, but, rather I'm being forthright is, has our party become short-staffed of good diplomats up to the extent of not having even one person left, who can handle this job efficiently?"

Dr. Lukas indicated negatively.

"The problem, my darling girl is, in every political party in this world, be it the conservative party, Democrats, Labour, Green, Extreme right parties, Trotskyites . . . centre or left . . . our own type of Social Democrat, or even hard-liners . . . the fact still remains that, there are powers that be and these sets of individuals believe they have absolute powers, or that they're the pillars of their respective parties, believing that, if and when they pulled out from the party, it will disintegrate" stated Dr. Lukas critically and emphatically, "yet, the naked truth is, most of these men in grey suits that think they're sort of colossal beings to their respective parties are nothing but political 'neophytes' and our bossy Minister is not different."

Regina looking a little bored by the speech, asked.

"But love, how are you sure it were the cops that these reporters are always quoting as their impeccable source close to the prison, are the 'Beamten' or the cops as you always refer to them, the only people working in the prison?. Aren't there any other people capable of leaking this information out to the press?"

She shifted her body a bit to enable the waitress dish out another sets of their meal. Two plates of greasy cheeseburgers with fries and magnum bottle of Rosé d'Anjou—rosé wine which she ordered in advance.

"Hm Oh" Dr. Lukas smiled at the blonde haired, model built waitress with a simply gorgeous face. "Excuse me! Please, can I have another glass of chilled beer?"

He turned to Regina.

"And, who do you suppose would do it apart from them?"

Fräulein Regina ignored his question and used her left fingers to squeeze his ear jealously as reprimandation for his behaviour, the way he lovely stared at the waitress, as she felt envious of the waitress's beauty.

She took a mouthful of the cheeseburger.

"I meant, there were other civilians attached to the prison, weren't there? Like the doctors or the nurses or the psychologist . . . even the reference officers or maybe the cookers themselves . . . couldn't these people reveal these information? Who knows if one or two of them were materially gaining from the present situation."

"Oh do you forget that they were all partly police officers? All the same, to tell the truth, my darling girl, the chief psychologist Mag. Rupp and the chief doctor, Dr. Rabl, who incidentally was a member of the ad-hoc committee; made it categorically clear to everyone in the conference hall today, that they were not happy with the commandant for taking such action without their consent (maybe they would've advised against it, thereby saving us from the scandal) In fact, the doctor seemed very much annoyed that she described the commander's orders as a fire brigade approach."

He took the last of his burger and licked his fingers, happy that he had just devoured every bit of it. He had not eaten much for the past three or four days since these problems first emerged. First, about the sudden death which has been termed by the tabloid community as the *last journey* and now the first official consequence, which was this hunger strike. It was his taste for whiskey and cold beers that keeps him moving. Thesedays he found solace in them just to keep fit, if not he might not be able to face this critical moment of his career—which, if he or everybody concern does not take time and find a solution to it quickly will augur badly for the future of their party. The Party to him had not reacted intelligently to the crisis. The actions taken so far by the party and the government had only exacerbated the situation. He was buried in dip thought, as he drank from his glass of beer.

"You might be correct, my darling girl, you've helped me clarify my thoughts. In fact, Dr. Rabl is the only one capable of doing that . . . but, why could she of all people do this kind of thing?"

"If she is the one . . . Dr. Lukas!" she uttered scornfully. The first time she had boldly called him his surname wantonly in three months they had known each other. "I mean you don't have to judge people like that. We're not sure, who these impeccable sources are. Judging and passing verdict on things we don't know or are assumed is always a big mistake. What, if I told you it was from my ministry the information leaked out. Can you accuse the ministry as you've been accusing the cops and now Dr. Rabl, after all, I can boast of hearing this news of hunger strike and the order of strict confinement imposed by our all powerful commandant, before any of you from your ministry, even before the Minister himself."

She raised her glass of wine to her mouth and drank from the fizzy drink.

"I'm the impeccable source! Can you punish me, my love?"

She blew him another of her wonderful mouth kiss, which he responded accordingly.

"I love you," she murmured.

"I love you, too," Dr. Lukas said.

They kissed each other passionately and stared at each other face for a moment.

"I want to thank you for giving me your clear-cut opinion and your support. Nobody has ever been honest and straight forward with me. I'm not used to tension like this" he said, feeling ashamed for once. "The fact is my tirelessly optimistic natural instincts are now somehow dispirited and depressed. Could you imagine that those fools, the prison commandant and some of his officers are still insisting on some kind of punishment for the inmates, without considering the political implications their actions are already causing. So, tell me how one will feel okay when deliberating with these fascists."

Regina commiserated with him.

"This problem I believe must be solved in time, or else, we'll have a disgraceful end to this crisis. The state of anarchy in the prison is approaching an intolerable level and it will be impossible for your ministry to ignore this ugly development. What did the meeting eventually agree on?"

"Well, I can say, nothing so far . . ."

"That's tremendous" she said in a mockery voice.

"What's tremendous?"

"What've you been discussing then? They've started it anyway and I don't think anybody can change the situation by being so hard on them. As I see it, there must be a way to release them step by step. They must be freed for their own good, for the good of the party and for the good of the country. There is never a breach without mend."

"But you should be very careful in assuming more than it's reasonable to assume my darling girl."

"I agreed" she smiled.

"Please keep your views confidential."

He appreciated her more than before, ever since he observed her candidness and mental capacity. He had to come to conclusion that she would be of great importance to the party in the future. In fact, she has the intellectual capacity and composure of her late father.

+++

This was what Dr. Lukas had been contemplating in the tiny WC of the Café Royal where he had excused himself from her to ease, for he was a bit intoxicated, having consumed about five glasses of beer, out of frustration. He had taken longer time in the lavatory when two men entered, discussing and expressing disgust over the government's handling of the Omofuma sage, before Dr. Lukas was able to discern that he had spent a hell of time there. He heard one of the men openly agitating for the resignation of the Interior Minister and the chief commandant of the prison. He had listened attentively to what both men were discussing with dismay. He felt the public and the electorate were already against their party, which will constitute a big problem in the upcoming election. He tried to peep with the corner of his eyes at the men who had dressed in black custom made suits with black shoes and blue ties to match, to know whether he has seen any of the faces before. The Café Bar is frequented by only politicians and some powerful individuals within the society. But he couldn't recognize their faces nor had he met any of them before. He strongly believed both men must have been members of the opposition parties, and as such, he basically dismissed their stands as that of political enemies. He then hurriedly returned to his cabin, where his darling Regina (who was also quite inebriated . . . for she had almost finished the magnum bottle of the Rosé d'Anjou, rosé wine, which was originally brought for both of them, but he preferred beer today)—was waiting longingly for him.

"Oh love, where have you been for so long? I thought you only went to visit the loo. I was just trying to call 133 (police emergency number) to help search for you . . ."

"Ha! Ha!! Ha!!! My darling girl, I'm with you. I'm not yet lost, much more, being found" he laughed, cuddling her and kissing her, this time around with even more emotion, which she reciprocated, arousing him sexually.

They remained like that for sometime.

"My darling girl, please, let's forget these 'useless politicians' and their dirty politics for a little while" he said, still holding her with both arms. "I want to ask you something; and this very thing had been in my mind for a long time, but, I felt now is the right moment to let it out. And please, do not laugh . . ."

"What? I do not understand, what you mean, love?"

"Just, promise you'll not laugh at me for saying it."

"Alright, love, I promise, I'll not," she said, her face smirtling. "Now, what is your question?"

"Will you marry me . . . my darling girl?" whispered Dr. Lukas, his voice full of passion and heart-felt anticipation.

Regina could not believe her ears. She thought she was in a dream-land. She waited for a moment and then whispered back.

"YES, I'LL MARRY YOU MY LOVE!"

She threw herself at him, as tears of joy streamed down her euphoric face.

"Then, my problems are diminished," said a delighted Dr. Lukas, "and this occasion, my darling calls for special celebration between . . . just two of us."

Dr. Lukas told his driver over the phone to make reservation for them at the Bristol Hotel and asked him to cancel out all other appointments for the day, and be ready to drive them to the hotel. He was too happy to promise Regina that after all these hassles were over, both of them will just take a long holiday and fly out to a secluded Island for their honeymoon.

"But for the moment, Bristol here we come!" he chanted and led her away to enjoy their first night as engaged couple.

CHAPTER TWELVE

"This is the living testimony of the past, who speak to us from slavery and segregation, telling us, among other things, that nothing—neither reactionaries nor temporary political and economic setbacks—can destroy us here if we keep the faith of our fathers and mothers and put our hands to the plow and hold on.

Hope: the voices of the past speak to us of hope, endurance and daring. They tell us that Langston Hughes was right when he said 'We have tomorrow bright before us like a flame.' They tell us that Countee Cullen was right when he said 'We were made eternally to weep.' They tell us that Alexander Crummell was right when he said 'We were a people God has preserved to do something with.'

This is the fundamental wager, and the fundamental hope of the voices of the Blacks chorus of affirmation. And what these voices tell us today is that is not enough to honour the dead; it is necessary also to redeem them by responding to the calls they address to us from the graves.

> Somebody's knockin' at yo' do'
> Somebody's knockin' at yo' do'
> O, sinners, why don't you answer?

> ===Lerone Bennett Jr.

The two young Africans fell down inside the tiny cell which in reality was built at the outset to be occupied by only two inmates . . . but, will today

151

have to hold four of them. They glanced around in disappointment. One of them was wearing a worn tweed jacket and a black T-shirt imprinted with 'I LOVE VIENNA' boldly on the chest side (which had been torn in some way with the jacket by the warders who accompanied them to prison cell). He also wore a pair of black jeans, a black Nike facing cap, with a pair of white-red-black stripped Nike sporting shoes to match. While the other short, dark, big boned with big eye-balls guy, dressed in a pullover, black coloured and grey, new but very creased trousers with a black flat shoes. The two of them looked roughly of the same age group with Hyman and Koso, between twenty and twenty-four years.

"Hi! I'm Hyman Otta" greeted Hyman formally, lending the tall, skinning brighter one, a helping hand to stand up. "I'm very sorry for this, brothers . . . I believe they'll eventually pay for all these atrocious cruelties . . . Don't mind them!" he consoled the new inmates.

"Oh! I'm Prince Eto . . . , thank you brothers" he introduced himself, as he stood in a vertical position, losing a bit balance. He removed his Facing cap using his hand to scratche his dreadlock hair. "Hello brothers, Yah bless your soul. I'm very grateful. Ireman! It's a pleasure meeting you" he said trusting out his hand to him.

"You're welcome!" Hyman replied, giving a helping hand to the other guy.

"Hi man, my name is Jean Kanombe" said the other, who was a very short, stubby man with bristly chin. It wasn't hard for him to stand up, because of his shortness. Still looking shocked and surprised he added "I am not 'saying' good English . . . but I can speak French very well. Thank you brothers for . . . kindness" he said unconvincingly in his adulterated English, grinning like a Cheshire cat. "These people are some crazy people. They think they can kill me . . . or quenched my heart in putting me here . . . No way, tell them 'man' that they make great mistake for bringing me in this fine place. Yes, I think here is 'five stars hotel', talking of where I come from or where I have be . . . before God save me and bring me to Europe . . . Brothers, look, these people don't know I have seen '99', and then what is '100'. No, they cannot shake me" he assured shrugging, as he shook the hands of the other Africans.

Koso, who was already enveloped with laughter for his murderous English and the manner with which he uttered it without fear or favour, stepped out from where he was still sitting, went towards Eto and stuck out his hand in greeting.

"I'm Koso Osei from the Gold Coast (Ghana) and presumably, you're from 'Down Town'" he asserts, grimly.

"Hey! Yea, Ireman" answered Eto, in his Rasta man accentuated English, looking conspicuously at him, "I man, is really from Down Town, man, precisely from the 'City of the Real Jah . . . the Abba Father . . . but, me man, how do you apprised this . . . or you're a sort of 'Jah' destined prophet in 'prios', Ireman? Are you he who is to come or shall we look for another? Man . . . who're you, can you identify yourself by your colour . . . man?"

His language simply amused Koso more.

"When one considered your dreadlock, Charlie, one would've assume you're from Gambia straightaway, but having mentioned your name one could make no mistake. 'Prince is as common in Nigeria as Smith is in England' "Koso said and added cogently, stroking at his scattered bearded chin (which have the inconsistent hall-marks of Sunday activities). "Besides, I can know any 'Down Town' guy whenever and wherever I see one. I'm a virtuoso, when it comes to depicting Blackman's ethnological specification and credos" he told Eto, and swung round facing Kanombe, he introduced himself in a very fluent French, and asked if he is from either Rwanda or Burundi . . . "But, for sure" he said to him "You're from one of the two."

"Mon Ami, you got it precisely" Kanombe truthfully replied back, also in French. "Why? You said, you're from Ghana, I supposed Ghana is a former British colony, if so, then, where did you learn how to speak French in this articulated form?" he interestingly demanded.

"Why, I learnt it at school back then in Ghana you know. French and his brother English, having been apportioned the lion share of the West African countries during the colonial era, are now compulsory subjects in all the schools within the community" Koso was saying, having a good time with his French, his tongue lapping rapidly like that of a dog. (For in three months or so, he left Africa, he had not got the opportunity to speak the language with anybody.)

All the while, his old roommate, Hyman was goggling at him in astonishment. And then Koso continued.

"Besides, I had a very lovely French girlfriend then in high school . . . Actually she was an Ivorian, I mean from Ivory Coast, you know we have a common 'frontier' with them from almost three angles."

"Charlie, this girl of yours must be beautiful . . . Ireman! 'Cos I heard Ivory coast produces the most beautiful *okpekes* in the whole of that region . . . maybe, that will be the first place I man will arrive when going back . . . to see with my own eyes and equally taste those Ivorian apples" Eto interrupted jokingly.

"Of course, you're correct, yet we still know from European level that your Nigerian-Benin girls are also very gorgeous, you know! I tasted one during my good days in the asylum camp" Koso retorted and to Kanombe he said. Mon-ami, you see why I'm partially speaking French".

"Then, I'll be happy to speak with you. It'll not be boring for me, after all" Kanombe said gleefully. "The cardinal obscured vendettas we always have with our British colonized neighbouring brothers are language barrier. It has been a very big demarcation problem which the Europeans knowingly embedded in Africans just to make us never to be one. They're ever afraid of African unity. I believe, if every African can integrate themselves, at least to speak and write these two European enforced 'lingo' and understand each other better . . . that Africa can become a world power one day . . . why not? . . . If not! Africa is the richest continent (in terms of natural resources). We have the men, we've the brain, we've the raw materials, but we do not have the unity . . . which is the most imortant ingredient in developing a continent. The quintessence of what spieling about are American's unity, the European (after many years of wars against themselves), and now the new wave of Chinese (powerful integration both economically and militarily) which the world is envisaging at the moment."

Koso happily narrated to Hyman and Eto, what he had said in English, somehow wishing that another *history wizard* had come their way after Omofuma.

"Tell me, how is the news. How did our people, I mean, Africans took in such dreadful news?" asked Hyman frettingly.

"What news?" asked Kanombe.

"I meant, about the death of Marcus Omofuma. You don't know him, do you?" Hyman asked nodding towards Eto.

"Oh! Ireman, I know the Jah Boy! Man! I didn't know you're asking about my own soul brother men . . . the 'Omoba' himself. Ireman, to tell you the Jah truth, we're from the same part in my country . . . I mean . . . from the same Edo state. 'The Heart Beat Of The Nation' (Nigeria) . . . from the same ethnic group, yeah, of course, we speak the same native tongue, the same dialect . . . man, but I'd only known him here in Austria . . . you know what I mean, Jah brothers . . ." Prince Eto said.

"Rastafarian, what he asked is, how's the atmosphere outside the world? We, of course knew he's from Down Town. If I tell you that less than one week ago we, Hyman and my-very-self . . . chattered and played poker card and draught with Omofuma, before he embarked on this disastrous *last journey?*" interjected Koso, his face gloomy and was overshadowed with grief.

"Hey! Ghanaian, man, you mean, 'Omoba' was here in this room with you guys? Or you were just playing man. Ire 'tell' me the Jah truth" Eto insisted, pain stitched across his forehead.

"Loo Charlie no, not in this very room, but in another room, we were together with him in the same cell for months . . . We only fetched up here for the past three days because of the action" Koso asserted.

Prince Eto glanced at Hyman, then at Koso, shook his head and shrugged. There were deep lines under his eyes and on each side of his cheeks.

"I saw some posters about him yesterday before my arrest . . . at *Karlsplatz* and at *Dr. Karl Renner-Ring,* near the Parliament building, when I was returning from work . . . you know, I work in the *Reklame* Company. I think, there's a very powerful demonstration being organized by some powerful civilians. Jah, brothers, to tell the Jah truth, Omoba's blood is a very powerful blood, and the gods of our native land 'Ogun, the god of Iron' must not allow his blood to be ditched without fighting for him. The gods are not asleep Ireman, you know . . . He who Jah ar' bless no man . . . ar' curse . . . and he who Jah ar' curse, no man ar' bless, and I can assured you that Jah has already ar' curse the police officers" he quoted in his Rastafarian voice, waggling his dreadlock to and fro, as sweats dripped down his face, due to stuffiness of the tiny cell room.

He wiped away the sweats with a paper handkerchief and said.

"Believe me Jah brothers! It wasn't only the Black community that are despondent with this news, Ireman. In fact, a lot of White Niggers were also down casted. The news is the talk of the town. Even in my company premises yesterday morning, the news was in everybody's lips both the 'Fake Oyibos'. No wonder. I remembered, yesterday afternoon when I entered a tram I saw a White guy and a Black sister giving out what looks like post-cards to many passengers." he said, bobbing his head.

"When, did they say the demonstration will be, which day is exactly the D-day?" Koso demanded, somehow grining.

"Jah bothers, I can't lie to you. I didn't know the dates. Before they could reach where I was sitting, at the back seats, I think, I dropped off."

"That doesn't really matter now" Hyman said.

"Oh yeah, man! Believe me."

He felt the stirring of wanderlust in his soul, his eyes sparking. He gave a barely perceptible nod, crimping his lips tightly.

"Organizing demonstration? That means Koso boy!, we're absolutely right in what we're doing . . . If people who didn't knew exactly what was

156

happening or rather, who doesn't know the type of suffering we suffered together here could be so angry, then, we're right and we've right to . . ." he was saying, looking emotional.

"Ireman, what're you talking about . . . man?" Eto asked feverishly, wondering about what Hyman might meant or was he speaking in tongues?"

"Yes, for your information, emm, Rastaman or you said Prince 'Uto'" he mispronounced. "Please . . . you two have to join us on this action. Because of the way Omofuma was killed, we've decided to go on hunger strike indefinitely. This particular action entails every prison inmate to abide by it in solidarity . . . almost all the inmates are complying with us . . . even the 'Whites' and other non-African . . . Chinese, Indians, Chileans and so on. To be precise, we've not eaten or drank anything since Sunday evening. We all, voluntarily resolved not to taste anything. There was a great feeling of solidarity between us all in protest against Omofuma's sudden death, and furthermore, we want to force the prison authority through this self-denial act to reconsider this law of imprisoning innocent people for nothing" he said in an obligatory voice, his eyes very red and troubled.

He looked at Koso, then at the newcomers and uttered in a soft farway tone.

"Please, brothers we'll expect you to co-operate."

"Hey 'Me' man . . . stop the 'please' man . . . Jah soul had already joined without knowing Ireman. You know one thing Jah brothers, these warders aren't fools after all. I man, was surprised . . . policemen came to where I was sitting . . . man . . . only me in the waiting room. You know what I mean man! The motha-fukas just opened the door and asked if I'd like to join my Black brothers man, you know, when I say, yeah man why not . . . all of a sudden, I saw about three more 'Fukas' just emerged from nowhere man . . . pushing and dragging me man. At first I resisted Jah brothers, but when they started hitting me like Mike Tyson . . . punching on my Jah-humble-body, I quietly followed them and that was how I eventually found my Jah soul here before these fukas will condemn it. Now I understood why these suckers were so angry with me all the while, man, I really understand now, brother men. They were too 'bellicose' man, abusing and telling me they don't give a damn when dealing with a Black man, you know, ,cos man, why, I asked them to take it easy with me man, that, I'm not an animal, but a fellow being and should be treated as such, man!. Now that, I've known the reason, they should go to blazes and burn to ashes. I'm safe here and I strongly belong to African unity . . . so you don't need to fear Ireman, I'll never become a problem at all. W-h-a-t-e-v-e-r Jah people have come together and decided in Jah mighty name had already been ordained by the almighty Jah-Jehovah, and then need to be carried out by his witnesses here on the earth" Eto preachified.

He used his hands to pack and retie his dreadlock hair with a yellow-green-red coloured muffler, glancing laboriously at Kanombe, and back into Koso's face.

"Ghanaian, you can help to explain to our friend in French what is going on here as for me am no asunder, I've no problem with that, man!"

There were amity glints in Koso's eyes and his gaze seemed so deeply penetrating Kanombe's thoughts, as he vividly explained everything and the present state of things—the act of hunger strike to him—in good lucid French and then asked if he would liaise with them.

THE JEAN KANOMBE'S STORY

PART ONE

I, Jean Kanombe came from Rwanda. I was 12 years of old, when the killings happened in Gikongoro 'mon au village'. Yes, 'mon ami', that was on April 7th 1994, the greatest genocide in human history you heard that happened in Rwanda . . . I myself, I lost all mon famille that very day, mon camarades you hear me . . . I lost, mon pere (father), ma mere (mother), ma grand soeur (elder sister), three grand frere (three elder brothers), la petite soeur (younger sister), le petit frere (younger brother), my uncle with his two children, and ma tante (aunt) . . . How many people mon ami? In one day, in one single moment, how many? Isn't it 12 people? For one day, and don't forget I was only 12 years old then. 12 minus 12

'Mon camarade' equal to zero. Yes, I became 0 year that day without my family. I am from Tutsi and we Tutsi are born to be strong no matter what happens. I don't know if you believe in oracles, but hear this . . . My father was always saying that a Soothsayer predicted that there will be a massacre of both the Hutus and the Tutsi in the 1990's. He said this Soothsayer (a woman) also warned about the terrible fate that was to strike Rwanda, the war that will come and that the then president of Rwanda Juvenal Habyarimana, would die a sudden death. My father used to take this very seriously, repeating it in our ears like a pastor preaching about the second coming of Jesus Christ, but my uncle, he was a doubting Thomas, he always called my father an oracle man, that he believe too much in oracles . . . until the very morning of that very day, believe me, it pains me that the two of them (my father and my uncle) did not survive to argue it anymore. I enjoyed when two of them argued about these predictions or other matters, sometimes . . . in fact, in many occasions they forgot their food because of argument, and my brothers you know what will happen to the food?

Kanombe asked to know if they were with him.

"We don't know" they echoed.

"But, of course, one will presume you'll have double ration in such occasions" Koso added, interestedly.

"You are very correct, Charlie and that was exactly my plan that morning, as they were still arguing about the oracle, when I see the group of Hutu extremist militia, with heavy guns and machetes and axes coming directly to our house, singing war songs . . . you know, my father is a very big man then, a big politician. You all know what it means to be a politician in Africa" he laughed.

Amist laughters that erupted, Kanombe continued:

He was one of the biggest politicians supporting the Tutsi rebels of Rwanda Patriotic Front (RPF) while his brother (my uncle, who was also a politician) was the general secretary of their party. As I was saying, when I first saw these bloodthirsty Hutu army coming, I ran to where they were sitting and told them. We have a very big compound in Gikongoro and we all lived in the compound. My father started immediately to shout in our local dialect, telling eveybody to run and hide, while my uncle was still busy, trying to clear a point he was making.

I myself for my part, I did not know what to do. I confusedly went back to the backyard of our house and confusedly climb one of the Mango trees . . . a big mango tree, the biggest of the five in our compound. You know, I started climbing these trees when I was only three years old and can boast of climbing faster than any monkey. I remembered how I used to climbed up the trees to hide sometimes sleeping there when any of my family member wants to beat me . . . You know what happened, I was on the top of the mango tree, my heart beating rapidly like that of a Lizard that fell down . . . I saw those bastards—my God will never forgive them—as they brought out all my family members after collecting them from various places of hidings, under the mango tree. I was on its top and started to shoot and butchered all of them . . . Yes, 'mon' comrades, they killed all of them in my presence there, without me having the gut to even cry for fear of being butchered too, and like the ethnic cleansing mission they came for, they later packed the whole dead bodies, throwing them back inside the house and burned down the whole compound.

Kanombe recollected, strings tears dropping down his cheeks.

"Oh! Oh!! Oh!!! 'Mon ami', please, it's ok, that's okay! We're very sorry. We can forget about this story and talk other things. It's painful" Hyman pleaded.

"No, I don't mean to cry and we're not going to talk other things for now, but 'KANOMBE'S STORY', because whenever I remembered that terrible fated day, I always feel sad and shivering, yet, somehow happy to God for saving my life. But, I survived it. I am one of the few Tutsis who happened to survive the genocide that . . . they say, about 20,000 people died that day alone within my village" Kanombe said, performing the sign of the cross.

"How did you survive till now, even coming to Europe?" Koso asked.
"You asked me how I survived till these days. It's yet another long story, the part two of Kanombe's story, so you better ease yourself and take your seats and listen attentively. I real hope that one day the whole of 'THE KANOMBE'S STORY' will be published as a book and acted as a movie

for the whole world to know and see what I went through." he admonished predictably, and left for the WC.

THE KANOMBE'S STORY

PART TWO

Because I can speak Tutsi and Hutu very well, in fact, no person who knows me well could say for certain if I am Tutsi or Hutu. So it happens that after the massacre, which the Historians estimated to have claimed millions of lives—many of us, Tutsis that survived went to get shelter at the compound of some White Reverend Fathers. I mean the priests of the Catholic missionary organization in my village. When I explained to them about myself and my family . . . what I past through they all knew my father, and the tragedy that befell his household; but they didn't know that anybody survived from our family, yet they gave me food to eat. Oh those fathers were very good. God will continue to bless them. One of them even gave me some strong wine that day to drink to calm me down, because I was even shaking and shivering all through—they also gave me many clothes, and showed me a big hall where I met other survivers like me and we started living like a big family together once again, every one of us trying to forget his or her ordeals . . . but one couldn't forget such plights so easily, can he?

"Not really" they echoed.

You know, because I was little then, and having confirmed that I was who I said I was, the fathers don't normally allow me to stay with the other people until in the night when I will go to sleep . . . so I don't talk with them much to know about many of them or their own stories.
When I was 14 years, I finally joined the Rwandan Army, and that was exactly when all my problems came back again . . . After I finished my training under Colonel Theeoneste Bagosora a Nazi Hutu, who took me to be Hutu, I was now matured for another war. A brutal war indeed, but this time around not in my country (Rwanda). No, it was in the neighbouring country, the Democratic Republic of Congo (DRC) which of course, was formally known as Zaire. We were sent to Kisangani in DRC

to go and help the rebels there and topple the government of President Laurent Desire Kabila, whom my government blamed for bleaching an agreement between them after he was helped to toppled the government of Mobutu by our (Rwandan) troops . . . My unit was one of the last units that was sent in March 1999 and you could imagine how happy I was then, that I was going outside Rwanda for the first time in my life, but, alias, that was where I saw death in my palm again.

"How?" Koso asked interestedly.

Kanombe shallowed, his eyes glinting and water running down his nose. He excused himself and went into the toilet and cleaned it up, bringing with him more tissue papers. He went on.

We used to fight along—together with the Uganda army, who were there also to help the rebels. One day, we were on patrol along the Uvira and other villages alongside Lake Tanganyika (near the boarder between Rwanda and Burundi in the East), when fate ran against us . . . but that same day, I believe that God really exists. Yes, that same day fate ran against us, was exactly the day I believed that 'God' is still living 'mon' camarades.

"Praised be to the living God . . . . praise the Lord! Hallelujah!" Hyman shouted at the top of his voice, with tears in his eyes, "I know that our God is a Mighty God even in battles. He is a miraculous God. He said in Isaiah 43:10-11 'that you may understand that I am the same one. Before me there was no God formed, and after me there continued to be none. I-I am Jehovah, and beside me there is no saviour" he quoted joyfully, raising his two hands upward in praises and adoration, and started waving them to and fro.

"Ireman Jah remain blessed for saving your soul" concored Eto. "Jah is Jah forever man. He changeth not. He's everywhere you look for him man."

"What really happened next on that day?" demanded Koso anxiously, his thought, wasn't God or Jah, as his fellow roommates acclaimed there when Kanombe's entire family were murdered in a cold-blooded, broad-day light.

He looked passed Eto and Hyman and said.

"Soldier man, this your story is a piteous story indeed, please, try to complete it . . . before, Pastor Hyman will come up with his 'gospels' . . . You never knew him, he can easily cut this 'gist' and start preaching from there . . . he's a man of opportunity, and always capitalized if he sees one."

Evey one of them laughed at his utterances. After which Kanombe continued.

My brothers, everything about God is good. Before I do not believe in miracle, but that very day I saw one with my two naked eyes. Mon Dieu', comrades, before I didn't go to church—even when I was living with the Rev. Fathers—but now I used to be the first person in the church on Sundays . . . As I told you we were on patrol with our military trucks. Maybe you have heard about the big war. You know, there were big problems in the DRC . . . like I said, there were three main Rebel groups fighting in and around the country. But our main station was in Goma town in the boarder between DRC and Uganda. My troops were fighting under the command of rebels, commanded by Emile Ilunga, who was strongly backed by the Rwandan army; there was another rebel group which was being commanded by Wamba Dia Wamba. They were based in Kisangani, and were being sponsored by the Ugandan army; and yet another group which they rumoured was being supported by the Americans and their allied brothers (Australia, British etc.) and its leader was Bemba.

"Why are all these foreign powers interested and so involved in DRC? Koso asked.

Kanombe stared Koso fixedly as he stood up tiredly and cimbed his bed. He wanted to protest about the long-windness of the story, but he was just pretending for he preferred the story to Hyman's preaching, which he knew he is eager to start at any time.

You asked me why these countries were all interested in DRC. This is a big question that has a very long and historical answer. We're going to treat them one by one before we will be able to understand the true situation of things happening there. I will come back to my story.

I was a small boy that time of the genocide in my country, but as a son of a big politician, I used to hear my father discussed the problems then with my uncle and some other big friends of theirs in our parlour. According to my father, the President of DRC then (Zaire) Mobutu Sese Seko was in support of 'the Hutu president of Rwanda then Juvenal Habyarimana. In fact, my father used to say that it was Mobutu that put Juvenal in power. The Rwanda Tutsis then had been very angry at the government of the DRC, and this led to the Tutsis rebels having grudges against Mobutu . . . Sorry I'm taking you people back, but this was what really happened. I forgot to add about the oracle and the prediction of the sudden dead of our president. He indeed died in a horrible way as the oracle say—My father had got a long phone call from his friend that morning of the killings, telling him how the plane carrying our president Habyarimana and the Burundi president Cyprien Ntaryamira was shut down and crashed over Kanombe Airport and . . ."

"You said Kanombe airport, I don't think it belongs to your family or was it named after any of your family member?" Koso asked interruptingly.

Kanombe smiled broodingly and answered thoughtfully, wiping away sweats from his baby face.

Oh! No, in fact, I don't know why it was named KANOMBE, but I know it has nothing to do with our family . . . just the same. So as I was saying, I overheard my father that morning repeating on the phone to one of his friends . . . 'The presidential plane is in flame at the airport . . . the president is dead. Remember what the oracle said about his death . . . Hm! I'm afraid for my family . . . I don't have anywhere to run to.' And that had been the beginning of the end of things for us. After the killings, Kabila and the Tutsi Rebels began to fight together for one single course. Not quite long, the Tutsis took over the government in Rwanda and started helping Kabila in his fighting against Mobutu in Zaire. Then on the 17th of May 1997 it was reported over the Radio that President Mobutu Sese Seko of Zaire was on the run and that the new strong man was Laurent Kabila . . . I can remember that day vividly, because our camp commander then, Colonel Tanganyika had assembled the whole units that morning and said 'Listen all you officers of the arms, the economic future of our government (has) as of today entered into new phase and I want all of you to be ready to serve your country and the course it has taken for its well being'. He had told us that any moment from that day that our main unit, which was then based in Kigali, will be moving over to Zaire (now DRC, because the name was changed by Kabila) to help fighting there. You see, the main purpose, we the soldiers know at that time for going to DRC is to help Kabila, who had helped the Tutsis took over in Rwanda and according to Colonel Tanganyika, for the economic future of our country. The problems that resulted in Rwanda Army fighting the government of DRC under Kabila (economy and political issues) was what most of us in the Army did not understood then. Of course you cannot blame us, we were professional soldiers and not politicians. As for the (USA or their allied brothers from the West) or the Ugandan government; or from the other side of the biggest war Africa has seen, those countries helping Kabila. Countries like, Zimbabwe, Angola and Namibia or the foreign countries that they said were supporting Kabila financially and by supplying of military equipments; like (China, Russia, North Korea and Cuba). When you look at the war and the various interests these countries have in DRC, I mean, their selfish, dubious financial interest, you'll know that it was like another 'World War' going on there. There was no doubt they were all there for economic reasons like my country and believe me, they turned it as a war of the titans . . . Capitalism verse Communism. As one of the richest countries in Africa, the DRC is abundantly endowed with so many mineral resources and vital developmental components. They have Aluminium, Cobalt, Copper, Gold, Iron, Magnesium, Mercury, Nickel, Niobium, Sodium, Uranium, Tin, Zinc, Diamond, and Oil; to name but a few. You asked me how I come to know all these facts. I lived most of my short military life in DRC. In fact, I knew 'Congo' politics more than that of Rwanda."

"Mon ami' Kanombe, if we allow you to talk, believe me you can talk till next year without getting tired . . . please tell us what happened that day you said God saved you and maybe another day you can complete your DRC political theories. It seems you acquired a PhD in Zairian politics" Hyman suggested as he tiredly straightened himself up from where he was sitting and started unbending his arms and legs, feeling exhausted.

Koso looked at Hyman dissatisfiedly, attacking him for his interference.

"Aboy Hyman, are you going out for work? Or do you want to go and meet that blonde of yours? We're not in a hurry here . . . my . . . man, and remember that not only we're in prison now, but 'inside a prison in prison'. Since Marcus left us, you know we haven't had any more entertainment . . . please cool down a bit and allow him to put the finishing touches to this story. I know you want to . . ." he said reminding Otta about the new confinement they happened to found themselves for the past three days.

"Pal, listen, this story is a very long story. You know that I'm from the same region (Sudan). So I knew this problem and I knew that he will not be able to finish it today" Hyman frankly maintained.

"But, Otta, agreed you knew the story well . . . but not from this young and brave soldier's point of view, man . . . he's telling us from his practical experience and not . . ." Koso interrupted.

"Brother, I don't mean to put asunder, but then, if we leave him to finalize everything today, what can we live with tomorrow and the next, as you rightly pointed out that we two have nothing new to tell each other . . . ." Hyman said more to Koso than the new comers.

"Ireman *Bitte* . . . I beg you in the name of Jah . . . allow him to complete this gist or is it because you already knew about it as you said . . . please we the Jah created souls want to know also . . . I man is learning a big history from this Jah man. What the Jews already knew let the Gentiles also know it man . . . for our Jah is one, and 'He' peaches one love . . . Relax man!" Rastaman Eto pleaded Hyman.

Kanombe smiled again. He cleared his throat of cough and expunged his snout, staring directly at Hyman Otta.

No, no, not like that Rastaman . . . Otta is very correct of how lengthy these conflicts are and it is true we can not finish it in one day, you know. It is not only in DRC we have war in that region. Yes, all the countries around Democratic Republic of Congo, are fighting for either economic, political or religious wars which have resulted in millions of lives being lavished and more millions being rendered homeless . . . just because of many foreign powers who happen to be interested in these countries, these wars have been going on without end. For example, in the west of DRC, you have Angola and Congo (Brazzaville) fighting; in the east, you have Tanzania, Rwanda, Burundi, Uganda etc, as you might have known, there's war in all the region (except in Tanzania). And not to talk of the bloody, brutal war of the Somalians or that of Eritrea and Ethiopia, two brothers for that matter; Then in the northern boarder, you have, Otta's country Sudan and the Central African Republic. As a matter of fact, there're religious and political war going on in Sudan, since 1983 between the Christian South and the Muslim North. Maybe Otta must have told you about this. He knows I am saying the truth about our stupid leaders and their selfish wars . . . Is that not true? I know, I am not a good Historian, but, I tried and learnt a lot of the regional politics in my army days especially in Goma.

"Brother, all you're saying are truth and nothing but the truth" Hyman answered him, a bit blissfully, for him to confirm what he had told Koso before, concerning the useless wars going on in the regions of Africa. "You even seem to know about the whole region more than I thought you knew . . . but do you speak Kiswahili or Kriundi dialects?"

Mon ami', when you are an army man at my age you must learn many languages especially when you travelled with the army to many places like in my case. We sometimes patrol the border areas from the Eastern part of DRC to the West-North. Wars can take you many places and wars can equally teach you many languages. At present, I can speak Kiswahili, Kriundi, Luganda, my dialect in Rwanda, a bit Kikongo and Lingala also in DRC . . . you see, I have to learn languages and about many people and their cultures in that region.

He had declared, pressing his fingers down in counting. And then he continued from where he stopped.

So, you see, also in the Central African Republic, there were problems everyday . . . Today you hear about 'Coup d'etat', tomorrow you hear it has been quenched by the French army and you start asking yourself; what were these Europeans still doing in African political affairs? Nothing but only causing chaos, because they were still the same people that promote these problems. Sometimes you heard the army was muting . . . another time you heard Coup de grace had been administered to the soldiers causing the muting. Day in, day out, it is one problem or the other in the whole of Africa, and all of them have many foreign powers behind it, who are interested in the internal conflicts . . . so, tell me how and why these conflicts will ever end. Not until 'we' Africans come together and seat at one table and solve our problems without these greedy foreign powers around.

"So, Ireman, you think when the foreigners go away, that there're going to be a lasting and Jah reigning peace around these regions of Africa . . . even in Sierra Leone and Liberia?" asked Eto riveted.

"Boy! Now you remember that our own region—West Africa, particularly in Sierra Leone where that 'Bloodthirsty Viking' Foda Sanko ordered his rebel troops to amputate the legs and arms of many little girls and boys, and even adults, just for the sake of diamond . . . could you imagine that? Of course, with the help of people like the former Liberian leader Charles Taylor and co, who used to exchange the diamonds for military equipments, it's being referred as the 'Blood Diamond Trade'" Koso contributed, nodding in the direction of Prince Eto.

"You mean . . . cutting off the legs and hands of people?" Hyman said, furiously. "Jesus Christ, the souls that perpetrated these acts must rotten in hell."

"Not only that many of these young ones were raped and later killed by the soldiers and rebels alike" Koso assured.

Kanombe cuts in like a professional lecturer he wasn't.

These were consequences of war . . . having said that, we have to blame these unprofessional soldiers that committed these atrocities, yet, we must also focus our anger at these foreign powers that are really fuelling these conflicts around Africa. For instance, if Jonas Savimbi of Angola do not see or do business of diamond with the Western countries, who in turn supplies him with sophisticated weapons to kill his people, do you think the war in Angola would've lasted that long? Or if all these countries in the Democratic Republic of Congo (which unfortunately my country Rwanda was among) move out from there and leave the rebels to settle their differences with their governments . . . don't you think that the wars would have ended for long? With my experience as a former Rwandan army lance corporal, who happened to fought along these rebels and who travelled around these bordering areas meeting other officers from many other countries until my recent predicament; I can tell you that in as much as these foreign governments are helping to escalate the problems, African plights are still in African hands! . . . Why? The main thing is, Africans have not for now got hold of God fearing leaders . . . I mean, leaders, who can serve Africa for African interest . . . not leaders who are now serving Africans for foreign interest . . . Greedy leaders who are only interested in enriching their foreign allies, themselves and their families without putting their people at their hearts, or at least trying to solve the problems of the common man. Until, we have such leaders or these present ones come to their senses, and think good of Africa . . . Africa will never know peace . . . take it from me, 'mon comrades.

"Hey! Ireman . . . what you just preach man, is the Jah truth . . . but, man, why do you say you do not speak good English man . . . you don't know you speak English more than most of us from the British colonies man?" Eto said teasingly. "And besides man, you're accustomed to this region 'hiccups' man! Believe me, you would've made a good politician back there . . . in your country . . . if not this 'fucking' genocide."

Kanombe smiled again happily and continued in a measured tone.

Oh! I thank you very much Rastaman . . . the fact is, whenever I spoke English very long like today, I speak better you know the more I discuss in English. I forgot to tell you guys, that I undertook one of my trainings under some American officers led by Major John Harris . . . He was a Black officer and a very good man. It was then I learnt some of the English I'm speaking today. He always encourages us to speak better English . . . but you know, English is not all that easy to learn, much more, this American English with their 'Hi men . . . Fuck yo' men . . . We're gonna men . . . Hey look here yo' mutha-fucker!

They all laughed at his American imitated accents.

And the political aspect of me, you've forgotten I told you I came from a very big political family . . . 'mon pere' being a politician, 'mon' uncle and 'ma *Tante*'; she was the chairperson of the women wing Rwanda Patriotic

Front . . . so you see that politics is inborn as far as I'm concerned, yet as you said all is now a forgotten issue, all things have now changed for me . . . What remains now is how to organize myself and become a man again here in Europe and have 'my family' if God helps me to get one here and live to enjoy the rest of my life.

"So, you don't pray to go back to Rwanda, whenever there would be peace . . . I mean, when all Africa will be truly democratic," Hyman asked grinning.

Kanombe interrupted Hyman, not really understanding his proposal.

God forbid! Mon ami, for me to pray God to go back to Africa is the same as to pray to go straight to hell fire when I die. You seem not to understand what I went through in that continent.

"I meant, when eventually Africa becomes a democratic and developed continent," Hyman said.

Kanombe inquired seriously.

When, do you think this will take place Hyman, in 'our' life time? Comrades, I'm not trying to sound discouraged, but with all these powers there. Don't you think that they knew what they're doing, in that, they always encourage these conflicts in Africa and not helping her to solve them, like they're doing in the Middle East or in Asian countries, they knew that if and when Africa will have true democracy as you said, and come together as one and truly united Africa, then they will find it hard to deal with her—that is, they'll not be dictating to Africa in areas like telling Africa how much or when to sell their God given mineral resources. Or do you think Americans, Europeans, Russians or some of the Asian countries would've been interested in affairs of Africa if not because of her raw materials? No, comrades, these people would've isolated Africa totally, and maybe Africa would've been living in peace today. So you can agree with me that Africa is very poor today because she was very rich yesterday. And I heard, you asked if I don't pray to go back to Rwanda when every problem is settled there. I tell you no time will everything be ok in that country. We've a very long sentimental issue in that country, I mean the

Tutsi and the Hutu tribes—and besides, who will I go back to . . . I don't have any relative alive in Rwanda. Everybody I know, even distant relatives had gone with the genocide . . . so tell me, who I'll go back to meet? You see that it will not be possible for me after God saved me twice and finally brought me to Europe.

"But, there's what you said about the foreigners isolating Africa if not for our mineral resources, I think I disagree with you on that point . . . because, looking at the history of their coming, you agree that the Europeans (the Portuguese, the Spanish) came first, and later the other countries like France, British, Belgium, German etc., all came to Africa some hundreds of years ago before we even discovered the mineral resources . . . if this part of history is correct, then why did you say that they wouldn't have been interested in African affairs if not because of our resources?" Hyman Otta queries deliberately, yearning for a heated sparring with Jean and to taste his historical knowledge as well.

The old 'child' soldier looked askance at Otta.

Now listen very carefully. I'm not a historian nor did I went to school much (apart from my primary education) as you would've known . . . but the little I was taught in my school days and the one 'mon pere' normally sat us down in the good old days and taught us concerning the Whitemen and their interests in Africa . . . I can tell you that the first Europeans that came to Africa, like the Portuguese and the Spanish as you rightly pointed out, did not come to bring the Christian religion as they claimed to have come for, but to prepare the road to slavery . . . just like 'John the Baptist' came to prepare the way of Christ Jesus, according to the Bible . . . So you'll believe me that after these sets of spies came and spied out Africa, then come the slave masters. Having succeeded in destabilizing the peace our forefathers were having before they came . . . mind you, I'm only talking of my country, I do not know what happened in the other countries or your country; then, we have what we called organized African traditional democracy. For example, our forefathers had kings and chiefs that everybody fears and always trust to take their problems to; who will in turn judge and render pure justice without fear or favour . . . We have the 'Munju' (gods) which everybody worship and are very afraid of, that time. There're no wars between our people at that time. People were very

171

contented with whatever they had at that time. As a matter of fact, our forefathers were used to living in peaceful atmosphere with each other . . . until these greedy slave masters came with their tricks and corruptions, which they've known for ages and which they've been dealing with in their own respective countries and cultures; and which we do not in anyway know in our own cultures before they came.

You see, that was when corruption entered Africa, that was when enmity entered Africa and that was when slavery entered Africa, to name but a few, thereby opening the way for African forceful emigration to Europe and later America. Now you see their main purpose of coming to Africa, my brothers. To corrupt African leaders who were very hard working for their people then; and who always respect and fear the Munju gods then; and whom their subjects used to respect without malice that time . . . Yes of course, because it was after their coming that these African kings and chiefs came to know about acquiring much riches for themselves. Judge for yourselves my brothers. Are the gods to be blame? No, the gods are not to be blamed, but the Europeans. They even forced the African leaders then. For some kings and chiefs who did not follow their corruptive ways and their religions, they were instantly killed without remorse. So, many of these African leaders afraid to be killed were enticed by their materialistic ways. And the leaders who were then being charmed with these material things—for example mirrors and foreign wines—would dance according to their wishes and started selling our forefathers, our mothers, our sisters and our bothers as slaves. That was not all, because after shipping these slaves to America for forceful plantation booms; then and having helped in every aspect of building the New World (USA), later, when America declared their independence from Britain (after the bloody war which the Black slaves were fully involved and millions of lives lost) on the 4th of July 1776, then these issues of slavery eventually came up again, this time around, not on how to buy more slaves, but how to stop slaves coming into the new world, and how to do away with the ones that were already inside. The same slaves who as it were, had used their manpower and sweats to help build America, and even shed their blood for her when the need arouse . . . Yes, they were thinking of deporting them from America, their arguments being that they (African slaves) were too barbaric to live in the New World, but they were not too timid and barbaric to help shaping the New World. You see what I mean, my brothers? They started planning where to deport the Black slaves. Of course, they were successful in deporting many of the slaves from America; which brought about the birth of countries like Liberia (Monrovia) and Sierra Leone (Freetown). Yes that was why they called the capital of Sierra Leone 'Freetown' where many Negroes of different origins were automatically sanctioned out of America and deported there forcefully—intentionally depriving them of their basic human rights. Some of the slaves, all black in faces, minds, and blood were taken to Brazil, Dominican Republic, Jamaica, Haiti etc.. Oh! Yes comrades, almost all the Black people in these countries are our African lost brothers and sisters. It was not yet over between Africa and these Europeans . . . I mean the atrocities did not stop in the slave trade. They started killing each other in Africa. Fighting against each other in a continent that wasn't theirs, in another man's backyard . . . They started scrambling for Africa in Africa. Not until Berlin conference of 1884-1885. Oh 'wee . . . wee' they agreed and went and seated on one conference table in Berlin (everyone putting down their weapons); and distributed 'Mother Africa' among themselves. They shared Africa at the Berlin conference like a mother sharing a loaf of bread to her children around the dinning table, or could I say, like soldiers sharing spoils of war among themselves. The British colonizing and intimidating South Africa, Nigeria, Ghana, Zimbabwe, Zambia, Botswana and many other countries; while France was given the taste of punishing, Central Africa Republic, Congo, Ivory Coast, Benin Republic, Chad, Niger, Burkina Faso with many other countries as their own colonial empire (of course, the French government sought and obtained the lion share among the other European countries because of its super military might then). Belgium under the leadership of King Leopold 11 at that time had in their possession, the Democratic Republic of Congo DRC, my country Rwanda which they colonized, sliced, imbibed tribal sentiments and hatred into and Burundi; Germany took Namibia; Portugal as small as they were in population had Angola, Mozambique, Guinea-Bissau, Cape Verde Island, Sao Tome and Principe; while Spain colonized Equatorial Guinea. That was how they scrambled and divided Africa on their own without one African sitting there that day with them. Yes, Africa had no representative, where her own issue was on board. Or, I better say where she was being slaughtered without committing any sin. Oh yes, comrades, the Berlin conference 'Hall' where the meeting was held was the slaughter-house for Africa, and that very day the meeting was concluded and agreement reached, signalled the death and burial date of Africa. It marked the beginning and the end of Africa's freedom. Believe me comrades it's not a laughing matter. Nor is it a matter Africa will be sitting crying and killing themselves. But, rather, it should be a matter Africa must sit together and think over and fight the injustice done so far against her. Because, I tell you, Africa was brought just like a sheep to the slaughtering, and like Ewe that was before her sharers, she has become mute. She also would not open her mouth to protest. But for sure, with time and by God's special grace and powers she will be resuscitate. She must resurrect with more powers. She will never depend on anybody again. Yet for now, her survival will be partially at the hands of these powers that be. It's a matter of, if and when they want Africa to become united; and then partially and most importantly in the hands of African leaders of today to come together and fight it together and know that it's either they fight now or they will leave it forever . . . but let the leaders of today have it in their minds that he who fights and run away, lives to fight another day. And, that instead of postponing the fighting for unity to the unborn children of Africa they will have to start it now. All Africans must come together and help these regions of Africa where there are still war . . . before peace will finally come.

"I supported you," Koso cuts in, "Africa must not wait for the United Nation which in the real sense is dis-united on many issues concerning her. One good example, being the 'reparation' issue or for the Europeans, and the Americans, who insistently eliminate any good African leader that stands against them."

Kanombe broadened his eyelids in appreciation. He glanced at his roommates from one face to the other and continued in his humorous, yet veracious vein.

And that brings us to the other side of their foreign policies which never varied. Well, the truth they say is very bitter. However, it must always have to be said so that one must be free. As Koso just said, what happened to the first elected Prime Minister of the Democratic Republic of Congo Patrice Lumumba was a typical case of this elimination tactics. Did any of you guys know exactly what happened to him?

"Yeah, he was killed" replied Hyman Otta.

"Any idea of how he was killed. Or, who killed him?"

"Well, I only heard he was killed during an uprising after the election, but I didn't know why he was killed or by whom?"

Kanombe smiled again, believing his newly acquired friends were getting along with him.

Then, listen and listen for good. On 17th of January 1961, barely two months and, after the first free and fair election in the whole of Africa and after almost six months and two weeks the government of Belgium granted the then Congo her independence on the 30th of June 1960; Patrice Lumumba, a self-made idealist was assassinated by a plot masterfully planned by the Belgium Secret Police Unit and the America's Central Intelligence Agency-CIA simply because he wanted to rule his country the other way round, and not their capitalist and monopolistic ways. He strongly believed in the political and economic freedom of his country and he dearly died for that cause. But, his innocent blood is still, up to this day in pursuit of those that killed him. The conspirators will never, never know peace.

"Ireman, you wouldn't have left Africa, man! Because, I believe, man! Africa really needs people like you . . . people who can help solve her problems man!" complimented Eto, the Jah Rastaman.

He turned and stared at Eto.

Naa wee, wee I would've. But for now, I happened to find myself here. Well, far, alive and save. It was quite unfortunate for Africa. I really believe I've contributed my own quota for her and her problems. I lost my whole family in a tribal and sentimental (Genocide). I suffered as an orphan from a very youthful age. I fought as a professional soldier in Africa's bloodiest, most dangerous and most senseless war in the DRC (for the leader's selfish reasons and enrichment). Twice I found myself very close to death, for no just cause. You know what that means my brothers for somebody to be in coma for almost 14 days. I've tried for Africa. Let others help her, too. I've left Africa for good. To tell the fact, I said bye, bye to Africa and forget about her and her troubles on the very day I boarded the plane.

175

"Now, please can you continue the story and tell us everything that took place that day you said God saved your life. It's a very interesting story and I believe every one of us is interested and eager to listen" interrupted Koso, staring at the radio clock. "Hee boy, it's almost 7 pm. You've spoken for nearly six hours without knowing . . . Oh! Charlie, you're super. You've made today one of the fastest days for us. Please, try to complete . . . or we could possibly adjourn for another day if you're tired already?"

Kanombe felt a bit proud for Koso's compliments.

For Christ's precious sake, you don't say please to me for talking. I am a professional talkative, just like I am a professional soldier. And besides what else can one do in this type of condition if one is not talking, your please makes me to remember one day last year, of course. We were drinking in one of my close pal's apartment inside the camp, in one of our military barracks. Oh he died in that accident which ended my career as a soldier. May his departed soul and the souls of others rest in perfect peace! Amen.

Kanombe prayed and made a sign of the cross, and constructively continued.

So as we were drinking that day, after we had smoked some quantities of grass and were trying to . . .

"Ire old soldier man, you also puff ganja? That's good of you . . . Oh! Man, I'm very happy you belonged . . . Ireman! . . . I for say . . . that's why you're wise and intelligent . . . that's the 'food' for the wise man!" uttered the Rastaman praisingly. "Yo man, when you take ganja . . . you think, eat, behave, meditate and see wisely. It's also the 'grandmother' of all medicine man! That's why the Indians call it the India hemp. In fact, it supposes to have been legalized by all the government of the world man! I'm a staunch supporter of the world wide campaign for the legalization of Marijuana. It remains the only politics I'm very very interested in . . . Ireman, you got me?"

Kanombe shook his head in agreement.

We used to call it 'dazza' in our barrack but one of my friends Tiko normally called it 'our father in the bush'. You 'gata' believe no soldier, be him or her

176

Westerners or Africans can go without dazza? And even many politicians and bigger guys in every segment of the society take ganja. And so, as I was saying before, we had just finished smoking and were soaking and drowning ourselves for hours—all the while I was giving them 'gist' about so many things, histories, politics, women affairs . . . when one other friend 'Johnson the black-Rover'—he was my friend since our days in the army training camp, and continued to be my roommate in the war camp—, asked me if I'm not tired yet, and suggested that we go back to our bunk and relax for the whole unit would be moving out the following morning. You couldn't believe what happened next. I sat up from where I was sitting, and wanted to depart with him, but the fellow hosting us refused and instead he organized others to push Johnny out of the place. As he was struggling with them, you know soldiers, how crazy they used to be, one of them just rushed and stabbed him with a broken bottle, while another drew his service pistol and shot him on the leg. Because of as he later told our commander the next day that Johnny the black Rover was disturbing the peace and trying to take away from them their only happiness in the death camp. Comrades forgive me for dragging you along, now I've to go back to that miraculous part of this story of my life.

+++

It was getting dark and the whistles of death huming, drawing us nearer to the land of the Spirits. The day started for every soldier in my unit as a happy bright day but towards evening, things started to change. First, it started to rain without any sign from the gods that rain will fall. It was on the 7th of April. Exactly five years of the genocide. As it were, I also lost more than ten trusted and close friends of mine. Some of them as close to me as my perished family. So, you see why this day would always remain special in my life.

Kanombe declared to his fellow cellmates eventually. They were all lying on their bunk-beds listening.

As we were patrolling with two full loaded trucks, it didn't occur to any of us that death was fast coming. Because I was feeling weak after much smoking and drinking the previous day, I went and took my position at the back of the last truck so as not to be disturbed by anyone. I was very tired up to the extent that I think I fell fast asleep before the accident happened. And that was all I could remember. The story later was that my patrol team felt upon the enemy's anti-tank mines and that brought to an abrupt end of my military career and the death of thirty-nine Rwandan army personnel. Believe me, up till today, I don't know how I escaped the fatal accident and anything I told you apart from this means I am basically lying. But one thing is, for sure, God saved me the second time in my life, and I believe He saved me for a purpose, so my duty now is to search for that purpose.

"What happened next, I meant, how did you later know about what had befallen you and your troops and how did you manage to come to Europe?" Koso enquired.

Kanombe made the sign of the cross once more, with his index finger and grimaced as he recollected the incident.

This is where I will ever remain grateful to God all my life . . . see what happened. As I was later told by the mademoiselle, the Ugandan girl that took care of me for almost two weeks before I travelled, after our trucks struck the anti-tank mine, nobody knew what happened to us immediately. Our central command could not be able to locate us or account for us because the truth was that we left our normal patrol route entirely to go as far as Bunia border in the Province Oriental (Haut Congo). At that time, after the Rwandan army had some misunderstanding with their Ugandan counterparts, which resulted in a brief military confrontation between the former two allies, a lot of mistrusts existed even when the problem was settled. From then on, we don't normally operate to that side of the border because it was entirely under the command of the Ugandan army and the rebel faction of Professor Wamba Dia Wamba. So it happened that on that very evening, our leader, second lieutenant Mbongo Bizigame was adamant by disobeying our general commander's standing order not to cross our strong position of the borders near Goma our main Base. Of course, our second lieutenant Mbongo was such a stubborn and strange guy, that none of us that day could question his order. The only one that reminded him of the commander's order, Sergeant Kizi was immediately reprimanded by him and he, Mbongo, threatened to punish him when we get back to the camp. He was so stubborn and pompous like a dog, that day—which made me to remember the adage of my people, 'that a dog destined to die is always blind and can't as usual sniff out the odour of stools'. Yeah, I was told by the nurse, Esther by name, a pretty and tender girl that her master, Brigadier Amin Sokoeveni brought me to his quarters after four days of the incident, when his troops had found our scattered trucks and later I, as the only surviving member of the patrol team, with the other thirty-nine dead bodies along their own side of the border. Brigadier Amin was from the Uganda army. She said that for almost ten days after I was brought to the house, that I could not open my eyes. But she asserted, that my last words before I finally drifted into coma, was to an Ugandan army personnel, who, as she said, I was able to give my personal data and courageously begged him not to let me die. When I lost consciousness, the officer, his name was Sergeant Kozium took me to their military hospital, probably a clinic, inside their camp and later I was brought to the quarters of the brigadier who happened to be the chief medical officer of the camp and who immediately arranged and put me in a special emergency unit of his quarters, where Esther was assigned to look after me twenty-fours hours of the day and that she . . .

"So Ire-old soldier, what happened after that?" interrupted the Rastaman Eto who had been enjoying the overlonged gist all along but became more interested when Kanombe mentioned about the 'bebe' and how pretty she looked. "Ireman, I mean about the *okpeke* . . . you . . . you screwed the shit out of her prettiness man! Didn't you? Ire, tell us the Jah truth man! You don't dare tell lie to Jah Rastaman, men."

"Trust the African man he can never miss such opportunity," Koso supported.

Kanombe shook his head to and fro and continued.

Oh! Rastaman, you guys are too fast. That was not the issue then, I wasn't myself that time. There's a saying that 'he, whose house is on fire, does not strive for, or pursue the rat'. I will come to that later. Don't run faster than your shadow, okay.

He glanced towards Hyman Otta, who nodded his head in agreement.

Well, as I was saying, after ten days, that's excluding the four days before we were found, I regained full consciousness and became able for the first time to speak with the people around me. I believed God brought me out from the association of the dead that day. Mademoiselle Esther also said that the brigadier-doctor, who was also a Rev. Father and the chief chaplain of the catholic mission in the camp, ordered her to give me some tranquillizer injections so that I would have more rest and energy. The story later was that Sergeant Kozium whom I nicknamed 'the Samaritan Sergeant', and his men were the fourth patrol team that passed across the scene of the accident, and that even when they stopped to check on us, he was the only one that came down from their vehicle. When he came to where I had tumbled over . . . about six poles from the trucks and from where my colleagues were scattered, then he saw that I was still breathing slowly. He was the person that suggested that I might have fallen out from one of the truck before the accident. His reasons were, from the scene of the accident to where he saw me and again the fact that the only injury in my body was so minor that he thought the AK 47 gun which I was carrying with me on that bittered day, might have discharged itself when I was sleeping and fell out of the truck and struck at my right thigh. I think everybody took this story as the truth of what really happened, because the doctor also confirmed that they extracted two bullets from my thigh. And these bullets were without doubt from my gun. Sergent Kozium told me that he had a hard time with his fellow officers before they could agree to help me. That they refused because he told them that I was a Rwandan soldier, that he better forget this monster soldier who was as good as a dead person. But that he persisted and begged them to help. All the while that he was carrying me on his shoulder. For over one hour, he was imploring on my behalf, until their leader, captain Mako Ndunga, who was well known throughout the Ugandan army circle as an anti-Rwanda-soldier, jumped down from their vehicle and helped even to put me in between himself and my good samaritan sergeant at the passenger's seat because they feared that some of the soldiers at the back might intentionally kill me if I was taken to the back. The captain according to the story automatically ordered the driver to drive straight to the hospital.

He indicated another sign of the cross, tears dripping down his over-sweated face, yet, he continued as the brave soldier he was.

My brothers, this is where I come to believe that it was with a special hand and for a special purpose 'mon Dieu' delivered me. The story continued.

When they reached the camp, they hurriedly summoned the Rev. Brigadier doctor, who left all he was doing and with the assistance of the soldiers I was rushed into the emergency room and the journey to revive me then started in earnest. This will marvel you, I know, but the thing that will marvel you most, was the fact, that captain Mako Ndunga of all people, as she told me, did not go back on patrols again with his troops that day. But that rather, he was serious helping to carry me around to the emergency unit and back to the military Ambulance Jeep when the doctor suggested that I should be taken to his quarters for a special care. She even professed she saw captain Mako shedding tears when he was told by the doctor initially that my chance of surviving was very slim. However, that (the doctor) believed that if God Almighty could sustained me for that long since the accident happened, without food, without water to drink, then he only bet on the power and the miraculous hand of God; and that captain Ndunga, who was thoroughly known in the camp as a drunker and a womanizer, refused to drink and even to sleep with his 'camp birds' . . . that he even went as far as to boast in the presence of officers and subordinates alike, that he would not drink or touch any woman until I regain mon consciousness . . . that when he was asked by one of his officer's friends 'what he would do if I did not regain consciousness, let say in one or two months or on the contrary, if I happen to die.' She said that captain Ndunga boldly and frankly told his friend that, that would mean the end of his drunkenness and womanizing, and that he would even decide to quit the army and retire to private life. So, you see what God has done for me. The stone which the builders rejected later turned to be the corner stone. Because, to tell the truth, this same captain Mako Ndunga, who was a self-declared enemy of the Rwandese and whom it took almost one hour to change his heart to save me later became my 'Godfather' and the architect of my coming to Europe. And please bear with me until you know his reasons for his hatred against the Rwandese, then you will agree with me that God's hand was really on all the things that happened to me.

Kanombe wiped the tears of joy from his face, as he started to sing.

'Thank you for saving me, thank you my Lord!,' raising his hands upwards and tears of joy flowing down freely from his eyes, and was joined by his roommates in praises, after which he went into the toilet to ease himself.

He told his roommates to get ready for the final part of the Kanombe's story.

++

They were in the mood of great expectation for him to come out and complete his long pathetic story. Kanombe took his time and washed his sweated face with water and having cleared it with the paper handkerchief, he came out looking fresher and expectantly continued from where he stopped, clearing his throat.

Yes, God used him to help me. He was all and all to me now, except God. He was 'mon pere, mon oncle, mon frere' . . . in fact, he was everything to me. As the story goes, captain Ndunga had organized a kind of party the day I regained my consciousness. And the truth as he swore, that was the day he started tasting anything alcoholic and true to his words his 'cramps of birds' started flowing back to his bed once more. So it happened that, after three days, when I finally recovered full, and was able to move around without clutches, Captain Ndunga and Rev. Brigadier Doctor Sokoeveni invited me to visit them at the office of the doctor. When I came inside, they were already drinking from Vodka and the Red-wine bottles on top of the desk, and there was an extra empty tumbler on the table and an extra office chair. So being a professional soldier, I saluted them, and stood attentively, but the captain ordered me to be at ease. Do you know what it means to tell a soldier to be at 'ease'?

Kanombe demanded from them, laughing broadly, just to get them along.

"Ireman, it is military slang! How do you think us bloody civilians to know about military orders or soldiers' lives! I think military languages and lives will ever remain for the military, man!; and the Rastaman slangs and Reggae lives be for the Jah Rastamen; so also, should the preacher man's gospels, his Bibles, his lingua franca and lives remain for him man!; and even the . . ." he murmured, glancing at Koso for a moment and added jokingly, "and so also, the Guru-man's languages, knowledge and lives will be for him and his fellow gurumen . . ." uttered the Rastaman Eto, as he yanked out some of his dreadlock that lost from their tie and covered his face. "Jah man had once suggested that until every living thing, human beings, animals or the birds of heaven of the same feathers locomotes according to their *Genuss-man!*, *Katzenjammer* can't be averted, Ireman!"

"Oh! Rastaman you always manufacture strange words, what's this 'Katjam' you said?" Kanombe laughed. He stared at Hyman and Koso, who were all laughing out of control. "I've never heard of this English word that resembled Russian or the Indian metropolic figure of speech like Indian referring the guruman as Acharya. Is that what you mean?"

"Ireman, that's one of those things we the Jah Rastafarians came to promote in this 'Jah Universe' man! *Katzenjammer* is another word for problems in the Rastafarian movement. It's an (inspirational) obstacle between man and Jah! Which all Rastafarians are fighting against, man! Jah did not create man to live with problems in the first place, man! But the sins of man brought problems to man . . . Ireman! Oh yeah, man, it were sins that brought these problems that fill the Jah world today."

"Rastaman, please, let him finish. It's almost mid-night" Koso said cogitatively, "I knew we've assorted preachers here . . . but let's hear this gist to its conclusion, before you or Rev. Father H. Otta begins, for I already knew it will finally end up to that."

"Koso, why do you always seem to be afraid of the gospel just like 'devil and the workers of iniquities who always fall down anytime the name of Jesus Christ is being mentioned? Or are you a devil-reincarnate?" Hyman demanded and turning to Kanombe, he said.

"Now old soldier, you asked if we knew what it meant to remain at 'ease'right? Let me remind you that I was a former commissioner of the boy's scouts in the whole of Southern Sudan. And as a para-military organization, I've passed through orders and I've issued it myself. Your captain ordered you to remain serene. That is, you should feel relaxed and comfortable. Isn't it so?"

"Well, Mr Otta, that's correct . . . but, you have to understand that many military terms are not the same things as to compare with your boy's scouts."

"Granted, but . . ."

"And for your information, Mr. Old soldier," Koso called out, "I was the former commandant of the 'man o' war', another powerful para-military group in the whole of Kumasi region and the fourth deputy commandant in Ghana. So you see that everybody was either an old soldier, or an old boy's scout, or an old man o' war . . . with the exception of Prince Eto, whom I never know whether he was the former 'President or an old Prime Minister of the Rastafarian movement in the 'whole' of Nigeria . . . Are you one?" Koso inquired from Eto, reciprocating his initial joke to him, when Eto called him the guru man.

"Ireman, to be lance corporal of this, or the commissioner of that, or the commandant of . . . . will never be the goal of the Jah Rastaman on earth, but rather, to preach about 'one love' and the love of Jah to all nation, man! And to worship Jah in holiness and listen to lyrics about Jah and his Highness, man!"

Kanombe was happy none of them appeared tired of his talkative manners.

Now, I understand you all said. Look guys, I only want to know if you're still following the gist. So the captain asked me to feel at home, that they only wanted to have a little chat with me and that I should rather tell them the truth of everything they wanted to know about me and my family, and that I should, please help myself as far as the drinks are concerned. Comrades, you know that for over two weeks I had not smelt any drink since the last one on the previous night of the last journey of my military career. Before the captain could finish what he was saying I had rushed down the first glass of Vodka which helped and made me feel bolder and relaxed. The captain asked me my name. I humbly told him my name. At first, when I pronounced my surname, the Brigadier looked absolutely shocked. He immediately asked if the KANOMBE of a name has any connection with Mr. Gobe Kanombe of the Gikongoro 'au village'; that perished with every member of his family in the 1994 genocide. I told them that I was his son and briefly narrated how I saw my family being massacred by the Hutu extremist from top of the mango tree and how I escaped later. The brigadier doctor Rev. Father abruptly made a very loud emotional shout and embraced me, crying openly like a baby, which made tears to drop from my already dried eyeballs. Later, after about ten minutes of crying somehow for joy, it was the captain, for the brigadier was short of words, who explained the whole mystery to me.

At that moment, there were noises from the warders on night duty who were going round the prison cells checking on the prisoners. They peeped through the opening on the center of the heavy iron-door. Kanombe paused for a moment and continued as the warders left for other cells.

To begin with, he told me how my father and both of them—the brigadier and himself, captain Mako and even my uncle attended the same high school in Rwanda—after which both of them returned to their country Uganda, how he joined the army immediately as a Lance Bombardier, and the Brigadier preferring the Seminary school, finished and was ordained as a Rev. Father, and went to further course as a medical doctor before joining the army. He said that all this while, they were communicating with my family up to that last day of the tragedy. He went on and narrated to me how four of them, my father, my uncle, the brigadier and himself were the backbone of their school's soccer team and how my father was later selected as the captain of their school team, even in deviation to the choice of the school's games master (Coach) but that the coach later bowed to pressure after four of them seriously threatened to change to a nearby rival school. He also professed to me how closed all of them were, in the sense that they were all present the very day my father first met my mother at an Inter-Denominational church crusade which was organized by the Rwandan Pentecostal Movement which the Principal of their school, Mr. Kakagama was the president. And that it was held at their school's big football field. He told me how my mother was very shy at first when my father approached her, and how they all later went to a local Bier-Parlour near their school that same evening and had some local brews-up-wine. The captain did not stop there, he went on and told me, how before one week the crusade lasted, my father and my mother had agreed to marry each other, and that the brigadier and himself, even later attended their wedding eventually after almost four years they'd left school. The captain took time to narrate to me many things—even the holidays they embarked together to America and Europe. He said that the most painful thing about the 1994 genocide, was the fact that the Brigadier and himself were in Rwanda visiting an old school mate in the Kiyovu village, a neighbourhood village near Kigali on that 7ᵗʰ day of April 1994, and that prior to their visit, they had telephoned my father and arranged to visit our house as their last port of call. And that the first person they recognized his picture in the national dailies was that of my father and the entire family, and according to him, he could not eat or drink anything for nearly five days and that it was the shock of the tragedy that even made him a drunk afterwards, because it was too much for him to bore as a friend; and that in fact, was the very day his hatred for the Hutus all over the world and the Rwandese in general started. And that he had carried this in his mind up to that very evening they rescued me. But that his hatred had subdued now. He professed to have erected a kind of shrine, a very big 'Ciborium', where he had putting up a grand monument in honour of my family at his compound in Kampala, the Ugandan capital, and that he had placed my family photograph (which he had snapped us on the fiftieth birthday of my father of which he attended in the company of the Rev. Brigadier doctor) visibly inside the shrine. He admitted that he had unknowingly counted me dead and even buried me in his heart together with my other family members. That it was now he really understood the physical and passionate emotions which boiled within him that day I was rescued, and why he did not as usual shoot the Samaritan sergeant for disobeying his orders, not to allow me die off. That the sergeant had insisted and told him (captain Ndunga) that God has ordered him to save this Rwandan man and that as a Christian, it was better for him to obey the voice of God, rather than obeying the voice of man. This had made the captain very annoyed and the devil had surely pushed him up to the extent that he brought out his revolver and unlocked it before the shivering began, his hands and entire body shaking like someone suffering from chronic Parkinson disease, and that there was a sort of instant seizure of his right hand where he held the gun. And that his instinct as a result, immediately told him to jump down and help the Samaritan sergeant. And so he continued to talk and talk and talk for more than five hours, proving to be more talkative than me, the professional talkative himself. Later when the doctor got himself he told his own part of the story which centred that he did not save me by his expertise, but that it was by God's power and mercy I'm alive today.

"The Lord is good all the time," Hyman said.

"All the time the Lord is good," replied Kanombe devotedly, as he performed the sign of the cross once more.

Kanombe straightened, feeling more tired, he continued in a very low voice for it had been nearly three o'clock in the morning, yet his roommates were still earger to listen, like his army friends were in the barrack back then.

If I continued to recount everything I discussed with them that day, I don't think we can sleep for the next five days. But the bottom line is that, it was that same meeting which later led to the decision of my coming to Europe. To cut everything short, listen to what happened. After the brigadier's aide, brought us the evening meal of porridge red-beans and fried plantain—which was very delicious. The Brigadier and Captain Ndunga excused theirselves and went out to discuss briefly. When they came back it was the Rev. Brigadier this time around who spoke first, asking me what I would like to do with my miraculous life, hence, it has been certain that I would not be going back to the Rwandan army and to the most senseless war again. Because, the captain had earlier in the afternoon during the course of our discussions, joked that God has adopted me to him, and that he would take a short leave the following day and use it to travel to his family house in Kampala, and erased my face from my family photograph in his shrine, as he said, 'a living man has no place in the land of the dead'. Well, I frankly answered them that, as a little boy then and the son of a well known politician I used to adore politicians, that later after the genocide as a young boy of fourteen years but matured man in suffering, I'd decided to enter the Rwandan army as my last chance hoping that one day I'll be able to grow in ranks and even become the most senior officer, then I would have the opportunity to revenge the cold-blooded massacre of my tribal men and women. But alias, to the two officers of the Ugandan army, and very close pals of my late father and my uncle, that seems to be history or 'June 12' as one of my Nigerian friend called my opinion after I narrated my story to him in the asylum camp.

"And what did he mean by this June 12?" asked Koso himself laughing.

"Rastaman Eto could you help with that? You must have known about . . ." Hyman said.

"Yeah Ireman, June, 12 1993 remains the darkest scene in the history of the Nigeria's political set-up man! It was a day no Nigerian will ever forget, man! A very free and fair election was held on that day. And M.K.O Abiola, a Yoruba from South-West part of Nigeria won a landslide victory man! But he was denied his chance to become president, man! By no other people, than our Northern brothers, who as it were had almost been ruling the country since Independence from Britain on October, 1st, 1960. Ireman, you can't believe it man! But it surely happened. Chief M.K.O. Abiola was later imprisoned by the dictatorial military government of Gen. Sanni Abacha in 1994 till July 8 1998, when he died yet in a mysterious circumstance in the prison, man! . . . So Ire-brothers, June 12 became history the moment MKO died" Eto asserted thoughtfully.

"Believe me, Nigerians are all funny people. They seem to have an apropos names for everything. Like they use to call fraudsters '419ers'" Koso jokingly assured. "But, look, old soldier, you must finish this story."

Kanombe choked as his fellow inmate's eager faces looked up and listened.

You don't need to worry, Charlie, the story has already entered into the extra-time any moment from now the referee will blow the final whistle. So, right-away there, in the office of the Rev. Doctor Brigadier-Gen. I was provided with a special 'pass' which automatically changed my name to Joseph Mago Ndunga meaning that I've been instantly adopted by the captain without too much protocol. Oh yes, comrades, I became the adopted son of captain Mako Ndunga in a twinkle of an eye. Something, we all know that would've taken up to three years in the West took only five minutes to complete in the office of an African army personnel. After all, they said 'that something new always comes from Africa and that everything is possible in Africa'. Later that night as three of us walked back towards the officer's mess, my step-father asked me to write down in a paper my size of shoe, shirt, trouser and everything I needed and send it to him that same night through the Brigadier's orderly. Boy! I was overjoyed at their kindnesses up to I immediately knelt down 'en route' (on the track road) and started to thank them even I spoke 'Luganda' without knowing, which surprised both of them more, for they didn't know I speak their native language. We had been all the while conversing in Kiswahili dialect, so when they heard me speaking their ethnic language, their love for me even increased. Could you imagine, making me somebody from nobody. The Brigadier came where I was kneeling and lifted me up and hugged me in happiness. When I later told them that I speak more than five of the regional languages in the whole of central and southern parts of Africa they became even more proud of me. I really know you are all feeling somehow exhausted and may be surprised on why this is taking too long to complete or why am I telling this part in details instead of narrating how I finally entered Europe. I beg you to be a bit more patient with me, please, don't be annoyed. Like I said in the beginning, this is the whole story of my life aka, 'the Kanombe's Story', and I derive pleasure and always feel emotionally strong and equally seem contented with my life whenever I'm retelling this story to anyone, because to me these acts of charity which these Ugandan army 'saints' showered on me is not only worthy of emulation, but it must be told and mentioned vividly to the Glory of God. To cut a long story short just like the 'special pass' was issued to me under five minutes so also the 'diplomatic passport' which I eventually used, appeared without notice. For once prior to that day I boarded the aeroplane my step-father did not mention anything concerning travelling in my presence, but rather, sometimes especially in the evenings, after he might have consumed some quantities of the locally brewed liquors or Vodka, the captain would under that influence tell me, that he was planning for me to be taken to Kampala, to go and help manage his chains of businesses there for him; and to stay close with his family which comprised his wife and three beautiful daughters, my step-sisters whom I didn't have the opportunity to see facially but their pictures, before I travelled. On such occasions, he would happily tell me that I was a special gift from God to him, that God has finally heard and answered his prayers and provided him with a 'son' at his old age because he had been earnestly requesting from him through his wife's child-bearing age but that God at that time did not want to listen to him or maybe He (God), didn't really understood how important a son is to an Arican man. However, he would always add, 'Just as God later blessed Abraham in his old age by giving him a son Isaac through his wife Sarah, so also God has blessed him by giving him Joseph (Isaac) Mago Ndunga, at his (the captain's) old age, but, unlike Abraham, not through his lovely wife, rather through

'the anti-tank mine' accident at Bunia border'. May His name always be praised', captain Ndunga would say.
Not until the very last minute I boarded the Swiss-Air at the Kinshasa International Airport that day did I know I was going abroad. Earlier that evening the captain had ordered his aide de camp and the driver of the Brigadier Rev. to drive me to the airport and told me that I was supposed to be in Kampala in a few hours time that he would call and make sure that I'd arrive there safely. As we arrived at the airport I was met by a tall White guy who handed the 'diplomatic passport' over to me with a boarding pass just a few minutes before we entered the plane. The same guy who looked a little bit older than me and who introduced himself in French as Jean Perry Edouard, a business representative and consultant of my step-father captain Mako Ndunga, in the whole of Western countries and North America (USA, Canada, Mexico etc), eventually escorted me to Europe and dumped me.

"So you did arrive in Europe as a legitimate son of Ugandan army captain, why, did you decide to seek for asylum without papers? Or, did you summit your pass along with other documents to the *Bundesministerium*?" Hyman asked him, unable to understand why he would be brought to the deportation camp unlike him and the others that had no papers to present to the authorities.

Kanombe stared at him for a moment, and continued, his voice cracking with emotion.

Here comes another big question which has a rather short answer attached to it. To start with, I've told you I didn't know where I was going in the first instance. I was told by the captain, I'm going to Kampala, later inside the aircraft, Mr Edouard told me that after he had listened to my sympathetic story from his business partner (captain Mako Ndunga) that he had tried to convince him that the best option for me is to go to abroad and obtain some basic education, after which I'd be taken over the management of their international firms, rather than going to Kampala. You know that I've no authority to ask where or to say no or yes since I was assured I'm not going to Rwanda or back to the bloody DRC war. I didn't bother to ask in any case. So when eventually the White guy added that he preferred me to be in Canada and we're in the air, I'd have no gut again to doubt his integrity. He said his reason for Canada was because of two things. Firstly, that he was always in Canada more than any other countries so he would be seeing me often, and secondly, that Canada would offer the type of basic education and business experience I need to acquire, because of the Lingual-franca nature . . . that is, that Canada and Swiss are the only countries in this world, where English and French are being spoken almost on equal basis, and that it would help my course of trying to master both languages without much stress. I thanked him and told him that I was very appreciative of his effort in arguing with my step-father of my being sent to Kampala and for his wise choice for me. Like I said before, to say the truth I did not for once suspect or question the honesty of anything the White man said to me. As I later recollected, as a matter of convincing me more, I think, immediately after we boarded not quite thirty minutes or so after the plane eventually had taken off as we unfastened the seat belt in order to relax ourselves well, Jean Perry Edouard, who was dressed in complete hugo-boss black business suit, with pure-white shirt, dark grey tie, a pair of black hugo-boss shoes probably or could I say intentionally brought out from under the seat, his golden-coated powerful civilian briefcase and opened it, I saw some shining and sparkling objects which I instantly perceived to be samples of gold, diamond and some pieces of precious stones and little containers of mercury which I recognized immediately because that was the business of our American army training officer friend, I believe you still remember him. You know these articles I saw in the briefcase made me to believe more about his genuineness in what he had claimed to have been and besides, we were on board the aircraft's first class lounge. So, tell me how I would've smelled a smoking gun? This was exactly the situation of things when we arrived at one airport, I think, somewhere here in Europe I didn't know exactly because we did not go down from the plane and equally we didn't waste up to one hour there only discharging and re-entering of the plane by some passengers mainly Whites, and few Blacks. And then, the plane once again took-off and not quite an hour or so, it touched down at . . . I mean, we arrived at the Vienna International airport. And that was where and when the third chapter of the story of my life began.

"What happened again?" Hyman asked attentively, surprised at how suddenly tears started dripping from Kanombe's eyes once again. Hyman stretched out his hand, tapping him by the shoulder. "I think . . . I think it is high time we stop this story maybe for another day . . . It's getting so emotional for you. That's Ok. That'll do for now Ok!!" Hyman pestered, shrugging his shoulders "We don't mean to . . . Instead, lets forget this part entirely."

THE KANOMBE'S STORY

PART THREE

He quickly glanced at the radio clock and the time was about 4:25 am, which meant he had talked for nearly 15 hours still without food or water and his stomach was already signalling that it was getting much more empty and the worms could not wait any longer as they started to protest vehemently, biting him harder, yet he wanted to complete this story, because according to him tomorrow might be too late. He wiped away the tears with his handkerchief which was by now as wet as the tongue of a cow.

Believe me it is not as if I am dismayed or depressed or something of that nature. No, no, it was emotional tears after all I was not stranded at an African airport or North Korean airport, but in Europe. In fact, in one of the best cities in the Western Europe, Vienna city, as the Viennese used to call it. You should have known by now that I was once a soldier and even before I had become a soldier, I had been a survivor, and as such there was no question of my shedding unnecessary tears or being disappointed in any situation in life, rather, it was my fate. I believe that whatever comes to a man is equal to a man. For very long time in my life, I've already learnt and sewed the coat of hopefulness, sobriety, grief-strickeness, survival and purposefulness and I always carried them and wore them along to any place I went to, or fate took me to.

The English says 'beggars cannot be choosers'. So I've no grudges. This was what really happened. Around ten or fifteen minutes before the plane finally taxied its way and parked at the Vienna airport, Mr. Jean Perry, for the first time since I first met him at the Kinshasa airport some hours before we embarked on this journey, happened to speak English to me. His English was very clear and very understandable even more than his perfect-oriented French. He had told me 'hey, boy, this is Europe where everybody's eyes are widely open and a land of great opportunities where many people became rich overnight at other people's expense, so I would like you to hand your passport and air fair ticket before these 'Romanian pick-pocketers' teach you some lesson . . . and don't forget you must open your eyes widely'. And I had as usual without questioning handed him the Oxblood-coloured diplomatic passport which accidentally bore one of the original passport size picture which I took in the office of the brigadier doctor that very day I conversed with the officers, and from which they used one of it to produce my special 'Pass' in the camp. And which as well bore my adopted name Joseph Mago Ndunga with my original date of birth 15-8-82. Mr. Edouard told me partially that we would be transiting for some hours at the airport we're about to land on . . . that he would prefer us to enter inside the old 'Hitler city' as he put it for some sightseeing and maybe shopping . . . that he had collected my passport and 'the sliver suitcase he had handed over to me at the airport in Kinshasa in case of unexpected. Oh! Yes, I forgot to mention about the suitcase. He had handed me the passport and boarding pass and the suitcase that was somehow heavier than it looked, and asked me not try to open it. And he had warned me to be careful with my little handbag which contains some of the things captain Ndunga had bought for me in Kampala. And had seriously cautioned me 'in case you miss contact with me, don't hesitate to hand yourself over to the police and explain your situation to them . . . 'All the while he was brain-washing and telling me all these 'European gospel' my little mind did not comprehend the fact that I had already arrived at his so much acclaimed lingua franca Canadian.

"Ireman, old soldier that was Mr. Perry's discharging code words to you but I bet you still won. It's not easy to come to Europe nowadays man! I mean, half bread is better than none, man!" Eto submitted. "But it's only Jah almighty that knows what were in that suitcase."

Kanombe still laughing and at the same time being thoughtful of what and what, were in this particular suitcase Mr. Jean Perry Edouard—if that was his real name—had ordered him not try to open decleared finally.

Mon comrades, to conclude the long story short and simple, the American, Canadian, Mexican, Frankard and general European representative and special chains of business consultant of mon step-father, captain Mako Ndunga of the Ugandan army, quick-wittedly disappeared through the throng of passengers at the Vienna International airport barely two minutes of our disembarkment from the flight leaving me stranded and no option than to hand myself over to the Viennese police as he advised without papers. 'Mon comrades', this is the end of the third part of the story of my life as I am beginning to record the fourth part from this 'five-star Hotel' accommodation—the prison cell room. So thank you very much, Mr. Scout Commissioner, Mr. Man O' War Commandant and the Honourable Prime Minster of Rastafarians for giving me your ears.

Kanombe ritually greeted his cellmates for their act of endurance to his pathetic long story.

"Bon arrive mon ami! *Und willkommen Kollege,*" Koso solicitously greeted in his lingua franca manner. "Old soldier, you're welcome to the European league of Nations—Black Hustlers Union. I can only thank sergeant Kozium, captain Ndunga and the Rev. Father, brigadier doctor Sokoeveni for your life. They are what the elders in my native Ghana used to call *Barima ne nea otua dua* (A man is he who has something between his thighs). And I bet you, these three men not only have something between their thighs but also they have something in their hearts. They're old friends that don't forget the good old days for many friends forgot so easily . . . your father must be happy for them and for you in his grave."
"Ire-Old Soldier, man! Jah loves you man! And you must not fail to worship Jah-Jehovah all the days of your life man! And don't ever cry that you're stranded here in Western part. For millions had died on the Niger-Algeria-Morocco-Spain desert route on their way to Europe, man! I mean young men and women trying to walk their ways to Europe, man! With only but few surviving from this hazardous journey of no return, of which I'm proudly one of them . . . Has any survivor happened to tell you about this story we nicknamed 'Europe by bidon'?" Rastaman Eto asked seriously.

"Not at all I haven't heard about it" Kanombe frankly replied.

"And none of you two?" Eto asked Hyman and Koso.

"No, never heard of it," Koso and Hyman echoed, shaking their heads to and fro.

194

"Then you guys have to prepare yourselves for another hazardous, pathetic and longest story ever experienced by any Black man in diaspora. In fact even longer than what we experienced today—Kanombe's story—then you will see that the grass is not greener on the other side after all, Ire-brothers! It's a funny old world, man! Where you can't say you're there until you're actually there! If you understand what I mean, Jah men?" Eto bravely declared.

"Oh my brothers, whatever be the case, whatever we individually and collectively might've experienced or are experiencing now together. What can we say than to give thanks and praises to the living God, who is and has beeen our personal Lord and Saviour for delivering everyone of us from 'those' bondages and darknesses in Africa; and sustaining all of us, and finally brought us out from far away countries of wars, of genocides, of depression, of intimidation, of suppressions, of nepotisms, and of tribal discriminations. And 'He' deposited us to this part of Europe, Austria, a land flowing with foreigner's hatred and pro-Nazi sentiments, with partial nepotism and police intimidations, with racial discriminations and with mass imprisonment of helpless immigrants. Yet, most importantly for we survivors, a fortuitous land of hopefulness and miraculous opportunities which we must embrace with fortitudes and find a way to fully integrate ourselves into its society" Hyman advised his fellow prisoners of conscience, still holding Kanombe in his arms. "Mon ami', you can now see, we're all survivors . . . yes, of course, every one of us here in this cell room tonight. It's either from endless wars, or genocide, or tribal, or social, economic, or political problems that warranted some of us to make the deadly escape from our respective countries of origins. And through God's special grace, we were assembled here today, to know, narrate, believe and share our various difficulties together and in turn encourage each other. And as the true survivors we are, I humbly pray that God's purpose of eventually bringing us to this 'land of hope' will come to fruition in the Mighty name of Jesus Christ, amen."

Hyman entreatied passionately, cleaninf his over sweated face.

"Amen! Amen!! Amen!!! Amen!!!! Amen!!!!!" echoed his cellmates, like parishioners faithfully riposting from a prayer of a clergyman.

++

195

"But, Ireman old-soldier Kanombe, if I tell you I didn't enjoy that story of your life, yester-night man! Every single part, you know I'm a Jah forsaken lier, man! But you had promised to include some certain actions in the second part yet, you had concluded the story and still omitted them Ireman! Why?" asked Eto the Rastaman the following afternoon, just to start off another round of gist for they had been sitting 'idle' since they had woken up.

"Like what and what?" retorted Kanombe,

"I mean, your angel Esther and the actions that followed after you regained your consciousness . . . or can you swear to me, you didn't 'dig the hole' for once man! Or have any contact . . . to do with her . . . I mean this is one of the most important parts I'm really eager to know, man! Please kindly elaborate on that a little more . . . old soldier . . ."

"And moreover, you asserted you tell everything in details but had by-passed the *omoge* part of the story, after all, she was an essential I meant, the person that really took care of you when you're in coma and when you were out of it, you know what I mean?" Koso maintained smiling.

"Oh! No, you also, Charlie? Oh! Ha, ha, ha, hm," Kanombe laughed out widely. "Rastaman Eto, you are the 'funniest man' on earth I've ever come in contact with. So, what you're trying to tell me is that making love and Esther alone are the most important events of the whole story of my life? Well, if that is what you guys want to hear. Yeah, we made love. I 'fornicated' with her many times than you could imagine. However, you have to agree with me that fornication is part of immoralities, and most of us nasty fornicators do not comprehend that it is an immoral behaviour. Rastaman and Mr. Commandant, this is exactly why I do not think it is a wise thing to be included 'orally' to these miraculous and precious events of my life which as I earlier said, I hope . . ."

"That's where you're wrong my buddy old-soldier. You think the Hollywood guys will ever be interested in your story without this vital part, as you said you hope it will be . . . ." Koso interrupted candidly. "The Hollywood doesn't act any 'bestselling film' without 'sex scene' my good old soldier."

"Ha! No, that's not what I mean, Ghanaian man, as I said earlier I hope to write and eventually publish this story, including the one my European sojourn will bring one day when everything will become good again. Oh! Yes *eni jour viendra,* (one day will come) when I'll publish my biography then you would read everything that prevailed between me and Esther, and maybe God's Will, you'll equally see it on movie. So until then, 'mon amis' Eto and Koso . . . try to exercise some patience . . . *Danke!*

HYMAN OTTA'S PREACHING TO HIS FELLOW CELLMATES

"The Croown of the Torah (Bible) is waiting and read for all Israel (Africans).

==== Rambam (Hilchos Talmud Torah 3:1).

Koso had expected Hyman and his preaching all along, knowing fully well that he could seize an opportunity like this which he knew was inevitable, but not their, two new roommates who did not know him well. He wanted to object but Hyman was quick on him.

"Praise the Lord" Hyman began.

"Hallelujah" shouted Kanombe.

"Oh! You're very, very correct, my brother" Hyman said to Kanombe expeditiously after he ceased speaking and then turning and staring at the directions of Eto, the Rastaman and at Koso, the commandant, he said:

"And you people should strive to safeguard your tongue against what's bad; and your lips against speaking deception. Yeah, brothers, haven't you ever come across in the Bible . . . In the book of Ephesians chapter four, from verses twenty-nine (4:29) . . . where and when St. Paul was admonishing the people of Ephesus. It says,

'Let a rotten saying not proceed out of your mouth, but whatever saying is good for building up as the need may be, that it may impart what is favourable to the hearers" he quoted off-head with his Bible firmly held in his right hand.

He added rather wisely in his patient and good nature tone.

"Which means, brothers you must respect Kanombe's reason of omitting these parts of his life story you were interested in, for I believe our friend Kanombe as somebody who has given his life to Jesus Christ, accepting him as his personal Lord and redeemer, who shed his precious blood on the cross of calvary for all—knows full well that these things you're interested in, and of which were burning your hearts with curiosity . . . are not even supposed to be remembered, much more, be mentioned from the mouth of a man who God in his infinite mercies and kindness, had delivered from his enemies in many occasions . . . both during the 'genocide' and at the war fronts, and even from the anti-tank-mine accident which claimed the lives of his other colleagues—about thirty-nine of them—mercifully surviving only him, just for a purpose. Again, in chapter five of the same Ephesians, verses three to five says:

'Let fornication and uncleanness of every sort or greediness not be mentioned among you, just as it befits holy people; neither shameful conduct nor foolish talking nor obscene jesting, things which are not becoming, but rather the giving of thanks. For you know this, recognizing it for yourselves, that no fornicator or unclean person or greedy person—which means being an Idolater—has any inheritance in the kingdom of the Christ and God.'

Hyman once again recited without glancing at his Bible, as he cleaned his face, which was drenched with sweat. He paused briefly and then continued.

"My brothers in Christ, you now see, that Kanombe was perfectly right by excluding these acts you now said is the most interesting thing to you, and which, as a matter of fact, we can not learn or gain anything meaningful from—than what we had learnt, adored and cherished from how God led him through these rough, dark and very dangerous roads, and even brought him out victoriously by sending him abroad to the promise land, Europe. No matter our present predicaments and hassles at the hands of the authorities. There's a Christian hymn that goes like this—

'Stand up, stand up, stand up for Jesus, you soldiers of the cross, this day the noise of the battle, the next (days) the victorious songs" he sang.

"Brothers, sorry . . . what I'm trying to say? My message to you this day, my fellow prisoners of conscience, is that, this day might prove to us a suffering day, but a day is coming . . . the day of the Lord . . . A day that Lord will say that enough is enough, that his children whom He delivered out of their bondages in Africa, have suffered enough, and uses his powerful hand to bring us out of this unwarranted and unwanted prison" Hyman stated predictably and in a very forceful and homily voice, as if he were to deliver a homily like a Priest he would've been.

He gave them a soulful glance.

"I believe that all of you brothers are conversant with the story of the Israelites in the Holy Bible . . . When God sent Moses to the land of Egypt to deliver his people (Israel) out of their bondage, after Moses had met God in the miraculous 'burning bush' and how Moses eventually went after trying to argue and disagree with God; stating that he was a stammerer and a wanted man, who had killed a soul in the land, which he must pay with his own life. And how God argued him out that no harm will befall him and besides, He has already prepared Aaron, his brother for the work and to help him out in matters of speech. How God seriously warned Moses and Aaron that their task is not going to be all that easy, that Pharaoh will sure be obstinate and will make his heart unreponsive to let the Israelites move out of his land and out of their suffering. How Mose and Aaron his brother, finally arrived in the land and gathered all the elders of Isreal as God had directed them and gave them all the messages from the God of their forefathers, concerning their deliverance from their bondages in Egypt. God had assured the people of Israel of their safety. Just as God has promise all of us in this cell room tonight and all our African brothers and sisters in the prisons all over the whole world and even our brothers and sisters who might have been in bondages and difficulties (even in the outside world, I mean those that were not in prison), as we saw ourselves at this moment that our miracles are on the way and that we'll soon be free, and be free indeed, in God's infinite name, amen!" he decleared. "So brothers, God had promised his people, when he said, I quote:

'And the blood must serve as a sign upon the house where you are; and I must see the blood and pass over you, and the plague will not come on you as a ruin when I strike at the land of Egypt' Exodus 12:13.

Hyman enunciated carefully, his eyes bubbling like a sparkling glass of wine, as he continued unflaggingly.

"Then, the true God has before hand told Moses and his brother Aaron to go for the last time and warn Pharaoh and his people about the impending perils. And Moses and Aaron had gone and warned pharaoh accordingly, but he had pompously replied them

'Get out from me! Watch yourself! Do not try to see my face again, because on the day of you seeing my face you will die. To this Moses said 'That is the way you have spoken. I shall not try to see your face anymore . . . Exodus 10:28-29"

Hyman recited again, portioning out in pellucid prose manner, his spiritual gift of the knowledge of the Bible and then he continued as lines of sweats dropped down his cheeks.

"Just as Pharaoh had threatened, Moses and Aaron did not return to persuade him anymore rather they went and prepared the Israelites for their long journey. It happened that as the true God has promised—because He is a God that promised and never fails, unlike other small gods that always fail to fulfil their promises. So it came to be that in the whole land of Egypt that very night, all the first born of every living thing, starting from Pharaoh's first son dropped dead as the true God has decreed and that became the last straw that would break the Camel's back in that in every household in the whole land of Egypt, there're lamentations, whining, wailing and gnashing of teeth, while joys and merriments and praises were heard from the households of the sons of Israel as Pharaoh ordered according to the book of Exodus 12:31-32. At once he (Pharaoh) called Moses and Aaron by night and said,

'Get up, get out from the midst of my people both you and the (other) sons of Israel, and go, serve Jehovah, just as you have stated. Take both your flocks and your herds, just as you have stated and go. And, you must bless me besides.'

Praise the Lord!" Hyman shouted once more.

"Hallelujah! Hallelujah!! . . . Amen and Amen!!" his roommates sang interestingly.

"Yes, brothers as Pharaoh could not linger, procrastinate, spurn or reject God's authority when it was finally made known to him, so also when God's time for us to be free here comes, nobody, not even the cops, the warders or the *Bundesministerium* will stop us. When God has decreed no man can hamstrung it" he stated happily and then continued "Now, my brothers what, then can we say to these things, our conditions and our well being here in the prison, if God be for us who, can be against us?"

"NOBODY!" they all devotedly replied, as they seemed to have overcome by Hyman's sermons.

"Then, brothers, believe me not even the devil can subdue us . . . one thing for sure is that, God has saved all of us for a purpose and we're survivors indeed, and while we hopefully and earnestly waiting for our release as we have proposed with endurance, let us have a total repentance and surrender our lives to Jesus Christ and to our God, who searches the hearts and knows everything. And He, who, I believe, has pre-ordained and called us to reach out to the world, the good news of his coming kingdom. For St.Paul was speaking to the people of Rome in Romana 8:35-38:

'Who will separate us from the love of Christ? Will tribulations or distress or persecution or hunger or nakedness or danger or sword?' Just as it is written, 'For your sake we are being put to death all the long, we have been accounted as sheep for slaughter . . . To the coutrary, in all these things we are coming off completely victorious through him that loved us. For I am convinced that neither death nor life nor angels nor governments nor things now here nor things to come nor powers nor height nor depth nor any other creation will be able to separate us from God's love that is in Christ Jesus . . . '

Hyman said flawlessly, once again, brushing and drying his permeated face, and then, he inspirationally ordered in a very placid voice . . .

"Let us pray!"

Motivatedly his three roommates obeyed and fell down on their knees quietly, while he remained standing, and closing his eyes he sang some adorational hymns after which he began:

"Abba Father, we thank and give 'You' praise. We honour and adore Your Holy name. We uplift and bless Your Holy name for 'You' are so good. You had been good since the creation. King David said that once he had been young and later he became old, but he has never seen the Lord changeth. You are sitting there in heavenly places, yet 'You' have made the earth your footstool. We ask you, Mighty God to receive in Your paradise our departed brothers and sisters, especially the family of our brother here with us . . . Kanombe and my own father and two younger brothers, and our former cellmate and good friend, Marcus Omofuma, who recently left us and who because of our grieve for him we're being detained in this inhuman condition today. We ask 'You' to bless and give his loved ones and his people over there in Nigeria, the heart and fortitude to bear his untimely death; we also ask 'You' to forgive all our iniquities and the iniquities of evey person who might have in one way or the other concerned in this case. For the Bible said in the book of Romans 3:23-24 'For all have sinned and fall short the glory of God and it is as a free gift that we are being declared righteous by your undeserved kindness through the release by ransom (paid by Christ Jesus)'. So we pour out our hearts to God, this very hour and thank God for the individual lives He has given us. We pray also for blessing to all our people in Africa, those whom we have left out of frustrations. We pray, omni-potent and omni-present God to use Your powerful hand and put an end to all wars, bad governance, tribalism, unnecessary killings, suffering and starvations around this world, especially in Africa, and to give Africa good and fearful leaders who will work for their people and not for their individual pockets. Finally, we pray God to see our conditions here in this prison and the conditions of all our people who might have found themselves in this same condition to-night, and to use Your mighty and saving hand with which 'You' used to deliver the Israelites out of their bondage in the land of Egypt and deliver us from our bondage in this Austrian prison. We hope and believe that 'You' heard and granted our requests, the ones we remember and the ones we did not remember . . . even before we uttered them. All these we pray and ask with the precious blood that Christ shed on the cross of calvary, and in His mighty name, amen!" Hyman declared, waving his hands upwards in adoration.

"Hallelujah! Ireman! Jah be praised forever and ever," Eto shouted at the top of his voice.

"Amen and amen," repeated Kanombe and Koso simultaneously, also raising their hands up towards heaven, singing and continuously praising God in his Holiness.

CHAPTER THIRTEEN

"A man who won't die for something is not fit to live'. We've got some difficult days ahead. But it doesn't matter with me now because I've been to the mountain top . . . And I've seen the promise land. I may not get there with you. But I want you to know tonight that we as a people will get there to the promise land."

===Martin Luther King Jr.

The following morning was a very happy and gorgeous day for the African inmates because as they prayed the previous night before they finally slept—making it two consecutive nights of long story—the Lord had started showing his mercies towards them.

Firstly, the day was very bright as never before and the sunlight came into view as early as five-thirty while they were still feeling drowsy. Kanombe was the first of them to wake up. He had just woken from a nightmare as the early morning—sun entered and shone towards his bed and directly in his eyes for he had slept on the upper-side of the doubled-bunk bed. As he didn't like to disturb his roommates, who were all tiredly lying in their beds, he tip-toed over the tiny fenestral of their mini-cell where the authority had pigeon-hold them.

As it were, the sun had been penetrating through the little porthole of a fenestral into the cell. He carefully drew one of the cell stools and stood on its top to look out and roistered at the early morning rays that beamed down through as he held his hands on the wire-gusted window to support himself. He always perceived the sun as the most beautiful creation of God. And so for him, it's a good omen that the sun had been the first thing that greeted his second (ever) morning inside a prison wall in all his nearly eighteen years of life. Since even as a soldier he did not commit or cause anything that would've brought him face to face with the law or which would've caused him to be court-martialled in the notorious Rwandan army. For once he had never before smelled the 'iron bar' as he was doing this morning neither as a civilian nor as a soldier. Once he looked out of the compassed window, the first thing he experienced was the little fresh air that was piercing in with the sun. He did not hear even a single sound except the noise of pigeons and other birds which were flying out from their resting places and perhaps the soft 'snoring' from inside their cell room where his cellmates and fellow prisoners of conscience were still sprawling on their beds. He was also enjoying the early morning quietness and tranquillity that seemed to have descended from heaven and he thought it was specially oriented towards him from the living God to console him in the prison. Because he had never experienced anything of this kind before the prison did not resemble anything this morning, but an atmosphere of a graveyard. He watched the birds for a moment as they perched down and started looking for what to eat and he thought it over his mind, whether these pigeons and birds were dead warders and wardresses, who had served their times in the prison and could not afford to miss the environment they had so much loved to work during their life time. He reasoned this fact, seriously and even laughed it out a bit. This earth is a very funny and strange planet to live on. How can he, a motherless, fatherless, brotherless, sisterless, uncleless and auntless boy, one of the worst orphane in this world, could've dreamt of even travelling out of Rwanda if not for the army and for war as it seemed. Just last month, about twenty-nine days to be precise, since that miraculous accident which 'sadly' had eliminated the last of his close friends on this earth and which in turn automatically had changed his entire life and purpose. He had been or had equally adjusted his life to that of a soldier and nothing else. In the early morning like today and at or even before this time he must have woken up from his camp bed—which the prison bed he had slept on is far portable and better than—and would've been getting ready for the early morning parade, which is a must for every soldier of his status. After the rigorous parade, he would immediately rush down to the camp's diminutive dinning hall for his ration of the black tea (Atai) they used to serve them sometimes with pieces of bread and sometimes without. He would have to gulp down everything while still standing. After which, he would either go straight to his assignment for the day or he would find himself at the war training zone, where nowadays, they were training practically with live ammunitions. He remembered one of his close friends in the army, Privte Kodo, whom they had nicknamed 'the black Kite' in the camp, because of his too much darkened skin and his ability to somersault three or four times in the air in acrobatic nature (He had been a professional acrobat entertainer before he entered the army). And whom just two days prior to that day of the accident, was buried in their temporary cemetery near their camp at Goma, after he suddenly fell to a single bullet shot where he was training. The shot had unknowingly came from the gun of another soldier, who accidentally hit and scattered the skull of 'the Kite' when he had aimed at another object. His death had been devastating blow to him, because both of them have been survivors of the worst genocide in the history of the world, since the ethnic cleansing of the Jews at the hand of Hitler and his subordinates. Even sometimes, it seems to him that it was more than that of the Jews because then and now were never the same. Then it seemed a bit harder for the world at large to prevent Hitler, but to him, the world had been aware of the imminent danger of the Rwandan genocide, yet they have failed to prevent it. He remembered what the Rev. Fathers he was staying with after the genocide used to say—that powers that be in the world at present, especially America and their European allies were very very aware before hand and that they were cautioned about the Hutu's plan. Now having survived the atrocities, himself with others like Kodo, who had also lost all family members his brain can remember, they had joined the army and risked their lives for a country that murdered their families, with 'the black Kite' even paying with his own blood. How could the world seem so difficult to man? Or in fact, how could God allow this type of death to happen to Kodo 'the black Kite' he thought. 'It's such a pious thing to happen. But man has no authority of his own to question God or any of his activities'. 'Maybe,' he said out aloud 'that was why King Solomon of all people concluded wisely that vanity upon vanity is vanity. So if a special 'wisdom ordained' man like King Solomon could summon up such declaration, a layman like himself has nothing to offer then, than to live according to what is destined to him.'

Kanombe had been contemplating on these issues while still standing on top of the stool that morning without much explanation. But then, it had nothing mystical or spiritual attached to it. Nor could there be anything so special concerning this short-time dream he had before he woke up. Where for the first time since the genocide he saw and spoke with his entire family members in the dream, they had all seemed happy for him and encouraged him, telling him to fear nothing about his imprisonment that they're with him and would follow him to anywhere he went. 'How could that be? Were the deads conscious of their being dead? Might it be true that they have been following him to everywhere he goes since they left him? If so, that meant, they had followed and even drew him out from the truck before it struck the anti-tank mine and finally followed him to this prison.

Perplexed by the spate of destructions, tragedies and unusual happenings he had undergone in recent years, a lot of myths had been surrounding his memory to a certain extent, about God's existence; His ways of allowing things that physically seem to do with the prowling demons? Where did the explanations lie of all these questions that had been beleaguering his mind for long?' he asked himself a bit despondently, still glancing outside the prison environment. But, having thought or even sometimes murmured it out to himself, he was optimistic that things would in due course ameliorate for him and, of course, even better than before.

The only problem he had for the moment was this partial hearing defect he had due to heavy artillery fire after almost three years in intensive war front in the DRC. Yet it seemed to him that his deaf ears were now recuperating since that deadly accident. Maybe God's hand had touched them, or his people who had boasted in his dream to have followed him everywhere were the ones that cured him . . . Confusion begets confusion!

This was the situation he found himself that morning when he suddenly heard noise at his back. He turned and looked. His roommates had just woken up and were a kind of straightening their legs and arms in form of exercise. He stared and waited for them to finish their press-ups before he jumped down from the stool. They exchanged greetings between themselves.

Then Hyman greeted and asked in a euphemistical voice. "Oh! Bon jour! How many minutes did you sleep 'mon ami' Kanombe? Or do you think you're still in the army camp?" he joked.

"Bon jour. Caver?" replied Kanombe, as he approached and extended his hand to Hyman.
"I couldn't sleep too much 'mon' ami. I had been over there at the window for the past one hour and thirty minutes or thereabout, enjoying and monitoring God's given natures for free of charge. How is everything, I hope you had a sound sleep?"

"Well, I thank God. I slept for only a few hours, you know when we eventually went to bed this morning. But, yet!" he shrugged, "our God has been good, and I had a very sound and congenial nap, that, it seemed like I slept for the whole day . . . What have you been thinking over there 'mon ami'? You have to take it easy with yourself . . . I pray and equally believe that everything will soon be okay" Hyman consoled.

"Oh! No. Not like that 'mon' comrade. I'm not that kind of person . . . I can only think about things when it is necessary to think them. It's only that for the first time since 'mon famille' perished five years ago . . . I saw all of them in a dream this morning and they were all encouraging me not to be afraid of anything, but to be strong and courageous that they were following and were always with me anywhere I'll find myself in this world, you understand what I'm saying?" Kanombe asked, a bit gloatingly.

"'Mon ami', listen, I know it is not so cushy for you, bearing all this alone. Yet, to tell you the gospel truth, we're in the same boat. I mean both of us. I told you yesterday that I'm from Sudan, but I don't think I mentioned my own predicament in Africa or what made me to flee from my country. I also lost my family in such tragedy like the one you witnessed. The only difference is that I still have my mother and two sisters alive today, irrespective of the fact that they were still living in that slave practising country, they called Sudan, you see what I mean," Hyman uttered politely, holding Kanombe by the shoulders.

Kanombe nodded in agreement.

"This is a very critical condition for all of us and I believe that God knows this, and will come to help us in shouldering it. It's true that both of us had in the past shouldered a lot of pains, but so far as our messiah lives, He will surely come to our rescue, save and in the fullness of time, reinvigorate us again both physically and spiritually," he assured him hopefully and comfortingly, "I think they're all resting easily and they've gone on to whatever's waiting for them, but they're still alive inside us, because we remember them always."

Hyman's words of heartening perceptiblely placated Kanombe. He thanked him for his concerns and then immediately changed to another subject entirely.

"You remember what I asked you yesterday evening, if it can be possible to start and organize our own demonstration inside this prison . . . 'mon' ami, Otta? Can't it be possible?" he demanded absorbingly, staring directly at his tiny eyes. "Don't you think, it will be an interesting thing, if we can try and stage one here, maybe it will fasten everything."

"We were contemplating to do that exactly, when all of a sudden we were transferred to this cell and prohibited from going out for *Spazieren*, so I don't think it will be all that easy now if you understand what I mean?"

"What's *Spazieren*?"

"Hm, I forgot you're JJC. They stopped us from going out for a walk" he said with a frown. "Before, we normally go out to walk around in a small caged park outside everyday for only one hour" he said, pointing out towards the window where there was a small park of thirty feet by thirty square field surrounded with thick barbed wire and an iron gate.

"Why should they?" Kanombe asked.

"I think maybe their ideas are that they do not want us to get in contact with each other but I strongly believe that now there's pressure coming from both inside and outside the prison, things might change, then we will know what to do next."

"Where are the others? I thought that you two were the only people confined to this dungeon. I mean, this type of strict confinement, isn't it?" Kanombe said surprisingly.

"We were many, mon ami!" grunted Hyman softly, his face folded in thought, "In fact, I believe all the prisoners here who are observing this hunger strike were all confined like us . . . and almost every inmate were for it with the execption of about five or six people."

"May I ask why?" murmured Kanombe, his eyes flew opened.

Hyman swallowed and remained silent for a moment. He thought in his mind that they had gone through this yesterday but all the same.

"According to the latest news I heard, one or two are suffering from stomach 'ulcer' complications, one I'm very sure is a diabetic patient, i.e. he has blood-sugar problems. Then, the remaining three, I couldn't tell for sure why they presumably don't want to."

"Do you know those three? Are they Whites or Blacks?" Kanombe asked suspectingly, imagining why some people will always be spoilers in every human setting. He had experienced this many times, even in the army barrack when they would organize mutiny in protest for the non-payment of their salaries, some of the original organizers would go behind their back and betray them to the officers. But this is different. A fellow had just died in an inhuman way and these actions, if organize in a spirited manner may even lead to imprisonment of many officers and officials alike.

"Well, apart from one Romanian, and another I couldn't say for sure where he came from . . . I mean his country of origin. But, the remaining one I'm very sure, is from Tunisia" Hyman asserted.

"An African for that matter" Kanombe snapped. "Who is he to have got the gut to disagree with others, especially when the issue at hand concerns a fellow African brother he must have been a bastard, man!"

"Or ass-sucker, man! Are you sure he is not a betrayer, Ireman?" questioned Eto who had just joined them where they've been sitting, discussing the problems.

"For sure, he is! But he always said he's a Whiteman and for that he doesn't believe in the struggle . . . that he doesn't give a damn when a Blackman has died . . . Yet the fact is, he doesn't know that they're all Usu, bats. I mean they don't belong to any race. He's neither White nor Black, like the bats that can't be counted among the birds or other animal group."

"That fellow must be a rotten mothafucker, man!" Eto cursed bitterly.

"He was" concored Kanombe irritably as he scooped some old newspapers and magazines—which the human rights groups normally brought for some of the prisoners, mainly printed in English—out of one stool and dumped them on the floor to make space for Koso, who had equally joined, "which means, if I may ask again, all the other remaining people inside this prison are Blacks or what can I say to these useless utterances."

"No, sir, not at all!" said Hyman indignantly, his chin lifted slightly. "Of course, we're about thirty Blacks here (out of almost hundred to hundred-and-fifty inmates in this small prison). All others are either Chinese, North Africans, or of Eastern Bloc origins. He only wished to be a white, which he is not and will never be!"

"But, that's a selfish hope . . . Isn't it" asked Kanombe bewileredly.

"Of course, it's a foolish hope" said Hyman, his jaw dropped.

He still could not think of anything appropriate to say. He paused for a moment and then declared.

"Anyway let's forget about that idiot. At the very least, all other inmates about sixty percent of them fake *oyibos*—who were even better than him in colour agreed and are still co-operating."

They were all gathered there at the far corner of their cell room contemplating, chatting and telling stories, when around nine o'clock that morning their cell's door unceremoniously flung open and abnormally standing outside near the doorway were four big prison-*Beamten* looking elegant in their skyblue shirts, black ties, with black barrets, blue-black trousers and shinning black boots, a complete Austrian prison warder's uniform.

CHAPTER FOURTEEN

"Then it was that Nebuchad.nezzer approached the door of the burning fiery furnace. He was answering and saying: 'Sha'drach, Me'shach and A.bed'ne.-go, you servants of the Most High God, step out and come here!' At that time Sha'drach, Me'shach and A.bed'ne-go were stepping out from the midst of the fire."

===DANIEL 3:26

One of the warders spoke in a well bred voice and told them that it had been ordered that they should pack up their belongings and move back to their former cell-room and that they had three or four minutes to do so. The Africans did not hesitate as they immediately started to pick their *bijuo* personal possessions lik radio, their clothes, shoes, new and old newspapers and magazines in the case of Koso and Hyman; while Kanombe and Eto who was had spent only two days helped them to pick some of their bags along. The *Beamten* escorted them through another door adjacent to theirs and into the hallway which automatically led the way to their former oubliette. As they approached the cell, they encountered some other inmates who were in the same process, among them comrade Volvaskov and Stoyanov, who regardless of the strict order they had been given not to talk to any other prisoners on their way-waved and greeted the Africans by raising their clenched fists in comradeship gesture.

First thing first, the most superior of the three men and a woman, who was at the head of them all inserted a key into the keyhole of the cell and opened the door widely before they were able to go inside. The superior officer Thomas Werner addressed them in a conciliatory manner.

"Look, it's understood that your individual human rights have been undermined but my advice is for you to please bear with us till further notice."

He told them that their complaints had been acknowledged by the authorities, and that they were being seriously considered.

"But, having said that," he continued, "the same authorities will also appreciate it most if you guys can now change your minds and start eating again, in order to help make their decisions in a better atmosphere. I personally believe that you . . . good chaps should abide by that" officer Thomas Werner said smiling.

Hyman Otta was about to open his mouth and say something, however, he quickly held himself back and used his eyebrows to indicate to his fellow inmates not to speak at all. After a few moment of silence between warders and the Africans, Hyman Otta, presented their response and promised that they would see what they can do.

"We thank you superior officer, sir, for your concern and I promise you, we'll compare and contrast these options before we can know what to say or do. But firstly, sir, when are the authorities proposing to lift the ban on our *Spazieren*?" he asked smartly.

"Yes, actually, that is another happy news" replied the superior officer Werner, as he was wrapped in thought of whether to tell them of the coming interview by John Nelson that same morning which had been arranged on their behalf by the prison commandant for his newspaper and which was also the main reason for this early morning act of politeness and main reason of changing of their cell so early. "As a matter of fact, you people should be preparing for the *Spazieren* this morning but, let's say around ten or eleven or in the later part of the afternoon as the case may be" he assured them and asked rather courteously, "I believe you're all happy now?"

"Oh! Yes sir!" Hyman Otta answered in a well mannered voice. "We're happy that some of our lost rights are coming back to us and we hope that all other right will follow suit soon, including our right to freedom, sir!" he said, and made a courtly bow to him, turned and entered into the cell.

The superior officer stood momentarily and regarded him briefly and smiled from ear to ear at him. And then he pushed the iron door back and locked the door behind the Africans.

+++

Once inside, Hyman Otta threw his belongings to one corner of the room, knelt down and opened his Bible which he had been holding in his left hand like one of the newly repented Pentecostal church acolytes. After reading from it silently as the other of his roommates knelt beside him and prayed a short subvocal prayer. He straightened up from where he was kneeling and shouted in a very loud voice.

"Praise the Lord!"

"Hallelujah! Hallelujah!! Hallelujah!!! Amen" his cellmates chanted.

"My brothers, let us praise the living God who has given us partial victory this day, and who has changed their obstinated minds. Who was that man that is questioning the existence of God, and where are those fools that said there's no God?" he asked to nobody in particular. "Now we all know and believe that our God is God that promised and inturn fulfilled his promises. And only such God is worthy to be worshipped and praised . . . all the days of our lives" he said jubilantly and started singing

'Kumbaya Lord Kumbaya! Kumbaya Lord Kumbaya! Kumbaya Lord Kumbaya! Oh Lord Kumbaya;

He has given us victory, we will lift him higher, Jehovah, we will lift you higher!!!!' And yet another song of praise,

'On the mountain, in the valley, on the land and in the sea . . . the Lord is my portion in the land of the living . . . '

And he was immediately joined by others, who did not know how to sing the first two songs, but not the third song which to them was universal hymn.

There were still in this melodious mood, clapping, chanting more melody hymns, as they danced in the Lord when there was a heavey pitter-patter at the door (which had been going on constantly for one or two minutes and was intended for the Africans to keep quiet before the door would be opened). But they continued their praises without minding who was there. One of the officer that escorted the team, bent and peeped through the centred peephole attached to the iron door . . . then followed by more pattering at the door, this time around more severe than ever . . . and immediately the noise finally died down.

There were fumbling and wrangling of keys, after a period of short time, the heavy iron door finally flung open. The Prison commandant, Christian Gospel, with official *Beamten*-safari-jacket, the shoulder part and the upper breast-pocket side being embellished with sliver coated lines and colourful ribbons, displaying his commander's rank and status; and with his Cambridge-blue trousers with cardinal-red strip straightened down by the edge of the pocket, a black official shoes, completed with his official ceremonious golden 'Eagle' officers cap led the group. Treading on the heel of the commandant was the chief *Beamte* Martin Baur, who, as well dressed him in the same official costume, but slightly altered on the embroidered ranks, then followed by the secretary, and personal assistance to the commandant *Fräulein* Lisa Egger, the journalist John Nelson and his lensman companion Peter Preiter.

As they entered the cell the two journalists were already at work glancing around the environs of the tiny room assessing and using their eyes to guess and register the size of the room. The commandant's sensory faculty immediately told him that the room was too small to contain all of them and as such it would be inconvenient for the journalists to conduct their interview in such an open space (in the arcade, in front of their cell). But by then, the first sensitive damage had been recorded by the two press men who did not like the structural condition of the room.

The interviews formally began, after the chief-*Beamte* Martin Baur introduced the entourage to the Africans.

"Good morning, gentlemen" he greeted them indulgently, looking commiseratingly at them for all they had been through. He noted the slimness of their bodies, especially that of Hyman and Koso who started the hunger strike five days ago and had lost a considerable weight. "As you might have heard, I'm John Nelson from the *Augustin* group, publishers of the *Augustin* newspapers and I've come to get some certain information concerning your friend and former cellmate, Marcus Omofuma, and I'd please like you to answer my questions detailed without any fear of anything or anybody, and yet, without much gilding the lily or rather exaggerations of your side" he said with a little smile, which exposed his buttermilk-yellow teeth. "I think you understand what I mean, you tell the truth and nothing but the truth, Ok!"

"Alright" they all echoed in one voice.

"First of all . . . which of you were with Mr. Omofuma before his fateful journey?"

"Oh! Yeah, sir, it was only the two of us Koso and myself," said Hyman sharply, pointing at Koso.

"For how long, had you been together with him before that day he left?"

"I think, I was in this same room with him for four months and some days, of course, I met him here with two other Black brothers, who had been released earlier."

"And, I met both of them here, I mean Omofuma and Hyman when I came three months ago," interrupted Koso unaware.

"Now, when was he summoned last and told that he must be deported did he discuss anything pertaining to his feelings about the deportation?" asked the journalist.

"Sir, to be truthful," replied Hyman, "they have been summoning all of us, including Omofuma almost on daily basis, but he, himself was last summoned on Thursday the 29th of April around mid-day . . . yes. He discussed with us about the . . . his summoning and what he discussed with his reference officer . . . Koso and I—because these two guys were brought to our prison two days ago."

He motioned at Prince Eto and Jean Kanombe, a bit smile in his face.

"He, Omofuma, emphatically told us when he came back to the room, that the reference officer Dr. Melzer told him that since he vehemently refused to be deported back to his country that the authority had now placed him on 'provisional release orders' which as he interpreted as he was told, meant, that he would be released at anytime and very soon . . . probably the following day (Friday, the very day he was eventually taken away). But it turned out to be a blunt lie."

John Nelson jotted some lines in his notebook and asked.

"Was he optimistic about the release order . . . or did he had any kind of disbelief on his part, when he was told that he was under this provisional release order?"

"Precisely, he was like, 'look Hyman, these people are trying to use a sort of trick on me, I don't trust them and I don't trust their promises, I'm totally afraid of all these setups'" Hyman recounted to the journlist frowning. "Sir, to be frank with you, he, Omofuma, saw everything that happened to him before hand . . . Yes . . . including his untimely demise" Hyman assured the journalist, and narrated to them in details, how Marcus woke up that very morning and how he related to them his dreams, what he, Hyman, told him and about Koso's jovial remarks and atheistic stance concerning the dreams.

Hyman also told them how distraught Omofuma seemed to be throughout the morning of that day and how he lost his appetite that morning. And he went on to narrate, how eventually that Friday afternoon after they had come back from *Spazieren* how the *Beamten*, about four of them, came and asked him to pack all his belonging, telling him that he had been released. When in reality he was being led to the land of 'Moriah like Isaac for sacrificial purpose—without him knowing it—by Abraham his father (but on God's purpose and order).

"And, when did you two . . . I mean, you and your friend Koso hear about the news of his death? And, how did you feel when you heard about it?" journalist Nelson asked, jotting more lines, as he gestured his colleague to help him replace the cassette on the mini-recorder they came with.

"The first time we got knowledge of it was when we tuned our radio on last Sunday morning, 2nd of May, to our normal nine o'clock African program on FM 94.0 (the Radio Orange). At first we didn't get the hang of what the presenter was saying. Later, we heard it clear" Hyman fidgeted and waffled. "Then we heard the presenter gave the flash news that a Nigerian national asylum seeker in Austria had been reported dead on board the Balkan airline flight . . . It was something that changed your whole life in a minute. They said that news like that put one and all his purpose and what he intend to achieve in life in perspective and sometimes jeopardizes every effort of a man. That exactly was my condition then" he said. "And of course, I cried the whole day and I'm still crying to date for him."

"As for me" said Koso concomitantly, "I didn't cry, because I'm not used to crying for the dead . . . not even when I lose my loved ones like when I lost my mother and sister in a car accident at the same day but at different times knowing fully well that death will come when it will come as Shakespeare once wrote: I'm not afraid of it, but rather, I'm afraid of its consequences. I strongly questioned the way and manner in which he died. Whether you believe that his death should be punitive, vindictive, educational and deterrant? I believe before carrying out such act on a defenceless and vulnerable asylum seeker like Marcus Omofuma that the authorities had considered the moral or political impact this death would have in the society at large and the electorates in particular. Because, it's part of anybody's concern, especially the ruling Party's moral responsibility to weigh these considerations and its consequences which we all know, will be disastrous."

"Very interesting perspectives" said the journalist, a bit gloating. "If I may ask where did you come from I mean, from which country or countries?"

"Oh! Sir, I'm from Ghana, from Kumasi region."

"And you?" asked the journalist nodding over his head at Hyman Otta.

"Why? Sir, I'm from Sudan . . . yes, from the Southern part."

The journalist wrote something in his hand held pad, nodding thoughtfully.

"Can you describe your friend's attitude and nature when he was with you?"

"He was a very good boy, congenial, gregarious and generous person. Generous to me in the sense that all the time I was here with him, he used to buy every 'provision' we needed to supplement for food here, with his own money for I have no money. Whatever his money would provide we would share them equally with everyone . . . I mean without any hard feelings. In fact, this radio which incidentally broadcasted his death to us . . . was bought by him yet, he knowingly left it for us when he was going out that day . . . What again can a good friend offer? As if that was not enough, now he had died for every one of us asylum seekers, those of us who are in this prison right now and for all who will later pass through this system in time to come, and for every asylum seeker all over the world, be he or her White or Black. I believe he was an idealist 'born' orator. He was involved in a certain amount of story telling, including history and politics to the inmates, who did not live the time to contribute his talents to the society. I believe that, from all we knew about him, he had fought a good fight and as Christians also we are of the opinion that he has received his rewards and should be in heaven with Christ right now to rest in perfect peace, amen."

"Sir, I think he was very unfeigned, honest and canny human being. Definitely one of the very best departed" Koso added bitterly.

"So, what you're trying to say is that not for one day throughout the few months you stayed with him, you did not quarrel, fight or I mean, had misunderstanding with each other" the journalist inquired, ethically digging to get the facts and to help establish a contrary view on the allegation that the African man was aggressive in nature. "How temperamental was he, Marcus Omofuma?"

"To be frank and precise, I think we're all humans. And as such, people will naturally not always agree when they're gathered together predominantly, especially when they were congregated and confined in this sort of restricted grotto" Hyman said thoughtfully, glancing towards where the commandant and the chief *Beamte* had shifted to at the corner of the corridor, enjoying their Cuban cigar and chatting something of most important to them. "Of course, you don't have grown up people who don't disagree with each other, one way or the other."

"That is the very truth, sir, sometimes we disagreed to agree. However, that's human nature, and with a human face. We don't argue to fight or in stupidity, but rather, we normally argue intelligently" he smiled, looking at Hyman from the corner of his eyes.

"When did you people start this hunger strike and are you still striking now? After all the authorities have done for you to change your minds?"

"This question, if I may say so, sir, is a poignant question and I believe it would continue to be so . . . until the authorities change their hard and obstinate hearts, and not us, mere poor and helpless immigrants who have suffered from every angle as it seems to be. Firstly, to answer your question, we all, the inmates, both Whites and Blacks here, agree to do this for our departed friend and comrade as a mark of honour to him and to mourn him and to air our grievances to this unjust and inhumane act meted to him and then, most importantly for our freedom. We have committed no crime other than being lawful immigrants—and didn't suppose to be in such dreadful situation we found ourselves, as you see for yourself" Hyman declared, looking directly at the far corner, where the big officers were still puffing their cigars.

"In my own opinion, sir, we started the strike action almost immediately we heard about the news on Sunday and I don't think that anything or anybody or any tough stance from the prison authority will help the issue or persude us to stop. It had been determined and so it will remain," Koso maintained, with a poker-face.

"On *Spazieren* accord we stand!"

"That is, to say?"

"Without objection, sir, it was during the *Spazieren* time and on the *Spazieren*-ground that we all agreed to it and even swore to it. That's why we refer to it as *Spazieren*-accord'," Koso bragged.

"And how many are you? How many inmates do you think are still observing the strike?" the journalist interestedly asked.

"There're about one hundred to hundred and fifty prisoners in this deportation prison camp alone, and we expect everybody to abide by the hunger strike orders . . . and to" Hyman was saying.

"Without exceptions?" interrupted the reputable *Augustin* reporter.

"Without exemption!" snapped Koso.

"Every one of us is happy and very proud to abide by the actions" Hyman lied.

"Even newcomers like our two brothers there, Prince Eto from Nigeria and Jean Kanombe and a lot of others. You know the authorities were still arresting and imprisoning immigrants on daily basis, sorry sir, Kanombe is from Rwanda, with a piteous genocide story" Koso said as John Nelson would've demanded. "They've all joined accordingly."

"So you're confident that these actions will finally liberate you from this prison? Do you think it will have an effect on the immediate future?" asked the journalist.

"We have hope in the power of the press," Hyman complimented, as he smiled at the pressmen, "and with God all things are possible, but having said this sir, believe it or not, we're not looking for another liberator. I believe Marcus Omofuma was the real liberator of our situation and course. Yet, that doesn't mean we're clusters of cowards and Idiots as the authorities might be thinking. I, in particular will apparently have to comply with my native land adage which says that 'death is better than shame', when and if needs arised. So I want the authorities to understand that, if it is a legitimate thing for them to destabilize our efforts and rights to live, it is also legitimate for us to wail to the loudest and resist. And we would resist with everything within our reach, including our right to hunger strike. Let's say it once and for all, that he, Marcus Omofuma, is seen by many of us as the epitome of inspiration."

"And to me, sir, it's and remains the only way to our freedom. We must thwart any attempt by the authority (Fremdenpolizei) to deport us back to the very problems we ran from . . . which in some cases, like my own case, back to instant death because of my problems with the hostile and racial instigated government in Ghana at present. We'll never be like a child, who knows when he's hungry, why he's hungry, but doesn't know how to feed himself. We knew where our breads were buttered and where our interestes lies!" Koso said.

"Sir, we know that this action and nothing else will bring about our freedom. There's no going back. Never! Nor could we back down for any threat. And let me say this, not from me, but the fact that any attempt to . . . or assault to any of us from the authorities will be dealt with squarely this time around. What we're clamouring for is our precious freedom which must be handed unconditionally; and justice to be done to everyone who has a hand in Marcus Omofuma's death, period! No more no less."

"Let me ask you" said the journalist, indicating with his pan at Hyman. "It's a personal question and as such should be off the record" he assured as he switched off the mini-recorder on the top of the tiny table the authority had arranged for them.

Hyman Otta nodded his head in agreement.

"Is it true you're the chief organizer of these actions" John Nelson demanded unprofessionally, still out of his uncontrolled curiosity for he had come to love the unorthodox views and outburst of these promising Africans.

"With due respect, sir, the fact is," replied Hyman Otta flabbergastedly, contemplating where and who might have told this man of whom he had heard about his powerfulness with the pen and whom every right-wing politician in Austria despied because of his pro-immigration writing and publications—"I can neither swear to be an organizer or one of a 'Roman Commoners' in all these . . . And, beside, I don't think it's necessary whether I'm the chief organizer or an ordinary sympathizer . . . as it is, we're all equal in the decision of these 'games' and we are all determined to abide by the rules of the game, that's that . . . but, if I too may ask sir, who made this allegation?" Hyman enquired wittyly.

"Well, it . . . I don't think it matters now" said Nelson. "You've answered my question and I believe I understood what you said!"

He made no bone about the fact that many Africa he had met in the past were all cunning and always fiddled with questions.

"Alright, if you said so, but let me say it's false allegation and I believe I'm not the first person that the authority are after, in this whole episode or in general course of things in this very world. If one remember that our Lord Jesus Christ was often accused and betrayed by someone who was very close to him and by many others who had seen him performing signs and wonders in their mist."

"I forgot to ask you," Nelson said, glancing through his notebook, "you made mention of 'being imprisoned' while you're still in prison . . . can you elaborate on that . . . young man?"

Hyman frowned, his face like that of a defrauded investor as he replied.

"Hm!, I don't think it's a big news any more, that we were removed and transferred out from our 'frying-pan abode to a fire abode' . . . that's, from our cell room to a more smaller dungeon of a cell, originally built for . . . perhaps one or at most two inmates, but we're four there . . . packed like 'sardines without oil. Neither do I now call it a big thing that we were released from that dungeon just this morning, just few minutes ago before you came . . . probably because of this interview. I've seen it and everything is now clear to me . . . but the fact still remains that we shall by the special grace of God overcome, someday! We'll never surrender until we've our liberty and we're asking the authority not to leave any stone unturn. They must fish out the main culprits of these acts against humanity. Let it be known that we cannot fold our arms and allow this issue to overwhelm us. We must eke out our stance, by 'keeping the wolf from the door'. I think that we as humans deserve the right to stay alive, irrespective of the fact that few people are actually living in this world, while many are just existing for life sake," Hyman asserted, still wanting to say everything he felt necessary, "to avert a looming crisis, all the perpetrators of these will either voluntarily tender their resignations or they will be forced to do so . . . be quickly fired . . . because, for peace to reign . . . these things must first take place or the consequences will be unavoidable. They say that 'blood is thicker than water, and I tell you, Marcus Omofuma's blood is thicker than even the thickest liquid—an innocent blood which must be atoned (for) by the authority."

"If I may add something, sir, we had been wronged in many ways. And the immediate remedy will be efforts by the authorities to grant us our freedom and then other compensations to follow," Koso suggested splendidly. "I'd like to quote a phrase from the former American President, late Franklin Delano Roosevelt when he said that 'the only limit to our realization of tomorrow will be our doubts of today. Let us move forward with strong and active faith" he reiterated faultlessly.

"Aren't you afraid? Or in other words, don't you think that the authorities will use everything within their arsenal to deprive you of your freedom . . . because of the allegations that all of you entered into Austria illegally and as such deserve this punishment? And again, don't you believe that, they can easily get anybody. I mean, one of you, to reveal to them or say something about the organizers of the hunger strike action and the coming actions you've just boasted about?" questioned the journalist intently, staring directly a *Fräulein* Lisa Egger, the PA of the commandant, a very fine, beautiful lady, who the *Augustin* reporter had been admiring secretly in his mind, and who in turn had been with them all through the entire interview, jotting everything down on her hand-note. She had been indeed fascinated by the brilliance of the two African . . . which she had heard about before, but did not believe. Now, she had seen and heard with her own eyes and ears. She smiled back at the journalist, and listened attentively for their replies.

"Sir, to begin with, as you said, they're the authority. They've many powers but not the almighty power. It's only God who can boast of having the unlimited power than the authority, because man's power is limited. They can invade and even crackdown on the rights of individuals. Yes, government can suppress the will-power and rights of its citizens or commoners, but it's only if, and when God allows that to happen . . . so, I don't think we're afraid of any of their new threat to us . . . they've tried one or two before and as the unfolding events would show, their move have proved to be a big mistake. No amount of their pressure will subdue us. I think that we all should by now know that the evil that men do live within them, and not after them, contrary to what Shakespeare suggested" Hyman stated.

"To me, I can only say that 'the boasting of the hunter is never repeated before the elephant'. I also believe that any attempt by those we believe to be fifth columnist of these acts in trying to infiltrate into, or rather trying to intimidate us again . . . will be met with a kind of suicidal defiance from many of us. A friend of mine once told me that they called it 'suppuku' in Japanese language and that many of their noble men, men of timber and caliber, men of honours choose to die in such ways, rather than being subjected to shame before dying like cowards. These whole mess and actions, I believe was in the verge of plunging into . . . even more dark abyss . . . If the authorities try any funny trick on us again . . . period! Let everyone be warned!"

The journalist had dealt with and known Africans like the back of his palm. He was not too keen on Koso's threat of suicidal act. He knew Africans, especially Black Africans as people that love life and value it to its extreme. He silently dismissed it as an empty threat, and instead he asked.

"Talking of the authorities, the perpetrators of these acts as you call them . . . who do you think they are? And how do you feel they can be identified and exposed?"

"The lion share of these faults obviously lies on the side of the government. They're to take the sole responsibilities and guilt of these actions . . . from the death to the last action of imprisoning us while we're in prison, and on the part of how to fish out the main culprits. An African adage says that, 'the robes knew the parcel and the parcel knew the packer'" he said, his upturned chin hoisted, narrow lips affixed in a contemptuous grin, bright eyes gleaming. "You see, sir, they all know and would equally find out if they want to. There are no two ways about that. And moreover, they're already known, so the only problem is how to punish them, for my Bible tells me that no sinner will go unpunished! On the other hand, it should be understood that the government is an institution and being an institution, they know everybody within their jurisdictions and they will know whatever action that is appropriate to be done. It's also important to note that the institution when it fails to do what was expected of it will be termed to have neglected its duties to its taxpayers, for that reason, it would be said to has deficient in its integrity and as such lost the confidence imposed on it by its voters."

Amidst laughter for the journalist's displeasure over Hyman's trait of prolonging his answers, Koso said.

"If I were ask to contribute a short response on this, I'll only add one thing, that there're many alternative strategies to haul out the transgressors . . . one good example being the immediate arrest and interrogation of the three police officers who had accompanied Marcus Omofuma and the officers would in turn name their accomplices. And coming to our present predicament, believe me that even a blind man can tell the players in this game without touching the score card . . . that should be understood. There're many ways to kill a rat . . ."

"You seem to be too confident in what you're saying, what are the things that are motivating you?" asked the journalist. "You don't seem to be afraid of anything or anybody?"

"Like I said before, Almighty God is the first motivator and the one who takes away fear in me. Yet, on the physical level, I think I've to mention it again that Marcus Omofuma's death has taught me that life is truely a bowl of agony to some people, and a bowl of cheeries to others, a virtual perpetual cabaret to few, and also an ineffective transitory cabaret to many. His death has been inspirational in many ways. At least it has helped me to understand beyond reasonable doubt that 'whatever a man is aspiring in life or has even attained can be doused in a twinkle of an eye by another man altogether." Hyman said philosophically.

226

"To me," said Koso, laughing once more. "It's been said that truth is stronger than fiction or rather, that truth is a total stranger to falsity. I've no strings, no ulterior motives attached . . . but only naked hatred to evil and its institution, period! I once read in a book somewhere that, there are other ways to assassinate a human being without being the one at the other end of the gun. However, my question is why are always the helpless ones victims? This question without answer had been stuck in my mind and will ever remain so to eternity, I fear. Coming to inspiration, I'll only say that I'm being inspired by reading radical novels and acquiring radical ideas about life and its meanings. My motto in life is strike while the iron is still hot! The world is a strange place."

"Don't you think that it might've been that this is the destiny of your friend, former roommate and fellow African brother Omofuma? For him to have died in this way?" the journalist probed further, much more interested with the level of answers he is getting from the Africans.

"Believe it or not, sir" Koso said quickly with his everything is-okay-smile. "I don't believe in destiny because I know that it doesn't exist, but even if it exists, does it mean that man is a sole determinator of another man's destiny?" he asked disgruntedly.

"Well, I strongly believe in destiny" Hyman cuts in, "but let it be made clear to everybody that, if it's true that it was his destiny, then it was just a destiny far more immediate than the owner knew. It's a destiny of a one-way-street, a destiny where the incapables are being sacrificed and the powerful holding back. It's a destiny of amalgamation of the good and the bad forces of human existence."

"You've been talking good of this friend of yours Marcus Omofuma, can you describe in a brief account how close you were together with him when he was here? Or did you happen to know him before you met him here in the deportation prison camp?" Nelson asked.

"I hadn't known him before I met him here. Of course, there was no way I should've known him outside this prison, for I believe that he was already in prison before I even came to Austria, yet, from all I knew, for the little period of time I happened to spend with him. I think he was a nice guy and the type of man you could share secrets with, without any fear. We tended to live peacefully in the little days. We shared everything together, including our restricted lives. If you know what I mean?" Koso attested.

"He was like a blood brother to me and I'll never forget him in my life now, and in the life to come. Remember I told you that we were almost four months together in this same cell room. And for two people, who were not from the same country, the same culture and who have different mentalities to live in one room such as we had—and in this embittered condition where you were forced to eat the same type of food, sleep the same type of sleep and see the same type of people on a daily basis—but we succeeded without problems. I mean, it's something worthy of emulation" Hyman declared as tears globuled from his eyes.

He paused and wiped it with his hanky and then added in a measured tone.

"It's good and positive things that use to bound people together, mainly, when they're in this kind of tempestuous place, you see what I mean! In fact, we became at a time like toddlers who managed to perforate their fingers and become blood brothers. Still, I'm somehow happy that my main wish for him happened before this *last journey* of his. Through our sharing of the word of God together, he was able to receive the Lord Jesus Christ as his personal Lord and Saviour, and became a born-again Christian . . . yes, sir, the knowledge of God is the most important of all knowledge; and the fear of God is the beginning of wisdom. I believe that he, Omofuma, tackled life with bravery and death with Christian aspirations . . ."

As Hyman was giving his long answer, Koso was afraid that this interview will be prolonged more than what the journalist bargained for . . . for he was of the opinion that if Hyman was given the opprtunity to start his preaching then the vistors will be ready to follow up.

'These people don't know him and what he is up to' Koso murmured thoughtfully to himself.

"Did Omofuma complain of being sick or rather, do you suspect he had an inborn illness or a sort of internal sickness . . . like being a sickler, or suffering from any kind of hepatitis or high blood pressure or heart problem before he embarked on this journey. Did you notice any signs prior to his . . . ?" Nelson interjected, jotting some words down in his notepad.

"Sir, I'd believe that a sick man can either go to the hospital or the hospital would come for him. Somebody cannot be sick up to the extent you've just mentioned without a neighbour or a cellmate knowing he was sick. An adage says that, it's he who is within the close range of the teeth that perceives its mal odour" Hyman contented. "What I'm trying to say in earnest is that Omofuma as far as I'm concerned was not sick for one day here . . . and he did not complain for any irregular feelings of which I can remember. I mean we're in Europe and not in Africa. He supposed to have . . . I think, he had a medical file like any of us asylum seeker which of course, is the only good thing the authorities are very good at. The *Bundesministerium* always makes sure that all asylum seekers are insured health-wisely. So the medical dossier would assert his medical conditions before he departed to his so called *last journey*."

"And, beside" Koso heckled, "deporting a sick man, if that's what the authorities were trying to drive at, wasn't that against the international law? Or is the Austrian law different in this? Let us look at it from this angle. One cannot be sick and healthy at the same time. And a pregnant woman cannot conceal her gestation period for nine months without someone being cognizant of it. Can she?" he asked to no one in particular.

"No, I don't think it's possible" replied the journalist, obviously curious of what's coming.

"Then that's absorbed, he couldn't be sick without we, his cellmates for months knowing about it. Let's try to be somehow emphatic and rational with reference to the true condition of things. Let's not be like the domestic fowl that jilts the blad that slaughtered it, but bent its neck for the *potjie*, a cooking utensil. He was not and hadn't been sick in our presence before that day as simple as ABCD" Koso strongly maintained.

"Do you think that Marcus Omofuma bore any responsibility or guilt for what happened? Because according to speculation, it seems as if he was somewhat obdurated, agitated and resistant which triggered the use of adhesive tape by the cops to bandage his body and mouth. Or, being somebody you knew well, he couldn't misbehave up to the extent of prompting the use of gagging?" queried Nelson.

"Why don't we wait for the outcome of the Interior Minister's promised committee of inquiring, if it will not be prejudiced rather than speculate?" Hyman said quick-wittedly as the journalist quickly jotted down few details. "Why do we like speculations before facts? Now, I don't have the facts of which you asked me about because as it were I'm not there when all these things were happening. And, so talking about them is to encourage speculations. Let's leave speculations until the facts come out, when the truth might've been ascertained. And then the devil will surely be abashed and crushed. But, having said that, I can only vouch for Omofuma I knew and not the Omofuma, whom I didn't know. And the gospel truth is the Omofuma I knew can never and will never do anything which would warrant such treatment meted out to him. Yet, the fact again is that, no matter how stubborn or strong-willed he could be under the circumstances he might've found himself, it was not enough to justify these gagging of the entire body and mouth, sir! You can only apprise a visually impaired man, a blind man, that there's no cooking oil in the soup but not salt for he will eventually taste the soup himself and discern the truth. It's only God who can tell the basic truth in all these allegations and counter allegations" Hyman pointedly remarked, using his hanky once more to blow his nose.

"Well, we're only reading some of these things in the newspapers and the newsmagazines like yours and others and yet, there's none of them which alleged this falsehood except one disgruntled government controlled newspaper which is well-known for its biased publications and adherents to its pay masters. They can write whatsoever they were being subjected to write, but let it be known that the tailless bull has its deity as curator from flies."

Journalist John Nelson would've liked to pin-point the Africans usages of adages and proverbs in almost every sentence but he had a pending question to ask. He glanced through the notepad on the table in front of him.

"Mr. Otta, sorry to take you back . . . you made mention of if it would not be prejudiced . . . if I were correct . . ." Nelson smiled, "could you throw more light on . . . ."

"I don't know much but I think that the objectivity of the committee has already been questioned, in that it includes many politicians who are all anti-immigration, hard-line nationalist like Dr. Mandl the chairman of the committee who was well known for his racist and prejudiced views, especially against African immigrants in Austria" Hyman asserted.

"And to add but a few words," said Koso somehow awkwardly that the question was not really directed to him in particular but to Hyman, "talking of the committee or committees, for we also heard that another committee was instigated by the foreign affairs ministry, let it be known that too many committees always end up with nothing. I'm of that school of thought that says that, the best way to kill an idea is to form too many committees who will in turn come out with different vibrant opinions."

"What consequences do you think these actions both that of the authorities and yours will result in, and how sure are you that these actions will help to liberate you from here?"

"I thought you've asked this before but for the benefit of doubt, I think for me, we're both driving to one place. And I believe it will be the last stop to all these mess. But for now it seems obvious that they have not come to know nor do they understand because their eyes have been besmeared so as not to see, their heart so as to have no insight, their whole sense of belonging have been trifled with . . . which has led them astray because of some political incentive enshrouded in these desperate straits we all found ourselves in" Hyman Otta attested, "for now, their hearts have been harder than flints . . . presumably, the authorities will later reconsider their stance . . . for us it's the game of the survival of the fittest!"

"The chimpanzee may be trapped by the snare, yet it the chimpanzee must move ahead. It's been said that everyday is for the thief, but one day is for the owner. I don't think that we're going to give up this, until our freedom is achieved" declared Koso joyfully, "sir, if you help for one thing, just tell them that our freedom is the answer. We're not at all apprehensive about their dubious tactics because it's only the end that justifies the means. And again let me add this African adage which says that who holds a child's cake in his hand upwards, will eventually bring his hand down when he starts feeling tired and the child will eventually grab his cake . . . if you know what I mean?"

"In a short sentence, what message do you have for your host governments, the European governments, and your unfortunate African brothers and sisters who may be aspiring to migrate over here considering your bitter experiences so far at the Austrian government?" Nelson said as he regarded *Fräulein* Lisa with a lovely stare. She seemed to have been exhausted and did not respond to him like before but Nelson is not the type that gives up so easily. He wanted her on his pay-roll and maybe for something else.

"My humble advice to the European government is that they should find a way to receive us with open-hand, and they should try to relax some of the policies and restrictions that hinder us from integrating into the society easily. They must look back at history between the two continents and tell themselves the basic truth that no man lives in peace when his neighbours languish in poverty. And to my fellow Africans I advise anyone that wants to come over here to be well-prepared because it's never a child's play. They may even fortify themselves with our African *Ju-ju* (Vodoo), for the Europeans had come with their own *Ju-ju*—guns and machetes and their cunning Bible—to annex Africa a long, long time ago. And I must say this, that even if they succeed to deport as many of us that are here now or even others in other European countries, millions of us are still coming. It is, 'soldier go, soldier come!' as my good friend, the legendary Fela Ransom Kuti—may his soul rest in peace—once sang. We Africans are not terrorists nor are we coming over here as suicidal bombers; like my very self Koso Osei came to Europe for my daily bread and the means to feed my poor and impoverished family over there in Ghana" Koso said.

"The only thing I can add to this is," Hyman laughed gently, a visible smile wreathed its way across his face, as he stroke at his chin, "if there were no problems in Africa as you would've known many of us would not want to spend one single day in these racist societies across Europe, from France to England to Spain and Portugal to Scandinavian countries and to Austria. The European government must understand this, that permanent interest policy, not permanent friends which is the foundation stone of their foreign policies is not acceptable to us anymore. They've been the friends of Africans for long and I would prefer them to remain just that. And being friends, the Europeans were expected to help Africa out of her problems, having been the sower and master-minders at the on-set. Having said this, I'll like to use this opportunity to remind my Black brothers and sisters who wish to come and live in Europe that there're many pleasurable experiences as well as many unpleasant moments awaiting them—among which were racial discriminations within all levels of the segments of the society and the prison cultures. The future of a free world—as they used to say—depends upon being in the forefront of controlling human behaviour . . . but, again, we will not forget that man's greatest unconscious nightmare is to become a slave or a prisoner, especially when as a prisoner he or she didn't commit any crime."

"Finally, guys on behalf of the editor, staff and entire members of *Augustin* publishers, I once again sympathize with you in the lost of your good and cherished friend, Marcus Omofuma, and I pray that God will give you, his friends and his families in Africa the valour and fortitude to bear his premature death in this earth and that 'you' also will live to see your freedom from here. I thank you for your co-operation and time spent" the journalist John Nelson expressed comfortedly as his colleague, Peter Preiter used his twin-lens reflex camera to get some snapshots of the Africans and the prison environment including their tiny cell room.

"I thank you very much, sir!" said Hyman Otta, his eyes shone also with happiness. "And on behalf of all the inmates of this deportation prison camp I convey our gratitude to the entire management and staff of the *Augustin* publishing house for commiserating with us at these darkest hours and you personally, sir, for this interview. I believe it's a golden opportunity for the world to hear about our plights; and to publicly reprimand the Austrian government for this illegal entry law. And also I'm using this golden opportunity to send a 'Save Our Soul' (SOS) message to Human Rights Organizations and the general public to please, come to our aid and rescue us from this unlawful incarceration. Once again, thanks and God bless you" Hyman smiled as the pressmen shook hands with him and Koso Osei, and waved at the other two Africans, Prince Eto and Jean Kanombe from where they were watching the interview.

Later, the prison commandant and the chief *Beamte* who had been away from the beginning of the interview sipping coffees and smoking cigars joined others. Nelson had finally succumbed to his heart's wish and asked *Fräulein* Lisa Egger for a date that evening at the *Willkommen* Chinese restaurant in the 9th district of Vienna which she accepted with much reservation. The newspapermen thanked their host, promising to keep getting in touch as the greatest dilemma of the Austrian deportation prison camp system unfolded before the watchful eye of the world.

CHAPTER FIFTEEN

"Our destiny is largely in our own hands. If we find, we shall have succeed in the race of life it must be by our own energies, and by our own exertions. Other may clear the road, but we must go forward, or be left behind in the race of life.

If we remain poor and dependent, the riches of the other men will not avail us. If we are ignorant, the intelligence of the other men will do but little for us. If we are foolish, the wisdom of the other men will not guide us. If we are wasteful of time and money, the economy of the other men will only make our destitution the more disgraceful and hurtful."

===Frederick Douglas.

And so with determination and hopefulness Hyman, Koso, Prince, Kanombe and their fellow prison inmates pushed forward. It had been five days today since these ordeals began and no one would be able to guess of when or if it will ever come to an end. But the situation must change somehow. It's either it changes for better or it changes for worst. The only thing that was constant in this world is change. It was only time which would tell. And to the prison inmates the last hope had not yet come or rather passed. Most of them had been in a position to talk to the journalist John Nelson and air their grievances. Yet, it's generally believed that words alone could not accomplish all their aims and objectives. Actions would have to supersede words. One thing with situation like this was that you did not know what would happen next. It's like a pregnant woman that doesn't actually know the very time her baby will be brought to bed, but she knew for sure what sex the baby would be and the exact day of its parturition because of the help of mordern technology. It had not been easy for many of them, going without food for days.

But as Hyman used to tell his cellmates, a hungry man who has hope of getting food don't always die easily. There's this glimpse of hope that their sufferings would soon end, but before then it would be good to try next action which hopefully would prompt the authorities to be apprised of the vast disparity between a dead man and a snoring man. For them, the prison inmates, all these issues started one day and surely it must come to an end one day.

Hyman and his companions were all inside their cell deliberating about their interviews with the *Augustin* reporter John Nelson who they had added his name to their official list of very good friends of which officer Nicole, O. C. Nico was the foremost. As they contemplated on what they had uttered, what and what they supposed to have added or shouldn't have mentioned at all, it seemed obvious that they had made some human common mistakes. For example, Hyman thought: 'I had mentioned about the coming action to the journalist. How could I be so stupid and imperious to have said that when we'd all planned this action to be surprisingly executed. I had with the help of my roommates managed to draft some circulars on which we'd detailed the next course of action' and O.C Nico had as expected helped them to secretly distribute the flyers among the other inmates. After all their efforts, what if the authorities discerned this now and probably the stopped them from going out for *Spazieren* again . . . Then, I'd have to blame myself and will be blamed by others. I, Hyman Otta', he thought, 'The so called chief organizer

'Sometimes the gods are not to blame but human beings and in this case, I, Otta would've to carry the cross if . . . I'll be taken for a fool by many of my comrades. Imagine that, the chief organizer, becoming the chief spoiler. God forbid!" he said out a bit louder, staring at his wristwatch in angry consternation.

The minutes hand of the watch was approaching 11:48 am, that was precisely twelve minutes to twelve mid-day and according to the prison's official house rules and regulations if it happened that they could not go out for the *Spazieren*—which the authority has promised—by twelve o'clock sharp they might end up not going again that day or, forever, if at all the prison commandant and his hard-liner subordinate officers—like the prison superintendent Michael Schuller who was also well-known for his racist and prejudiced stance against the African immigrants in the prison—already knew about impending action.

Full of anxiety, Hyman called out to Kanombe and demanded from him what exactly the superior officer had told them in the morning about going out for *Spazieren*. Kanombe reassured him that the superior officer had promised them for 'walk' but that he, Kanombe, did not know when the *Spazieren* usually took place. His anxiety grew as he remembered the carton-cut *Spazieren* and food—*Menü*—time-table which he had written himself and which he neatly placed by the side of his prison's wooden-cupboard when he initially arrived at the prison. It was then after glancing quickly at the time-table he became less anxious for that day was Friday which meant that if they'd go at all it's not yet time. He had forgotten that because Fridays are half-working days the authority had mandated that *Spazieren* would be after the day's work was officially over. 'In fact, they'd have thirty-five to forty minutes . . . more than half an hour' Hyman thought as he stared fixedly at the paper. It was written bodly: On Friday, *Spazieren* at 12:30 pm and finish by 1:30 pm, then comes the evening meals immediately.

He opened the cabinet which he used as his wardrobe, cocktail cabinet, pantry and also as bookshelf and brought out his writing and drawing materials which he had begged Omofuma to help him buy just last week when he, Omofuma, had the last shopping. And Omofuma had as usual bought it for him without questioning. Hyman had been a very good artist—from his primary school days up till when he had proceeded to the senior seminary where his main courses ranged from philosophy to theology, up to the extent that one of his reverend father friend had once joked that he believed that he would've made a very good fine artist star instead of his priesthood aspiration.

Hyman carefully selected the drawing books and the crayons out of the entire package of painting materials. As he selected, he remembered Omofuma and was even illusioned to think that he saw Omofuma's face appearing before him from the drawing booklet.

'What can one say about life and its preconceptions' he asked himself. 'Why're humans so anxious and so unrepentant? And what was the need of striving to have riches or why do we exist at all? If everything we have and are will remain in this world while we just extinguish like fire and die forever. No man has ever died and taken-away with him any of his properties not even a single pin' Hyman hissed as he deposited the materials on top of the tiny wooden table that supposed to be their dinning table. He opened the centre page of one of the drawing books where he had been teaching Omofuma how to draw a day before he died. He emotionally invited Kanombe and Eto and showed them the drawings and explained to them how the pencil sketchings of their cell room came about. The ones he had drawn and that of Omofuma. His eyes moistened as he put the entire booklet aside. He took another drawing book and from the centre, he tore out about ten double plain pages, and started writing defiance slogans on them. In one of the plain sheet paper, he wrote, very boldly:

NO PEACE UNTIL OUR FREEDOM IS ACHIEVED!!!!! he painted it with the crayons. Yet, in another page, he wrote again

IF ONE IS MURDERED ALL ARE EQUALLY EAGER TO BE MURDERED TOO
And in another he wrote

WE WILL NEVER SURRENDER, WE WILL NEVER RETREAT WE WILL NEVER GIVE UP!!!!! WE WILL FIGHT NOW OR NEVER!!!!!
And yet,

THE WIZARD WE LOVED YOU, YET, IT'S NEVER YOUR FAULT, BUT, THAT OF A FELLOW HUMAN BEING. HOWEVER, WE BELIEVE GOD LOVES YOU MOST. WE BID YOU FAREWELL, ADIEU! ADIEU!! ADIEU!!! COMRADE OMOFUMA! And lastly he wrote,

BROTHER OMOFUMA, THEY'VE NO REMORSE FOR YOU BUT GOD WILL KINDLY GIVE YOU TRUE REPOSE IN HEAVEN. WE BELIEVE YOU ARE THERE RIGHT NOW!!!!!!!! MAY HIS SOUL REST IN PERFECT PEACE, AMEN!!!!

All these and many other slogans that touched the heart he had written. He also sketchily painted Omofuma's portrait, one of which showed how he was gagged with the adhesive tape which he painted in Austrian red-white-red national flag colour with the Hitler's Nazi insignia patently attached at far end, covering his mouth and the nose. And yet another poster was displaying how he was strapped with more tapes to the seat and with a plastic belt across his chest and abdomen on board the Balkan airline twin-engined Tupolev flight. All this while he was being helped by his fellow African brothers, especially Prince Eto, the Rastaman, who claimed to have learnt how to draw back in his primary school days in Nigeria. In all, they were able to arrange more that took place before his *last journey.* The Africans had each folded the placards and hid them into their trouser pockets, covering it with their shirts which they stuck out on purpose. As Hyman glanced at his time-piece again, it was 12:29 pm, and instantly without notice, the iron door of their cell unbarred. A warder immediately shouted:

"*Fertig machen zum Spazieren!* (Get ready for walk around!)"

"Oh! Yeah, we're coming please . . . Hey guys!" Hyman yelled from inside, urging others to double up. "*Bitte, wir kommen sofort! Wir kommen schon!* (Please, we are coming immediately. We are coming soon!)"

They hurried and moved out from the cell room as fast as they could, leaving the *Beamte* behind to lock the door back before he came after them.

On emerging from the corner of the aisle, they met the other inmates whom they hadn't seen nor spoken with face to face since their last *Spazieren* together on that Sunday afternoon. The only mode of communications between them had been the unofficial window to window verbal discourse among the prisoners which normally took place later in the evenings when many prison officials might had closed and gone home, leaving very few low-ranking officers to take control. In this way also the inmates sometimes with the help of long ropes can easily transfer coded letters from stock to stock through the window. O.C. Nico had also in the few days he was on duty been their emissary.

Hyman and Koso were proffering their hands and at same time introducing the newcomers Kanombe and Eto to the other prison inmates. When all the prisoners finally flocked together, they were countered one by one as usual by the four warders escorting them to the *Spazieren* ground. One of the prison warders opened the gate and out flung the inmates for the first time since five days.

Without hesitation, Hyman approached comrade Andreas Volvaskov who seemed to have lost ten pounds of his formerly hundred-and-sixty pound weight with his pot belly drastically reducing to more flattened human form. After conversing momentarily with him and telling him all the schemes he had planned before-hand concerning the demonstration and even showed him some of the placards they have designed for the occasion comrade Volvaskov became immensely satisfied. He praised Hyman for his muse and better organizational skills and outlined some other ways which would help their course more and more. After which he signalled to comrade Ognyan Stoyanov whom he always spoke with in Russian dialect and who as it were was discussing with Wakil Muhamet, the Afghanistian national. Both men at once left to join Volvaskov and Hyman Otta where they had already been encircled by other inmates. They consulted with each other and Hyman and his roommates dipped their hands and from their pockets, they produced the protest placards and distributed them among the prisoners.

Comrade Volvaskov instantaneously asked Hyman Otta to lead them in a short prayer.

Hyman prayed, entreating God to protect all of them in whatsoever their action might turn to either for better or for worse.

"Father, we praise and adore your holy name because you're so good and merciful. And you're worthy to be praised. You know the heart of man and know we're doing this not for violence or cruelty, but for solidarity and in honour of our untimely departed friend and brother Marcus Omofuma, who died as a result of man's inhumanity to his fellow man and also for you God, to help us achieve our freedom from this prison. All these and many other things . . . we ask through Christ our Lord, amen!"

"AMEN AND AMEN!!!!!!" re-echoed all the other inmates.

As the prisoners encircled comrade Volvaskov he once again asked them to observe a one minute silence in Omofuma's honor. When the one minute silence had passed he now automatically declared the peaceful protest officially opened by first raising his own placard up over his head and immediately the other inmates follow suit and did the same.

When they'd all hoisted up their posters and placards comrade Stoyanov then led them in a chant of

"ALL WE ARE SAYING IS GIVES US OUR FREEDOM!!!!!
ALL WE ARE SAYING IS GIVES US OUR FREEDOM!!!!!
ALL WE ARE SAYING IS WE MUST BE FREE!!!!!!!!
ALL WE ARE SAYING IS WE MUST BE FREE!!!!!!!!
ALL WE ARE SAYING CLOSE DOWN THIS DEPORTATION
PRISON CAMP!!!!!!!!!
ALL WE ARE SAYING CLOSE DOWN ALL DEPORTATION
CAMPS!!"

These chants which they all chorusly sang on top of their hungry orientated voices was what instantly called the attention of the *Beamten* who had escorted them to the *Spazieren*-ground. They were inside the laminated-glass partitioned look-out tower where they always sit back, enjoying their cigarettes, while still overlooking the prisoners. Sensing what the inmates had started doing, three of the *Beamten* immediately rushed out, startled, they began shouting orders to the prisoners to quiet them down.

Meanwhile, the leader of the escort *Beamten* was still inside, furiously making phone calls. First, he dialled the office of the prison commandant Christian Gospel, then to the chief-*Beamte* Martin Baur and that of the superior officer Thomas Werner who happened to be the only one he could speak with directly on the line for the personal secretaries of the commandant and the chief-*Beamte* had already told him that they could not be reached because they were still in the conference hall meeting with other officials and committee members.

All this while, the protest was gaining momentum. Their chanting became more blaring with about three or four inmates exasperatingly throwing stones and anything their hands could grab towards the look-out tower, smashing one side of the laminated glass. At that very minute, comrade Volvaskov raised his hands up in an attempt to calm the raring crowd.

About one or two minutes later and with the help of comrades Hyman, Ognyan, Wakil and Koso, he was able to accomplish that as the stoning and the roars of the crowd abruptly came to a halt.

Comrade Volvaskov cleared his throat and started to address the inmates.

"My fellow humble comrades, it will prove to be provocative and senseless efforts to all of us if we could allow ourselves to be destructive and noxious" he spouted to the crowded prisoners of conscience and also prisoners of the Austrian illegal entry law as he raised his folded right fist in gesture of more support and strongness, and then he continued in a more tactical voice, "let us remember our main aims and objectives of organizing this protest. Let every comrade try and remember that we're doing all this in solidarity of our former colleague and prison associate; who we all know as a very peaceful, harmonious and gentle being . . . yet, a gallant and outspoken critic of the inhuman treatments which we're receiving daily at the hands of the prison authorities . . . A freedom fighter of a virtuoso stature and a static, staunched, and an extraordinary orator and zealous censurer of these diurnal events . . . series breachings of our basic and fundamental entitlements which have been perpetrated against us—so as to diminish our fighting spirits—by the callous and wicked government of Austria?" he shouted, thrusting his clenched hand more and more upwards, "yes, of course, as human beings I strongly believe that we should be given our basic entitlements, irrespective of our conditions today. Our rights should not be sacrificed. Nor could we be put in an invidious position by some disgruntled elements. I mean, disgruntled politicians for their own selfish, hard-headed and hard-hearted reasonings which had made it possible for you and me to be incarcerated today . . . We must give honor to whom honor is due and peace to whom peace is due . . . And for our lovely brother and comrade Marcus Omofuma to be absence from us today in body but not in spirit, let us honour him by being thoughtful and never provocative in our actions for I know as well as you know also that he, Omofuma, will be proud and happy today, wherever he might be now, when he sees our actions today and the ones we've organized on his behalf since his departure from us" comrade Volvaskov declared as he bent his neck towards Hyman Otta who had approached and whispered something to him. "So, let me once again remind every comrade that our main intention is to sit it out here today, for our liberty and for our supports in upholding the esprit de corps of our departed comrade. I think, I'll call it off, for the meantime but before we continue our peaceful 'sit in' revolt, let us please listen briefly to one of our comrade in arms' comrade Hyman Otta, who I believe has a little thing to tell us. Thank you all" he bowed, extending his stretched hand towards Otta.

There was a very big hand of applause, and whistling from among the prisoners for sometime and as it died down, Hyman Otta coughed, blocking his mouth with his palm and began in a hoarse voice, for his voice had became worn from shouting, he was the loudest of the day.

"Friends, comrades and fellow inmates, I thank you all for giving me this great opportunity to address you on this historic day of this deportation prison camp, and of our unjustified imprisonment. Before I continue, I'd like to quote my idol and one of the world's greatest freedom fighter for human rights of our modern times, Malcolm X of blessed memory who once said that our people have made the mistake of confusing the methods with the objectives. As long as we agree on objective, we should never fall out with each other just because we believe in different methods or tactics or strategies to reach a common objective. We have to keep in mind at all times that we are not fighting for separation. We are fighting for recognition as free humans in this society . . ." Hyman enumerated, his tone becoming clearer and louder as he spoke.

"Oh wee . . . Oh wee" applaued the prisoners as he spoke.

"Violence and ruin my fellow comrades, would never, I repeat, never help our course of action, but rather, it would help to stigmatize us as being inimical, barbarians and antagonistic to our courses which would make some of our supporters to become unsympathetic towards us and our course. You might be thinking that nobody or no group has come to our aid since the beginning of these episodes. But let me make it clear today to everyone who has ears that man and God have heard our desperate out cries and prayers . . . And I believe that it will never be news any more to majority of us that the press world were cognitant of what is happening and that most importantly our people in the outside world' are preparing for a very big demonstration in honour of Marcus Omofuma, the majority of whom in the practical sense, do not know him, but who believe that it's high time when we have to come together and condemn racism, discrimination, and brutality in this world. And to collectively declare that man's inhumanity to man is poisonous and sinful act which should be eradicated . . . by all God fearing people. It's said, that this kind of difficult situation we found ourselves these days usually help to bring out a man's most tiresome side . . . we all know that this very journey we have chosen to follow will never be too easy but there's no harm in trial. And I'm assuring you today that our God is never asleep and that He must answer us today or we will never leave him . . . unless He blesses and sets us free from this prison. Comrades, as we all know and believe that, if a peaceful change or solution is rejected, then a calculated violent approach and solution became inevitable . . . but for now I pray every comrade to abide by this peaceful sit-in action we all seem to have agreed to . . . As defenceless and helpless prisoners of illegal entry law, let us not allow the masses who must in due time hear about these actions to turn against us but rather for us. The authorities must not deny us any longer. There's a saying that when a man dies, all his thoughts and actions die with him . . . but, I tell you in reality that we're not yet dead and every one of our hope in life will eventually have to come to fruition. However, we must fight today in order to enjoy tomorrow. We must work today in order to eat tomorrow . . ." Hyman Otta forcefully asserted as he glanced at the direction of the *Spazieren*-ground where many *Beamten* whom had been invited by the superior officer Thomas Werner to come and force the prisoners out of the *Spazieren*-ground, were planning how to undertake such task without causing commotion. But he was not in anyway shaken by their presence, as he returned his gaze nor did any of the prison inmates, who were busy listening attentively and who even urged him to forget the officers and continue his speech.

He paused for a moment and then went on.

"Comrades, united will continue to be our only watchword because it's only in unity we can fight and keep our rightful hopes alive . . . but, in disunity we'll lose more of our rights and will be equally defeated at long last. I want to make it very clear to all comrades here with us today that Austrian government is not going to yield what rightfully belongs to us without a struggle kept up by us this very day and at this very *Spazieren*-ground. Remember, my fellow prisoners of conscience that it all started here and it's going to end here. Do not fear or be agitated, for our God is with us and He is going to perform His miraculous works for all of us today and we'll see and will come to believe more in Him. Today, our God is going to bring down the wall of racism like He scattered the Walls of Jerico . . . so, my comrades and fellow inmates, let our rally cry be . . .

FREEDOM! FREEDOM!! FREEDOM!!! POWER! POWER!! POWER!!!
FREEDOM! FREEDOM!! FREEDOM!!! POWER! POWER!!

"And I'd like every comrade to join me in singing this song of spiritual, comfort. Please, repeat after me . . . Member, don't get weary,
        Member, don't get weary,
        Member, don't get weary,
        For the works almost't done"

And this was the very song, the song of spiritual . . . which they were singing, shouting, yelling, whistling, clapping and dancing without anymore violence when they heard over their voices, a louder noise but the inmates continued to hallow in unison.

The banging persisted as comrade Volvaskov turned and looked towards the main gate of the *Spazieren*-ground, and standing there with a megaphone in his hand was the prison commandant, Christian Gospel who looked weary and anxious as he shouted at the prisoners to stop and listen to him. Standing beside him were Dr. Lukas, Mag. Berger, chief-*Beamte* Martin Baur, Dr. Rabl, Susanne Mayer and Dr. Luger. They had all abandoned their ad-hoc committee meeting, and rushed to the scene of the demonstration with the exception of Superintendent Michael

Schuller, who had been insisting that the prison authority had been too lenient and magnanimous in handling the whole issue and the inmates whom he always branded as criminals.

After a momentary hesitation comrade Volvaskov once again raised his hand and beckoned to his fellow prisoners to stop their singing as they started clamouring for immediate resignation of the prison commandant and his hard-core officers. The commandant invited them to approach and come nearer to the gate which was by now widely opened but still heavily guided by many *Beamten*-commandos who were dressed in complete dark-green khaki uniforms. The inmates were adamant about his offer to them and the continual increase of more *Beamten* and in addition of special anti-riot units who were invited in case the demonstration turned riotous. They had instead sat each man tirelessly on the grass while still hoisted their placards upwards to enable the guests to read for themselves. On the side of the officials outside the *Spazieren*-ground there was a heated argument among them on the best approach to follow. While the politicians were calling for a peaceful dialogue with the prison inmates, the officers led by the chief *Beamte* Martin Baur and Lieutenant Hermann of the anti-riot special unit were on the other hand insisting harsh measures, one of which called for forceful evacuation of the inmates from their positions by the 50 members of the anti-riot troop who had already stationed themselves around the *Spazieren*-ground with their full riot gears.

The argument lasted for some minutes before finally Dr. Lukas moved forward and slowly approached the inmates, looking suave in a wine coloured Armani suit, with a brown tie, brown sunglasses and brown shoes to match. He barely moved five meters towards the prisoners in anticipation of at least to partially initiate a kind of an informal discussion with them—when they began to shout out his own name asking him to leave them alone.

ALL WE ARE SAYING LEAVE US ALONE! ALL WE ARE SAYING, DR. LUKAS PLEASE LEAVE US ALONE!!!! ALL WE ARE SAYING!!!!!!!!!

He passionately called out to them to drop their posters and placards and listen attentively to what he wanted to say. It was then, with his raised eyebrows that comrade Volvaskov gestured and pleaded his fellow freedom fighters to stop their shoutings and to kindly drop their placards. At once, the inmates obeyed and the atmosphere had quietened as Dr. Lukas, able to regain his composure, began to address them:

"Good afternoon, gentlemen, please, I want you to give me your ears for just a few minutes and listen very carefully," he desperately entreated with them for calmness as he smiled his typical sunshine smiles. "I'm Dr. Paulus Lukas from the ministry of Internal affairs as you might have known."

He pause a little to contemplate on what he had just said. How could he claim that these prisoners had known him when he had not met any one of them before, or was it that the same person who had earlier on leaked this hunger strike information to the press had been the same to leak, he believed, all the names of the members of the ad-hoc committee, as it were, if that was the case, then this insider of a person is up to something. But all the same he have to try and see what he could do for now. He glanced around the faces of the hunger-stricken prisoners, and as a human being, he for once had pity on them, and shook his head in ultaral contemplation as to what and what he could say that would not be too offensive to the souls of this already wounded prisoners. He continued pathetically.

"And I'm here to represent the Minister of Interior. The ministry has heard about your problems and has directed me to come and speak directly to you . . . if you all will be quiet and non-violent" he lied and added rather solicitously as a result of his immediate compassionate concern for the inmates. "Now can any of you tell us the reason why you should not humbly go inside your cells and wait for the final decisions of the Minister . . . which I believe, will pave the way for final and meaningful settlement of this mess? I'm quite confident that all of you will once again have your smiles, hope and aspirations returned to you but the basic thing now will be marked by your willingness to accept the new circumstances and promise . . . and then try to adapt to them by agreeing to go back to your various rooms voluntarily. The authorities believed that all of you would easily be acquiesced to this simple instruction which is the key to any favourable solution . . . Do you understand me?" asked Dr. Lukas, in expectation of getting one of them to speak-up.

"Well done, sir," commended comrade Andreas Volvaskov still standing where he had been since the man approached them. "Let me begin by saying this, sir, a nation without knowledge of its history is like a big tree which knows nothing about its tapped roots. Sir, this adage is indirectly applicable to our plights here in this prison. I can assure you that we all know our problems like we are familiar with our private parts. Individually and collectively, we knew how it all started and when it all started. We knew when problems have got out of the hand and automatically we've all agreed to see the end of it all, for we know that what goes up must surely come down. We're not in anyway afraid or worried on how it will end for as far as nature is concerned, it will either change for good or for worse. And let me quickly add this, that we're all very determined and courageous that it will be either now or never as we have promised ourselves not to be destructive or violent but to stick it out by peacefully organizing ourselves and staging this sit-in-strike. We've been maintaining that and we are going to maintain that until our demands are met. Sir, we're not proving to be selfish people but rather sensible and law—abiding individuals who know when the violation of their fundamental rights have become proportionally unacceptable and as such, try to put an end to it," comrade Volvaskov was saying in his articulated manner of a former labour leader.

He glanced through the faces of the officers and civilian officials alike who had all approached nearer to hear his long but tactical speech, and likewise he turned and glanced around the frowned but consciously happy and determined inmates he is representing.
Satisfied with the level of co-operation he had so far got from them, he continued.

"Sir, we all need our freedom and we want it right now. Here in this *Spazieren*-ground! It's either today or no more! We can't be fools any more. You can fool the people sometimes but you cannot fool them every time. We're a people like all of you standing there today as officials of your government and as representatives of various ministries and offices. We aren't animals or starked illiterates as you might've be thinking" he proclaimed, glancing around once more at his fellow prisoners of conscience as the heated sun and the five days of hunger strike had forced many of them to become too tired and straightened themselves on the field in a manner of sleeping but his instincts told him that they were just pretending as was originally planned.

He shook his head to and fro and continued after a little pausing.

"What we're doing now and what we'll be doing in due course, if and when necessary, as the need may arise, is nothing, than more or less taking an extreme step and measure to protect an equally extreme emergency, which we've found to be bigger than what we as human beings can. We decided to act now because we're not sure how much longer we can bear the pain," comrade Volvaskov deduced at long last, looking cheerful and fulfilled as some of his fellow comrades who were still fit applauded to his long speech.

As it were, more and more people had joined the officials, including most importantly for the prisoners, journalist John Nelson who had received an emergency phone call from his trusted source in the prison, O. C. Nico. He had hurriedly packed his journalistic instruments without having the opportunity to call upon his cameraman but had rushed down to the prison to cover at least the later part of the scene. Because he had been duely accredited, it had not been too hard for him to secure entrance into the prison yard. And fortunately *Fräulein* Lisa Egger who was equally on duty had made it easier for him when some of the *Beamten* had tried to refuse him entrance, as he approached them the look of many of the officials and *Beamten* had changed to nothing but unpleasant.

Dr. Lukas after conversing briefly with the prison chief psychologist Mag. Rupp who had joined him, said with a mild tone.

"I'm very happy to hear you speak out your mind and equally happy that, not only you're able to speak sensibly but that you can also control and call your fellow inmates to order. So, I'd be very happy if you can, for the interest of peace and for your benefit and that of your fellow prisoners and friends, advise them to gradually go back to their cells and gently wait for what is in store for you."

"Excuse me, sir" comrade Volvaskov interrupted, staring directly at the two men. "The fact that I speak out cannot be misunderstood by you to mean that I'm the leader of these meek and gentle people or that I can order them around as my subordinates" he said in his low, mellifluous, but firm voice. "I'm really disappointed with what you've just uttered and whatever you're intending to say anymore. Throughout modern history we have witnessed state repression, suppression and denial of individual rights, but these had all taken place under fascist or semi-fascist or totalitarian states . . . and never in a democratic government like we can assume to have here. I mean, why wouldn't you ask the *Fremdenpolizei* and the prison authority and the politicians, why they are so hell bent on holding most of us here as criminals . . . subjecting and treating us day by day as condemned criminals when in actuality we were only running away from life-threatening problems in our various countries? How come you haven't questioned these heartless people on the way they've broken both local and international laws by 'imprisoning us while we are still in prison?" comrade Volvaskov seriously asked, unable to hide his unfailing courtesy and forbearance under provocation.

He cleaned his glasses with a handkerchief he took from his trouser pocket, scowled at the officials and the prison officers standing in front of them defiantly.

"Now, what you're trying to tell us is that, we don't have any right to stage a common peaceful demonstration" he said and turned his back at Dr. Lukas and Mag. Rupp, and facing squarely his fellow inmates.

"Now, you're to tell us that Dr. Nelson Mandela, Steve Biko, Dr. Martin Luther King Jr., Malcolm X and many other human rights activists and freedom fighters were unwise to have fought for their rights and the rights of their people. Now you want to teach us that we 'as' people have no will-power to fight for our rights and that peaceful and non-violence demonstration have been totally wrong and excluded from us . . . Well, sirs!, to say the fact, I've no right or power to order these helpless citizens, who have been going without food or water for many days to stop their self-contained defiance . . . nor will I stand here promising you that I've the gut to do the unthinkable of invading any of their individual rights. I know, my position and previous activities have always put me at odds with the law enforcement agents but I hereby confess my helplessness in this and therefore I resign to speak anymore on anybody's behalf but for myself," comrade Volvaskov defensively maintained.

"But, Mr. Volvaskov you can't just do that, you've been their spokesman and I rather want you to continue being . . ." said Dr. Lukas who had earlier asked the chief psychologist Mag. Rupp if he knew the name of speaker as Volvaskov uttered his speech and had been assured of his name and what he had claimed to be in his country Ukraine—a labour union leader. But he was rather interrupted by this oriented speaker of a man whom he had come to believe he was really what he said he was.

"I think every one of them has the right to say yes or no to your proposals," comrade Volvaskov cut in once more, "but why're you ashamed to answer my questions?"

"What's your question again?"

"Why are we being held here against our will, against international laws on immigration, like we were dangerous criminals? Why are the authorities hell-bent on imprisoning us while in prison?"

Dr Lukas already knew the implication of answering his questions, especially his second question which had caused commotions in their last committee meeting. He chose his words and deliberated a moment.

"Sir," said Dr. Lukas reflectively, "I think that's a good question and fair question indeed. As an ordinary lesser official in my ministry, I don't think I've such power you might've supposed as to solving these problems. And let me say it openly that the ministry as a matter of fact doesn't well know about these things you just alleged" he lied again. "So, my candid advice to you'll be . . . accept what I've just proposed with good faith and go back to your individual rooms. You've done your part in proclaiming what I thought is basically your rights; however, if you would be so good as to pay attention to my counselling and allow the ministry to carry out a full-scale inquiry into these allegations, single out the perpetrators . . . of course, meted out punishment to everyone involved . . ."

"Your Minister's committee of inquiry is like 'transferring old wine in a new bottle in that it includes the main culprits of these acts . . ." comrade Volvaskov discreetly remarked.

"And, sir, how do you come to know about this appointment? Who gave you this false information? What gave you the impression that . . ." Dr. Lukas asked.

"I wouldn't be so indiscreet as to reveal my source, but can you deny this?"

"Listen, I would rather avoid entering into unnecessary argument with you because it will do us no good" Dr. Lukas explained. "Once more, I ask you to control your boys and peacefully march them in . . . I believe it will be much more accomplishment on your part than sitting here under the open sun, endangering your health and at the same time, jeopardizing your chances" he admonished as he stared and nodded at Mag. Rupp and the other committee members.

And at that instant some dramatic and incredible things started to unveil. Firstly, something clicked. Then a wilt flapping sound followed, comrade Volvaskov immediately turned his head to look at his fellow inmates. At the rear of the gathering, two of his colleagues were slipping into unconsciousness. While Wakil Muhamet had collapsed already, his mouth opened like that of a slaughtered goat, Andrew Peters on his own was just driving away to a state of stupor like someone given overdose of soporific drugs as his breathing became faster and furious. There was a kind of confusion everywhere. Some of the prisoners were colliding with each other as they rushed and rallied around their unconscious friends. Comrade Volvaskov shoved his way through the crowd and bent down at where Wakil laid and started to try everything possible to resuscitate him. Being someone who was experienced in that field—having worked as an adjuvant staff at many hospitals in and around Kiev—he thumbed and slowly thumbed at Wakil Muhamet's chest and finally, he gave him the kiss of life in an attempt to revive him in less than one minute Muhamet regained his consciousness and started to breath audibly and still coughing, like he was struggling for breathing, his eyebrows seemed to be swallening up and the eyeballs pirouetting. With a pious hope, comrade Volvaskov left Wakil and rushed towards Peters and compassionately he acquitted himself of the same adroit chore and gracefully achieved the same splendid result.

As he tiredly straightened himself up to look around and see if another of his comrades was in trouble, there and then, he was shoved off by four members of the special anti-riot police squad. They forcefully handcuffed him and dragged him away with his two legs kicking restlessly in the air.

All this while, journalist John Nelson had been taking pictures of the officials as they stood entreating the inmates and had equally took as many pictures as he can as these episodes unfolded. He turned and rushed to a scene—somewhere across the *Spazieren*-ground main gate another prisoner had collapsed to the floor fainting, while being dragged by three commandos who had covered their faces with black masks.

Further down the ground Jean Kanombe and two special unit officers were battling it out as they wanted to arrest and handcuff him. In less than two minutes Kanombe winced as one of the cops kicked him on the right thigh where he had his old wound and with the help of another three commando officers they finally pined him down, handcuffed and took him away from the scene. Not quite long after he was taken away, about ten nurses who were dressed in pristine-white work jacket, all in hand gloves arrived at the scene, carrying with them five stretchers. They immediately stretched three of the stretchers out at different locations. One for Wakil Muhamet, one for Andrew Peters and the last one for Ojo Madukwem, a Nigerian of Igbo origin, who had just arrived at the deportation prison camp that same morning as the inmates were about to go out for the *Spazieren*. Unlike Wakil and Peters who had fainted as a result of the hunger strike and blazing hot weather, he was hit at the back of his head with a truncheon by a commando officer. They were hurriedly strapped on the stretchers with its belts and quickly taken out in front of the prison compound where about five emergency ambulance vans parked. They were immediately rushed into the waiting hospital's egg-like coloured, with red stripped ring round vehicle and were speedily, with the help of the siren driven straight to the ALLGEMEINES KRANKENHAUS (AKH), the general hospital in the 9th district of Vienna.

Inside the prison yards and back to the *Spazieren*-ground, the policemen and their commando counterpart were still shoving, beating and kicking many of the prisoners while on handcuffs. As they approached their cells, they were released from their handcuffs and forcibly flung into their cell rooms. Koso, Eto and Kanombe were made to remain outside their cell room for nearly two hours as an intensive search of their cell was being conducted by four civil-dressed criminal police officers. The officers took away many written materials and prison diaries belonging to Hyman Otta and Koso Osei. They had earlier found Hyman's personal memo jotter where he has been recording his personal and collective experiences since he arrived in Austria and most importantly, the ones he had written since he came to the deportation prison camp.

Meanwhile, journalist John Nelson had professionally taken pictures as Andreas Volvaskov, Ogayan Stoyanov and Hyman Otta were specially singled out and being led into a nearby office. As they were forced inside the special detention room, there were more cudgelling and bashing by some of the commandos. They were later told that this special treatment, VIP treatment as one of the cop mockingly said were as a result of their organizing and inciting all the rebellious acts the prisoners had taken so far against the authorities. Three of them were later taken away and locked up, each man in a one-man cell on the order of the prison commandant Christian Gospel.

++

At the AKH, inside the intensive care unit room number four, a room forty-by-forty square, which was strictly guarded by three civil policemen on a special duty; Wakil Muhamet, Andrew Peters and Ojo Madukwem had being immediately been on arrival wheeled in, and were attended to. Three doctors were dispatched to them each, after they had been briefed by the mobile medical personnel who happened to be in one of the ambulance vans that rushed to the prison when the emergency call came.

The emergency room had two side windows which were covered with whitelace curtains. And the walls right-round were decorated with posters showing the most important building sites—among them, the Austrian Parliamental building and premises, and the United Nation Centre, (UNO City).

Peters was laid on one of the blue painted bed at the corner of one of the windows, Wakil at the extreme corner, while Madukwem was in the centre bed. Their bodies were fully draped. The doctors, after examining, started shouting orders to the nurses. After some minutes, Ojo Madukwem was able to regain himself, and he was ordered to be transferred by the doctors to another ward with full security.

At the same time, the IV standing near each of the beds, were affixed with different bottles of fluids, each merging in a single line that led straight under their body cover. Two nurses were sitting near the beds, their eyes locking on the electrocardiograph read out over the heads of Peter and Wakil. Earlier on, an oxygen mask had been used to cover their noses and faces. Five hours after they were brought to the hospital, neither of them had opened his eyes, nor had they regained consciousness. They remained insensate, and showed signs of serious malnutrition.

What had begun as a beautiful day for all the prisoners later changed to a dreadful and deplorable day, with two of their colleagues desperately fighting for their lives.

CHAPTER SIXTEEN

"Who makes a distinction between holy and profane?
Your pride and your haughtiness have brought about that
this ruling will not be repeated in your name."

===Rabbi Yehuda Pesachim 104b.

Regina left her office a bit later than she usually did. She had been going through so many files—both for her job and in keeping herself in position to help her man, Dr. Lukas in finding an end to all this mess his ministry had found itself in. To her, she must do something to help him and his career, now that they're trying to be one soul in marriage.

That morning, before he had left the hotel for the day's business, he seemed to be asking himself when would these ordeals come to an end, so that he and his fiancé would be able to leave these daily bureaucratic wars for some weeks to a more suitable area, maybe at the Bahamas, as he had been proposing. Now, she thought that morning before leaving the hotel, she had decided she must help, but only if he would agree to her proposals and confronts the Minister to square it out once and for all . . . and then, patiently wait for the consequences, which she believed would be favourable for him and his ministry.'

Regina came out of the old fashioned building under which she had her office at 12:15 pm precisely, fifteen minutes later than usual but firstly she had remembered to put in her hand purse all the notes she has jotted from many of the files. Because she felt she was already late for she shouldn't have been, she promised herself yesterday evening that things had changed for her now. She must be keeping time and start behaving more matured and resposible now than before. She couldn't wait for her normal taxi chauffeur who has just told her over her mobile phone to linger for another five minutes to enable him to reach her office—he was caught up in a traffic jam. She dashed out of her office and flagged down the first taxi she saw. Once the driver ushered her into the Mercedes Benz V-Boot 300 model car, she opened her calculator-shaped Nokia phone and dialled Dr. Lukas who told her that he himself was just trying to dial her and excused himself for the inconveniences he may have cause her, that he was on his way. She couldn't tell him that she was on her way, too. She felt a bit relaxed on her own and yet, tensed for him for the way he sounded on the phone it seemed that the problems had escalated somehow for him and his ministry.

In less than ten minutes the taxi was at the Café Royal. The driver rushed out as usual for that had been the manner of many Viennese taxi drivers, especially their male counterparts, whenever they chauffeured a lady passenger, they go to her side of the car and unlocked the door. Regina flounced out of the car like the sophisticated woman she was, extracted some Schilling notes from her cobral-skin purse and put it in the hand of the driver, who was grinning at her admiringly.

She waved her fingers at him in anticipation of telling him to forget the change he was supposed to give her. And once again she extracted from her handbag, black sun-shade-glasses putting it to cover her eyes from the brightening sun of the day. She placed the spectacles in between her forehead to give her a *jauntty mien* and smirked back at the driver, jostling her way into the Café Royal.

The waiter appearing in a canary-yellow shirt and well tailored lincoln-green trousers, with a shining black shoes and a light-yellow tie to match, greeted her warm-heartedly and escorted her to their choice table. She told him to bring her usual bottle of *Mineralwasser* before Dr. Lukas arrive when she would be able to know if she can order their usual Rosé wine for she didn't want to make mistake like the previous day she drank a whole bottle only her when he said he preferred beer instead, and she had been somehow intoxicated. She slumped into the chair thinking of her betrothal, his problems and how far they had come in the three months of their relationship. To her, this Café and this corner to be specific would ever be the most unforgettable corner of her entire life.

She heard his voice extending greetings to some of the waiters and waitresses and hurriedly packed her make-up case back into her purse. Dr. Lukas hastily sat down near her, jerking at his wristwatch but without his usual pleasant disposition. She noticed it on his face that things had not been better today. In short, from the way she saw the looks of his face, it was even worse today than yesterday. He moved closer trying to be cheering in a way but to no avail and was followed immediately by the waiter, who was carrying his beer and a packet of Cuban cigar.

He looked sober to an extend that made her ask.

"What is it, honey? What have been the problems this time around? Has the situation escalated, deteriorating?" All in quick succession herself feeling more tensed for him now than before.

Without words, he drew her closer and kissed her tenderly, caressing lovingly, his face appearing on the verge of tears. He turned to his beer and took a mouthful of it, downed his beer glass and lit his cigar and puffed intently and then, exhaled a cloud of the smoke through his mouth and nostrils. That was when he was able to speak out for the first time since entering the love corner.

"My darling Uxorial," he said, taking another drag of his cigar, "today, I saw and believe that there're still fiends roaming around in this God-forsaken world. You couldn't imagine what I saw with my two eyes this afternoon . . . and still have the guts to say we're in a developed world or that we've even learnt some lessons from our past. In fact, to be plain and clear, our commandant Christian Gospel with all his subordinates and their advisory board are all brutes. Can you imagine what happened this afternoon in my presence?"

"What happened" she asked curiously.

"Believe me it was like we were still in the Nazi era . . . or to be more polite, like what you saw over the television from dictatorial regimes in

Africa and middle-east countries, my dear. I was motionless, as a statue, trying to grasp what was happening. All of their actions seemed starkly cruel and viscous to me. Yet, it was so planned, very brutal that I began to question our harsh methods of handling this crisis. The commandant was corrupted by the feeling of power and brutality" Dr. Lukas tried to recall without pausing, "as far as I'm concern, he committed a *faux pas* which I'll never put out of my mind," he swore, sipping from his glass beer and took another drag of the cigar, "I'm all . . . disturbed about the future of our country and its human rights violations in the hands of these callous people . . . and to say the fact, there's fear as well for everyone concerned if these sort of atrocities are not stamped out, my darling. The hope of eradicating basic rights violation will never be achieved in this country, if such people are still part and parcel of the system. He has shown me his color today and his color to me is absolutely 'nefarious' in nature. His color is not only morbid, but is black and brown" he uttered, his furrowed lips slited in a misery scowl.

"I'm very disappointed in all of them, including your so called Minister." she said.

"A commandant I believe is supposed to be a model exemplary in all his decisions, but this one has shown that he is deficient in being a leader."

"Then, what do you think, will have to be the solution," Regina asked in muted tone, giving out a weak smile. "Love, I've never known you to be as disillusioned as you seem to be today" she said, in a serious voice.

For once, she thought, he had now come to realize what she was preaching all along and that he had finally come to his senses by calling a spade a spade.

"I don't know what to recommend now, or what to say . . . in fact" he frowned his face. "I rather, don't utter any word out of contempt I have for him this afternoon, starting from the onset of today's meeting—than uttering and later feeling repentant about whatever I might say. In situation like these, I like to be calculative before biting" he said, his febriled mouth moved swiftly, because of his sobriety which he always avoid getting into but can't help it this time. "I would've prefered us to talk about other things, than reminding myself of these" he suggested with a hiss and drank from his glass.

"Other things, like what and what, love?" she inquired with a faint smile.

"Like our love. Like talking about our future together . . . like discussing what and what will bring harmony and happiness in our lives" Dr. Lukas opined his sunny smile appearing briefly on his face.

"But, love, I'm . . ." she wanted to interject.

"Listen, my darling, I'm tired and fed up with the whole situation. How could one be associating himself with these stone-hearted and indurated sets of people? People who behave just like what we used to read in history book about Hitler and his generals in the olden days. Look, we're almost in the 21st century, and I tell you, we have to behave ourselves as new generation of Austrians not like the old Nazi generation that painted our name and history in infamy" he expressed, mainly to himself as Regina stared at him in utter amazement.

And she smiled.

"Which brings us back to where my position had always being in these issues, what I've to say now, my recommendations and why we must talk it over and find common solutions and put an end to these dilemmas, my love. Let's be truthful, all the people that are involved in these mix-ups have failed, starting from the Minister, down to the prison commandant and his so-called ardent supporters and advisers. And, as it is the rule, they must all step down straight away without any delay and pave the way for others to step in and solve the problems" she said advisingly. "All these mess started as a result of man's deficiency in his duties, which he had sworen to exercise in all instances. Why, then, should we be protracting the inevitable? Or seem to be blinded from the complexities?" she asked wearily.

"Because, as I told you the other day, my darling, the powers that be are blocking the truth, and instead, they're bent on politicising the whole thing and . . ."

"Then, I think they must be openly confronted before things run out of hand."

"By whom?" he questioned suspiciously.

"By you, my love!, by me!, by any true loving citizen of this country . . . the power that be, must comprehend this, that they must take positive steps now or else, it will cost them more than a fortune to repair the situation later, and by then, it may be too late. Understand me love, I'm not trying to be dictating to you, however, you'll have to listen to what I've to say . . . after all, you're one of the advisers to the Minister and ministry."

"Go on, darling, I'm listening. I want to be part of the solution, not part of the problem" he smiled. "Like your father used to say then that we will feel and accept responsibility in the playing process, not just the paying process (when he was striving to help promote our interests abroad, during those trying periods of our country after the war). Speak for thy lover is paying attention" he said, and for the first time that day his smile reappeared fully as he gave her a peek in the cheek.

"I'm so happy you're alive again," she smiled back at him and returned his kiss, "in fact, when I reached my office this morning, I was so sad that I couldn't do any work . . . but, just thinking how we can help to retrieve the situation. So, I went through some written documents of the United Nations committee against torture and other cruel, inhuman or degrading treatment or punishment (convention against torture) which our country is a state party to and what they say concerning these situations. To start with, according to the document, 'article 2, 11 and 16 of the convention against torture required each state party to take effective legislative, administrative, judicial or other measures to prevent torture and ill-treatment and to keep under systematic review interrogative rules and practices, and other arrangements for overseeing the custody and treatment of detainees, in order to prevent acts of torture and other cruel, inhuman or degrading treatments, and also, articles 12, 13, and 16 of the UN convention against torture required that each state party shall ensure that there is a prompt and impartial investigation when there is reasonable ground to believe an act of torture or other cruel, inhuman or degrading treatment have been committed. Article 12 makes it very clear that this duty is not dependent on a formal complaint by a detainee. Each state party, it says, shall ensure that its competent authorities proceed to a prompt and impartial investigation, where ever there is reasonable ground to believe that an act of torture has been committed in any territory under its jurisdiction" she excerpted from her jotter, which she has since wrenched out from her handbag, staring at her man in the face. "Love, you see why we must do something at this point in time?"

"But, who told you that . . . some thing of this nature has taken place already. I'm quite sure I've not said anything like that to you today . . . Have I?" he asked, very proud of her reasoning.

"Love, I don't think we need any soothsayer or fortune-teller to interpret your thoughts of views on what happened today. One thing is I've been learning all through you these months we've known each other. You're not the type of man who hides his feelings. And, that was exactly the sort of man I prayed for and have got," she said, planting a short wave kiss on him. "So, as I said before, I'm most concerned that although our hard-line Minister has created a structure to investigate these acts I'm not convinced yet that this will be effective in preventing the continuous violation of rights, and ill-treatment of these prisoners—like what happened this afternoon on the *Spazieren*—ground. Yes, of course, I've heard about the stupid actions that took place as these people were . . ."

"Who told you about it, my darling?" he demanded anxiously.

"I've my source in the prison and besides the story is all over the place at the External ministry compound as many people are concerned about the recent happenings" she murmured. "But that is just part of the issue . . . that's by the way! I strongly believe that it has reached the boiling point when the powers that be as you used to call them, would take immediate steps to stop and prevent further molestation of these illegal prisoners by releasing every one of them unconditionally and with immediate effect from custody. To say the fact, my father would've been enraged and full of condemnation of these actions were he to be alive today. I remember vividly what he said then when he granted an interview on the subject concerning these issues, that is, the detention and torture of asylum seekers . . . that he was concerned that there is no definition of torture in our country's penal code as provided by Article 1 of the convention against torture . . . that due to the absence of this definition in the penal code, he was afraid that the offence of torture does not appear as punishable by the appropriate penalties as required by Article 4, paragraph 2 of the convention against torture. And yet, in a separate interview, he had totally condemned the attitude of our government on asylum policies, stating that Austria as a nation has its citizens as the highest population of asylum seekers especially in America and Australia during and immediately after the Second World war, and I echoed his views on these facts" she said, grinning as she glanced through her jotter, sipping her *Mineralwasser.*

All the while he was nodding thoughtfully in agreement.

"And, as indicated in these documents, there was a strong recommendation to all state parties to incorporate the definition of Article 1 of the convention as punishable offence in accordance with Article 4, paragraph 2 of the convention against torture. For instance, in the pivot of these problems, that is, the sudden death of Marcus Omofuma, I bet, it's going to provoke a widespread condemnation because of the way the whole issue is being handled so far . . . There is concern about insufficient measures of protection in cases of individuals under an order of deportation, which are not in conformity with the provision of Article 3 and 11 of the convention. And there is also strong recommendation from the convention, that provision concerning the protection of asylum seeker should fully conformed with the relevant international standards . . . in particular Article 3 and 11 of the convention both in law and practice. Moreover, Article 10 and 16 of the convention against torture required that education and information regarding the prohibition against torture and other cruel, inhuman or degrading treatment, or punishment be fully included in the training of law enforcement personnel—unlike what your commandos and the special anti-riot officers atrociously committed this afternoon in the name of security" she accused. "The convention fully recommended that this education and information should be included in the rules or instructions issued in regard to the duties and functions of such personnel. Instruction should emphasize the importance of such education, that ill-treatment by law enforcement officials shall not be tolerated and shall be promptly investigated and punished in case of violation according to law" Regina recited from her notebook wearily.

"Oh yeah" was what he could only uttered. "Go on my pretty angel."

"With the conduct of your Minister and your ministry so far I would only say our country is at a cross-road, but not with the drivers it really needs to pass her through, I'm afraid. I don't think these ordeals are annoying anyone else but, me and I'm never the sort, who would hide her feelings especially from you. I must say this, all of you have failed to oblige and handle these problems under existing international law, my love! I don't mean to make you feel inferior, but outspokenness is part of my life and I want you to at least, understand whom you want to marry, before it will be too late. I would support you when you're right in things, and tell you when you were wrong" she said, smiling broadly at him. "Accept me if you can?"

"And I've accepted you my darling" Dr. Lukas replied reassuredly. "And according to articles 111 and 112 of lover's convention, I hereby suggest that the game of politics would be postponed indefinitely and the game of love applied immediately" he maintained in a voice filled with surprising aplomb as he slowly inerted the twenty-four carat gold engagement ring he had earlier bought (before going for the meeting) for the occasion and kissed her tenderly on the mouth.

Regina drew her hand back, took a quick look at the tiny satin ring and glanced briefly at Dr. Lukas as tears of joy rolled down her cheeks. She grabbed him with both hands, his cheeks nearer to hers and before you can say Jack Robinson she plugged her fevered lips to his equally fevered lips. They were in that position for some minutes. As she unplugged her lips, she emotionally summoned up.

"I thought I would have nothing out of it. But, look what these problems have brought to me . . . An everlasting love for my life and for my soul. Now I believe the saying that one person's lost is another person's gain, and moreover, that even the worst situations may produce the best event. I thank you Dr. Lukas for loving me" she voiced floatingly, plugging her lips to his once more as they cuddled themselves.

CHAPTER SEVENTEEN

"He who starts behind in the great race of life must forever
remain behind or run faster than the man in front."

===Benjamine E. Mays.

Since that very moment *Fräulein* Lisa Egger had accepted his invitation
for a dinner date, she'd been pondering it all. How could he of all people
seems to be the one to ask her for a date, after what had been to her a long
time without a man. Men to her are like a scarce commodity. In almost
her twenty years experience of men and their sexual promiscuity, she had
come to the conclusion that men are all chameleonic in nature. When
they want you, they can go to any length you seem to be pushing them
to. And they can equally dance to any tune you play. Tell them you don't
have time next week, they would ask what of next month? Apply any
excuse or sort of trick you can give to abscond from them and they would
always be patient with you. Ask them to go one mile with you they're
ready to go ten miles. Of course, no amount of intimidation could scare
them from following you like a male goat follows the female goat. Just like
the wolf who can't keep away from the sheeps, yet, when they eventually
got you; and sometimes women are so weak and so stupid to accept them
on face value, without questioning their integrity or the sincerity of the
'hell' they're getting themselves into only to be dumped and deserted
before they know it after they might've tasted their Eve's apple. Oh! Yes, of
course, she knew what she was thinking about, for she was a living witness
of men's insincerity and bad deportment or rather, men's inhumanity
to women. In the last two years alone, by her reckoning, she had got

involved with four men and not even one of them was interested in any commital relationship. They all seemed to believe in hit and run game. She remembered the most recent of these short time affairs which ended six months ago with a bitter experience and which agitated her more than anything she could think of.

'Well' she pondered, 'it's not going to cost me anything, but a little time I would be with him. If at all he said anything concerning being intimate, I'll only laugh it off and better admonish him to forget about it, because I'm already tired of men and have nothing to do with them anymore in my life, hence, they're all heart-breakers who have nothing to lose in any break-up relationship, but many things to gain, because they can easily move on with their lives and continue their lothariotic way with much satisfaction without remorse on how the other party feels.'

"But, wait a minute" she seemed to have said to herself a bit aloud, "why am I being too presumptuous while I have not known for sure what this man is looking for? Does it mean that every time a man asks a woman for a date that he must be talking of an affair? What if, all this man is trying to get from me is information about the recent events? After all, I overheard the prison commandant telling another officer that this John Nelson is a nasty son of a bitch journalist, the very type who could easily go to any length in course of his story in order to uncover every single truth and ascertain the facts, even if it warrants interviewing a madman. "Well, in that case," she chuckled to herself as she was rearranging her office bureau, signalling the end of the day's work, "I'll equally apprise him that he has chosen the wrong person, and that I wouldn't even contemplate snitching on an enemy, much more my boss. And besides, it's totally against my professional moral conduct. Anyway till I know why that 'inquisitor of a journalist' is after me," she smiled.

The phone rang as Lisa was scooping up her white strew handbag to leave the office. The commandant had just left, bidding her a good and pleasant evening as if he knew about her dinner date. She hesitated for a moment before picking up the hand set.

"Hello! Office of the prison commandant" she said curtly, hoping that whoever was on the other end would instinctively grasp that she had officially closed for the day and is only anxious to get home, relax a bit and hopefully get ready for this funny date which had occupied most of her thoughts for the better part of the day.

"Pronto Lisa!" the voice from the other end responded promptly. "Of course, I suppose you'll not recognize the voice. I'm John . . . John Nelson, the journalist. I hope you still remember about 'our' dinner appointment. Please, forgive me for being rude. I just remember I didn't tell you how to find the Restaurant. Do you know how to get to the Restaurant?" he asked, obvious that he was looking forward to the evening.

"What . . . restaurant?"

"Yeah the *Willkommen Restaurant* in the *Währingerstrasse*, of course, it's a Chinese restaurant, one of the best in town. You will love their . . ."

"No, I don't know how to get there, anyway!" she replied nonchalantly.

"Can you tell me where to pick you up and the exact time, please? I mean, which part of the city you're living" John asked, scrutinizingly.

"No, I can't do that either, I'm very sorry . . . But, meanwhile, Mr. John Nelson, why can't we postpone this date or even forget about it hence I didn't know where the . . . I mean your world—best Chinese restaurant is or how to get there?" she suggested widening her eyes in a pretended astonishment for she was very sure of what his reply would look like.

"I think my humble answer to that . . . fine-lady, is: no. We can't postpone it even for few minutes, Ma'ma!" John smiled to himself. "There's no cause for alarm, or do you think otherwise?"

She hesitated again as her hand on the handset started to shake. She wanted to say 'I am not ready for any relation now', but she shrugged.

"I don't think there's any cause for alarm only that I'm feeling tired after this hectic work schedules" she feigned once more.

"Good! I've already booked a reservation for us. Now listen," he said, and went on to describe to her how she would be able to locate the restaurant, asking her to board a taxi from any area she might be residing in, with the hope of footing the bill. He hoped the company would always pay such bills as far as he spent it in the course of his duty. "Will you do as I said, Ma'ma!?" he demanded in foist tiny voice. "Please, tell me yes!"

Fräulein Egger breathed heavily and paused for some few seconds.

"Hm, well yeah . . . yes, I'll have to find my way. I'll try my best . . . Bye for now" Lisa told him before plonking down the receiver, accepting the invitation with feigned enthusiasm and made her way nimbly out of her office, saying good bye to her duty for the day.

++

Fräulein Lisa Egger was startlingly eager for the evening outing. She took a long time settling on what to wear at least to look glamorous. She finally selected a long black cocktail gown with matching pumps. She softly applied the new 'full 'n'soft mascara' which gave her outrageously full, soft, healthy looking lashes. She added to her lips a cherry 'crush' lipstick, looking sexy with a touch of sweetness. A bit later, she was looking herself over from her love-shaped standing mirror, after she applied the rest of her make-up. She felt she appeared attractive and somehow more than she used to be, with her auburn hair which she wore long. She was smiling to herself, thanking her stars for her recent loss of weight through exercise. She had registered herself at a physical training centre near her house, where she normally go to do some light jogging and aerobics, after she was teased by her best friend Linda, who had told her, her problem of being jilted by men was her fault, for being overweight, suggesting that men always adore and stay with slim women. And she had taken her advice and had been very serious visiting the fitness centre almost on a daily basis after she came back from work or on weekends in the morning hours.

She left her apartment at around 6:45 pm that evening bearing in mind that they'd agreed to meet by eight o'clock in the Restaurant. But of course, she had to find the street and the actual location of the restaurant, irrespective of the fact that she was born and brought-up in Vienna, she didn't know her way. 'That has been her problem and the problems of most Viennese grown-ups who do not go anywhere apart from going to their offices and back straight to their homes after work,' she thought.

She didn't want to enter any taxi as he proposed to her for reasons. From her *Philadelphia Brücke* residential area it would cost not less than one-hundred-and-fifty Schilling by taxi which she thought would be too much money for him to pay. The second and most important reason was that she was just too happy to ride the trams and besides, what sort of cheap woman she would look to the journalist at their first meeting. She never knew what he was up to nor did she know his spending capabilities.

Lisa entered the bus 59A which would take her all the way to *Karlsplatz* where it would finally stop. She almost started revelling in herself, when the driver of the bus greeted her by complimenting her on the way she looked. Later she caught sight of the driver still peeking at her through the overhead rear-view mirror of the bus.

Meanwhile, sitting with her and other passengers inside the bus, was one of the *Wiener Linien* ticket controller, a huge, tall man of about 40 years old. As the bus left the station, he stood up immediately, going straight away towards the seats adjacent to where Lisa was sitting and started controlling two Black men sitting together and another Black woman who seemed to be with them. They all gently showed their tickets, which he collected, scrutinized and handed back. She continued to watch him as he by-passed numerous passengers and went directly to the rear seats of the bus where about three or four *Ausländer* (foreigners) were sitting. They were presumably from the Northern part of Africa, Arabs from Algeria or Morroco. After controlling them he came back straight and sat down on his seat. For the first time this evening, Fraulein Lisa Egger felt herself despondent. She had known that racism and discrimination existed in every segment of the society, especially in the prison yard where she worked but she had never seen it on this scale the controller seemed to have exhibited in her presence this evening.

"How on earth can this God-forsaken controller single out only six or seven people in a bus full of passengers . . . more than thirty passengers?" she thought.

Her friend Linda used to tell her about her every day experiences of racial discrimination, nepotism, police inhuman treatments and many other anti-semitic acts against foreigners in the streets of Vienna, but never had she related anything as chauvinistic and xenophobic as the one she had just witnessed. Couldn't this man used his common sense at least and control maybe two or three other White passengers just to cover his ass, that would at least give the pretence of not being biased. She watched the Black men and the Black woman as they were discussing . . . maybe in their native language and staring towards her. No towards the Hitler-cousin of a controller; their faces frown at him. 'Yes, I think, he deserved whatever insults or abusive remarks they might be hurling at him. I would've advised them to even use their African Voodoo (*Ju-ju*) on him, for he really deserved it' she murmured to herself.

She glanced at her back, gawking discomfortably at a middle-aged couple. They were supportive of the controller's racist action and the way he conducted it. She overheard the middle-aged man telling his wife or perhaps his girlfriend "Yeah look, cherry! These Niggers don't normally pay for anything. Not even the underwear they wear. I think the man knew what he was doing," the man had said.

But it irritated Lisa more than anything else because she thought, these self-assured patriots might not even have their own tickets, yet the foolish controller had surmised all of them to have their tickets with the exception of the *Ausländers*. And yet they had proved him wrong. She bet that if he were to control every other passenger in this bus, he might apprehend more than three people without a ticket. Ticket defrauders as they were being called and the purse of the government would've swelling up this evening. She wanted to tell the middle-aged man at her back to shut-up his dirty mouth and mind his own business and stop being in support of this ass-hole controller and that she's quite sure he wouldn't be able to show his own ticket right away if he's controlled. But instead she turned to face the controller, chivalrously asking him why he thought that it was only these Blacks and the other *Ausländer* over there at the back of the bus that'd be without tickets, and she promptly told him that this attitude of his towards these people was nothing but an absurd idea which deserved outright condemnation.

"That's the worst discriminative act I've ever seen . . ." she told the controller.

"Oh! Fine, ma'ma, I don't think it's any of your business, is it?" he answered, grinning and at the same time stroking at his walrus moustache. "And besides, who are you to tell me whom and who to control. I know my job well and I did my job well, ma'ma, is that okay?" he said frowning at her.

"I think, yes, Mr. biased controller. It's as well my business in as much as it was your business to discriminate. I think we're in a free world and should have been treated as equal human being" she vehemently protested, doubting herself as being too outspoken on a human right issue like this.

Or she thought otherwise whether this journalist of a person she was going to meet who she had heard was a pro-human rights writer had already got hold of her without even a word of convert from him.

"How can you justify what you just did? Is this what you call productive work by controlling only six or seven selected people in a bus full of passengers? How're you sure that every other passenger has a ticket?" she poised at him sharply, staring towards the Black passengers who were all happy that at least somebody has come to their defence, for they had bitterly cursed the controller in their own language calling him an idiot.

"Nasty job, indeed" added another lady who was sitting at the opposite side of where Lisa sat. She had been watching them closely as the commotion unfolded. "Sir, I think your main work and sole duty is to control everybody on board except the driver. Not controlling people based on racial difference . . . got me" the lady snapped at him.

"Oh! Old ladies, I could see you're all nigger lovers . . . white niggers or can I say, *Ausländer*-defenders" he chuckled as he said it aloud. "But what I can't understand is who made you people judge over my duty?" he enquired turning to face the second woman. "Are you from the Green party or the Liberal forum? Which of them do you represent?" he asked, enjoying himself. "Yes, which of them do you belong to, because I really know it's only people from your party who'll be bold enough to defend these *Ausländer* who are all nothing but uncouth people . . ."

271

Amidst laughter from the middle-aged couple at their back, the middle-aged woman who was having a nose ring on her snout enjoined.

"You're very right, Mr. Controller. They all seem to be liberals nowadays, they think they're in the Netherlands which claims to be champions of human rights in European Union" she was laughing as she added "By their fruits we shall know them . . ."

"Now, you have to mind how you talk, Mr. Controller" the lady said dismissing the middle-aged woman and her man as junkies who did not know what the time is. "You're the one that is uncouth now . . . for singling them out to show their tickets. By producing their tickets, they showed you 'up' in front of everybody. Now what do you say to that, Mr. Controller? Or are they members of the Green party or the Liberal forum by being patriotic in holding their tickets?" she queried significantly.

"You might be whatever you chose to be . . . my old lady; a human right crusader, a 'nigger' apologist, a reformist . . . name them" the controller remonstrated angrily. "But, one thing you're not and would never be, at least not for now is, being a *Wiener Linien* supervisor . . . So you dare not instruct me on what to do or how to go about my own fucking business . . . you fucking asshole! Is that okay with you?" he expostulated further with her as he stired out of his seat, budging his way towards the egress of the bus, "I've done my duty the way I love doing it. As far as I'm concerned, you can go and jump in the sea . . . you and your other apologist," the *Wiener Linien* man was shouting back at Lisa, his voice deepening to a husky growl as the bus driver was pulling up the bus at the bus stop *Kettenbrückengasse.* "Don't forget to hop in the canal when you pass one on your way home."

"I've heard you, Mr. biased controller . . . And I think, with your attitude tonight, your sterling duty, your manner, you're a complete quack . . . and stack racist."

++

Fräulein Lisa Egger approached the woman as they disembarked from the bus. She was about the same age as herself. She was also almost as tall as her, about 5ft 7 whereas she was 5ft 8, just one inch taller. The only perceptible distinction between them was that she's fat and paunchy, just exactly like her some months ago, she thought. She was in fact what one could refer as an obese woman, yet she's full of life or rather she was looking healthy so to say. All smile and full of herself as Lisa had seen in the little moment.

"Oh, Ma'ma, I think you'd put that nasty fellow to where he righty belong without fear or favour. And I believe it serves him right!" Lisa acknowledged stretching out her hand to her as her face lightened in a grin. "I'm Lisa Egger. I'm very happy that there're still few good and decent people left in our society, who can vagorously call a madman a madman!" Lisa said happily.

They were standing along the tram route heading towards *Schottentor*.

"Sabina Rudas" said the fat woman, grinning back at her. "It's pleasure meeting you! Well, of course, I think it's my duty, the duty of every peace loving citizen of this country to speak out against these racist acts. Yeoo! We all must raise our voices ardently in unity against such racial discrimination and xenophobic behaviour encroaching on every segment of our society. Could you imagine what this man had just done and unfortunately he was very proud and pompous to call that doing his duty very well, when what he has done is nothing but an eyesore."

"I saw it, and I think . . . so did everybody in the bus, were all against his attitude, with the exception of those two . . ."

"No, no, my girl, not everybody, I'd not agree with you on this. If everybody thought it was bad as you suggested why didn't everybody speak out against it and censure him for his ugly behaviour, except you and my self? Did they? No, rather, they all kept quiet, maybe it didn't concern them. That has been the response of our people whenever and wherever it concern *Ausländer*. And that exactly where their attitudes then, when Hitler would've been stopped at the initial stage when he started his movement and campaign to extinguish the whole Jews around us. Listen, the society needs people like you and me who'll never allow another Hitler or any of their Nazi beliefs to spring up again. And believe me we'll never eradicate these acts by keeping quiet. Obviously this exactly is what my organization stands for. And this is what we're . . ."

"What organization are you talking about" enquired *Fräulein* Egger, seeing herself, interested to what the woman was saying.

"You mean my group?" she asked gleefully, like a Pentecostal church acolyte talking with a would-be member.

"Yes," she nodded.

Her instinct immediately told her she is on the verge of winning a new convert over.

"The name is 'Association for Human Rights of Immigrants' abbreviated (GEMMI)," she announced delightedly. "It is an organization which is clamouring for the protection, integration and total respect of all immigrants' human rights. We're also against any cruel, inhuman or degrading treatment or punishment of immigrants in any form. The association is also against any kind of racism, nepotism or favouritism, such as the one we witnessed this evening . . ."

"Is this organization only for the immigrants?" Lisa asked.

"No. Apart from the immigrants, we as well represent the interest of non-caucasian Austrian nationals and that of many Austrian citizens whose rights may have been infringed by the authorities. So, my charming lady, you can see for yourself that the association has a broad range of issues to tackle, because, to be rational, the war against racism and nepotism is not, and will never be an easy task. It needs people like you and me to openly speak out against it and openly denounce it, and openly protest against it wherever and whenever we encounter it" Sabina Rudas said convincingly.

Lisa was looking out through the glass window of the tram 1 that went around the *Kärntner Ring*. The tram had just passed fare stage at the tram-stop near the Austrian Parliamental building. Lisa followed suit and glancing through, she was able to recognize where they were. For some minutes she had forgotten about her date with Nelson and was so interested in the human rights preaching of the fat lady whom she had come to admire for her uprightness in the course of defending the rights of the immigrants communities in Austria who were being branded and blackmailed daily as criminals by the police and some disgruntled citizens, especially the *Omas* and the *Opas*. In all her almost thirty-five years of life, nobody has ever outlined the truth to her on these sensitive immigration issues, that always took half of the Parliamentary season every year, like this woman has done in this unforgettable day of her life.

Lisa Egger glanced at her wristwatch, it was 7:35 pm precisely which meant she had about twenty-five minutes left. She's still on course, she thought. From there to *Schottentor* would take maybe four to five minutes interval, that mean, she has almost twenty minutes to look for and reach the 'world's best Chinese restaurant' according John, the journalist.

"As I was saying," continued the woman, as Lisa turned to look at her, and saw that she was busy staring at a small booklet in her hand, "we're thriving in our efforts to make our society a non-racist society, where equality and rights for every individual regardless of his or her colour or character would be respected. However, as you can see, it needs a lot of labour and a lot of labourers to cultivate, plough, water before the fruits of labour would finally be harvested . . . you would agree with me that Rome was not built in a day, my fine lady!"

"Of course, that is a basic truth!" Lisa shook her head in agreement.

"And that brings me to my next point. Our association is looking for new members, people who can help to redress the wrongs of our country's past" she preached solicitingly. "And I'd be personally happy if you should consider joining . . . As you would've known, it's a non-partisan organization which welcomes its members from all walks of life . . . if you understand what I mean? No matter your position in the society, you're free to become a member. It doesn't cost you anything more than your spare time."

"Only my spare time" Lisa repeated askingly.

"Absolutely"

"Then, I think I'll consider the pros and cons of this free association! If I may ask, how does one attend the meeting and where?" Lisa inquired interestedly.

"Oh! Yes ma'ma, we've our office and meeting place at the *Stiftgasse* 8; and you're always welcome. The association needs open-minded people like you to grow" Sabina commended, smiling as she searched her handbag.

"Ya before I forget" she said, and handed Lisa a flyer.

"What's this," she asked surprisingly.

"Ah! It's one of the forthcoming activities of our association. We're organizing a series of peaceful demonstration in alliance with other human rights groups . . . tell you what, I've been on the road since three o'clock this afternoon sharing these flyers and posters after my office work and I'm on my way to one of our meetings."

All the while she was talking about her being on the road and so on, Lisa was not listening anymore, but rather, she was overcome by the picture in the poster. She saw in the poster, a sketched portrait of Marcus Omofuma with an adhesive tape gagged around his entire mouth and proboscis. She calmly read the slogan under the picture, which says.

IN HONOR OF MARCUS OMOFUMA, A NIGERIAN
NATIONAL; WHO DIED AT THE HAND OF THE AUSTRIAN
POLICE ON BOARD THE BALKAN AIRLINE FLIGHT TO
LAGOS VIA SOFIA ON THE 1ST OF MAY 1999.
AGED: 25 YEARS 1974-1999
ADIEU OMOFUMA. WE WILL NEVER FORGET YOU.
BYE! BYE!!! BYE!!!

When she picked up her head, tears had circled her eyes as she remembered how this very young man's death had overwhelmed her office work and all her joy nowadays. And she believed that this same topic would not overshadow her dinner with the journalist. The more she thought about it all, the more she felt enraged and loathing for those that perpetrated this horrendous act. Instantly, Lisa became aware of full soul transformation that went through her mind as she stared fixedly at the picture in her hand. And as the tram approached *Schottentor*, she stood up from her seat and extended her hand once more to Frau Sabina Rudas.

"I'm very happy to have met you, madam! You've helped me to found my lost soul. See you in one of your meetings one of these days" she promised as she finally disembarked from the tram.

"With all respect," Sabina Rudas smiled, happy that she probably had added one follower to their human rights fold. "We would be happy to welcome you!"

CHAPTER EIGHTEEN

"Anyone who has learned—let him come and teach.
Anyone who has not learned—let him come and learn.
They all assembled and discussed all that was necessary."

===(Midrash Rabbah to Shir Hashirim 2:5).

Inside the *Willkommen* Chinese restaurant at the *Währingerstrasse* in the 9th district of Vienna, John Nelson led *Fräulein* Lisa Egger to the table which had been reserved for them. Their table was at the extreme corner of the upper storey of the restaurant. John had motioned her to sit before he sat beside her.

On the side of where she was, stood the rolled-up almaco flint window glass that made the outside view very pleasant. A typical Chinese restaurant, with a red and white table cloth spread uniformly at every table. There were many Chinese traditional artifices at every corner of the wall which was beautifully covered with sensuous wall-papers and different glazed earthenware pots filled with Chinaberry and Chinese lanterns placed on top of every table. The whole atmosphere inside the restaurant looked good to her taste and everything was perfectly in order.

'Maybe this is really the world's-best Chinese restaurant' she thought at first sight.

"*Guten Abend!*" greeted a slim, average height waitress, who had come to take their orders, as she smiled and handed over to them an oxblood colored-covered menu-booklet.

Lisa opened the menu-booklet, scanning the pages in search of any diet food to request for. Across from where they were sitting sat a couple with their three children. They seemed to have been of Asian origin, maybe from China. A waitress approached them and they made their orders, speaking in their palpitated manner. Their third child, still a sibling, was crying frantically. 'Maybe, not so hot, not so cool ambience of the restaurant was making the child freful' Lisa thought. Immediately the mother reached out for her handbag and fished for a chocolate pack. She placed one of it inside the child's mouth. But just after a few seconds the child cried out again, until the mother gently unpacked her breast and breast-fed the child and then, just like one on sleeping substance, the child slept off.

'Oh! Sibling with their sensibilities' Lisa thought again. 'They know how to ask for things and get it. But how can any reasonable mother go against the rule of breast-feeding? Just look at the magic it has worked in a twinkle of an eye' she murmured thoughtfully.

"I heard the Chinese do not normally have more than one child?" she said out aloud, looking at John.

"Well, I've heard that also. I think that primitive law stands only for those of them within their communist territory they call China" he answered, glancing towards the couple and their children. "By mere looking, one could easily assume that if they were really Chinese, they're living here in the West, so to say. Their attires, of course, look western and maybe their children are Americans or Europeans by birth."

"By the way" the journalist said changing the subject. "I . . . I think, I've ordered a delicious dinner for us. You can only worry about what to drink, ma'ma! And I must comment, your dressing, it looks gorgeous you know! And equally it's befitting for your status, which suited the occasion" John Nelson compliments.

"Hm! Thank you!" she uttered as she tossed him a fetching look and said "Haa really? What've you ordered?"

She couldn't hide her feelings on what he had just commended, for no man had said such a thing to her in the last twenty years or so. Once more, she was very happy for her new found shape and thanked Linda for her constructive criticism against her former tubby figure. She had bought this black gown she was wearing with many other clothes just last week, after she had disposed her former dresses and gave them out to other fat friends and the remaining to the Caritas charity home.

"I've ordered what will be good for, you ma'ma! I knew you don't like fatty food anymore . . . And I believe you'll like the food when the order arrives!"

"How do you know I don't want fat food?" she asked suspiciously, astonished at how people read her thoughts these days.

"I use to read minds" he answered nonchalantly. "Beside, I can see you're trying to put down some weight, judging from the first time I saw you a few days ago" John lied convincingly.

The waitress came with his orders. She neatly deposited them on the table and made a bow and left. The food, served on sliver-trimmed plates, was simple, but appetizing. Boiled white rice, cole-slaw, creamed salad and savoury roasted dried red meat. Another waitress appeared and began to put down drinks including a bottle of red-wine and mineral water.

John did not waste time as he dished some cole-slaw and salad onto a flat plate and with a knife he chopped some of the meat, adding it to the plate, he deposited it in front of her. He portioned out the same in his plate and placed it before himself. Reaching across the table, he poured the red-wine into her glass, then in his.

Journalist John Nelson ceremoniously raised his wineglass.

"For the future!" he toasted.

And *Fräulein* Lisa Egger followed in the same suit and tiltered her glass at his.

"For the future" she iterated, not understanding what he meant by that.

At his request, the light from the chandiler affixed on the vaulting directly above them, had been dimmed. A flickering candle illuminated their faces as they started eating.

He picked at his food, pondering on how to get her to talk about herself. He wanted to know all there was to know; her family background, in fact, her life in general. Moreover, he wanted but not yet, to know about every damn thing happening in and around her place of work.

They continued to eat in silence. Finally, he said.

"I was thinking you'll never make it when my handy began to ring and, wow! there you were."

She turned her head and cast amorousing eyes at him. She wanted to tell him the truth but instead.

"Well, I decided to come at long last" she shrugged, sipping her wine. The wine had heavy dry-sweet taste that made her to smack her lips. "What's this wine called?" she asked.

"Ah! Ma'ma, this is Promessa Salento wine, specially made for red meat consumption. I like it much. Not good for your taste?" he asked curiously.

"Oh! It's so good!" was her curt reply.

"You can order your choice. Please, forgive me for being rude. That has been the bad side of me. I always think that the things I like would equally be liked by others, forgetting that another man's food, might be another man's poison, as they say . . . Of course, I'm always wrong about others choices . . ."

"Hmm, 'No' it's okay, I don't mean . . ."

"I know, I know," he said, lowering his voice, "it's just that . . . I don't know . . . it's bad of me assuming that . . . I forgot to ask you in time about your own taste" he uttered, guilt-ridden, giving the bridge of his nose a pinch.

Lisa did not hesitate.

"Of course," she replied crisply, "you might be right to think so but in this case, you're wrong. Your choice is good for me" she smiled, draining her glass, swallowing hard.

At that very moment, there was chanting, trumpeting and shouting outside the restaurant. Many people, men, young boys, girls, and women of different sizes and ages were rallying, beating drums, dancing and whistling their ways along the *Währingerstrasse*. The majority of them carried placards with slogans that read:

THE CIA AND THE MOSSAD ARE INVOLVED
AMERICANS ARE CONSPIRATORS
THE ISRAELIS ARE CONSPIRATORS
ABDULLAH ÖCALAN IS A HERO
LONG LIVE THE KURDISH PEOLE
LONG LIVE THE PKK
THE TURKS ARE MURDERERS NOT HIM.

As the demonstrators who were numbering in thousands marched passing, coming down from *Währingerstrasse* and heading towards *Schottentor*, there were heavy police presence, some of the police officers in full gear were moving ahead of the procession while many more officers followed from behind. There seemed to be police-siren sounding from all angles. From the *Landesgerichtstrasse* down to *Schwarzspanierstrasse*, down to *Türkenstrasse* where the *Afro-Asiatisches Institut* was situated, the protesters were shouting curses on the Turkish government and their co-conspirators.

"What were all those people chanting about and who are they?" Lisa asked fascinatedly, bending her head down to look through the window by her side. Her eyes were fixed on the demonstrators as they passed by the restaurant "I mean, why would they be disturbing people's peace and tranquillity by this hour of the day for Immanuel's sake!" she said, glancing at her golden watch. It's almost 20:55 pm. "Oh! God, these people must allow people to have their deserved rest . . ."

"I know why they're demonstrating" John answered smilingly, revealing his fractured centre teeth. "But I don't think there's any difference between a night demonstration and a day time demonstration. The most important thing is that in a democratic society, people have the right to protest provided their protests are legal and peaceful" journalist John Nelson lectured.

One of the protest marchers forcefully bulldozed his way through the police barricade, jostling into the restaurant. And started shouting in his native language. Two police officers immediately rushed after him and dragged him away by his shirt.

On the outside of the restaurant, a young girl of about 17 years, with long hair, that touched her shoulders was trying to ignite herself on fire with a cigarette lighter after drenching her clothes with gasoline, but the police was quick on her. A police woman had rushed and shoved the lighter away from her, preventing her from carrying out her threat as others started booing the police woman, while chanting the name of the 'pretty' girl calling a living 'Martyr', praising and admiring her courage and saintliness.

As they gradually passed-by, Lisa estimated them to be between five thousand and ten thousand, with the last line of the protesters mainly older men and women, screaming at the top of their voices.

LONG LIVE ABDULLA! LONG LIVE ABDULLAH!! LONG LIVE ÖCALAN!!! LONG LIVE KURDISH PEOPLE AROUND THE WORLD!!! ALLAHU AKBAR! ALLAHU AKBAR!!! ALLAHU AKBAR!!!

"Why should a young girl want to kill herself?" Lisa inquisitively asked.

"Oh! Now I think I know who they were and why they're staging these demonstrations" said John triumphantly, as if announcing a new scientific discovering, "and why the young pretty girl wanted to sacrifice her life."

"And who're they and why're they disturbing our peace?" she asked with a faint smile, taken a mouthful of the salad.

"They're ethnic Kurdish people, probably living in Vienna and across Austria. On the 15ᵗʰ of February this year, Abdullah Öcalan, their acclaimed leader who was on the run for a very long time, and whom the Turkish secret service had been hunting for, was finally tracked and captured, with the help of the CIA and some other international bodies as alleged by the Kurdish national Congress. He was later repatriated back to Turkey from Nairobi (Kenya) where he was arrested and blind-folded while on board. He's now somewhere in one of the prisons in Ankara awaiting trial. And there's fear that he might be hanged by the Turkish government. You see" John continued, looking down into his wine glass. "The Kurdish national congress felt disgusted and disappointed by this arrest and the involvement of some of the international community's secret services in tracking him down; and the subsequent ill-treatment he's been subjected to at the hand of his enemy . . . so, they called for these demonstrations throughout the cities of the world where their people are living. You know they're scattered all over the world like the Jews" the journalist asserted, as he drank from his wine and used the *Willkommen Restaurant's* emblazoned paper handkerchief to wipe his mouth and gave Lisa a lovely smile. "So, as it stands, being humans, their actions had been too aggressive in some cities, I tell you. I recently read from the *London Express* that a young lady and her mother burned themselves to death in London . . . could you imagine that" he said dryly.

"But the question is, why were they setting themselves on fire? That alone would not release the man from prison, will it?" she asked, a trace of anger in her shrill voice. "People would not be so stupid to take their own lives."

"I don't know, but presumably they seem to be sending a message to the authorities that revolutions might take place if . . . You know the Turkish government still has capital punishment in their constitution" John lectured.

"So, you mean, he might be condemned to death?"

"Exactly that's their fear . . ."

"And what was his crime?"

"For trying to win consensus from the Turkish government through terror, as they claimed" the journalist retorted.

"But, was he really a terrorist?"

"That, I don't know! Ma'ma!"

"Hmm! you're a journalist . . . an over ambitious and articulated one for that matter. You are supposed to know!" she said, not a question but a compliment.

"Thanks Ma . . . Oh yes! However, I'm not an expert on the Turkish-Kurdish problems" he replied calmly. "Point of correction, ma'ma, being a journalist does not make one an almighty as far as histories and current events and affairs are concerned. Journalism as any other establishment has branches. And many different journalist plays in different fields" he declared, wanting to use the opportunity to enter into the main reason for organizing the dinner date, yet, his instinct told him no, not yet time. "Actually, I don't know if he was a terrorist or not . . . . you know that these powers that be can and could label you anything especially when 'you' fell out with them . . ."

"Still, you know about him and you've read much about him these days, so what's your opinion on him?" *Fräulein* Lisa persisted.

"Well, my humble opinion may not echo the other opinion, but of course it's my personal . . . I think, he's just a leader of a tribal group of people who are striving to be given their full rights and to be recognized . . . in the society. And the truth is, it's not all that easy some time to fight these wars of suppressions and injustice without many ugly things happening from both sides . . . the case of Northern Ireland being a good example of what I'm saying, you see? Whatever one's opinion on these global wars and fight for freedom by individuals and races, there would always be a counter allegation to and fro . . . but having said these, you will believe me that throughtout history freedom is not given but freedom is earned . . . you must fight for it or it will elude you forever."

"Aren't they independent yet?" Lisa asked, interestedly, as she held out her empty glass to him to refill.

She glanced opposite their table and saw two young black Africans with their African girlfriends or their wives as the case may be, taking their seats and Lisa thought and prayed that these Chinese people would not be so rude as to discriminate against these sets of clients, fearing if they would be asked to look for another restaurant . . . as this stupid controller had demonstrated this evening in her presence. She watched awkwardly as two waitresses approached and took their orders smiling openely at the Africans and even joked with them in friendly manners. She felt a little bit happy that the contrary of her early thought had happened. She wanted to use the opportunity to narrate the controller's action to this inquisitive journalist, but decided to do that later, for now let him continue to lecture her on this current affair which in the actual sense she was supposed to have known about as a civil servant she was. She couldn't blame herself. She was not the only person in this shoe for she knows lots of her colleagues in her place of work don't even know the name of the mayor of Vienna. It's a big problem to many of them because they were not used to travelling nor were they interested in other people's affairs. Talking about travelling, she always felt dismayed that at her almost thirty-five years she had never travelled outside Austria. The widest journey she had undertaken was when she went to Graz to visit one of her old boyfriends. Travel they say is part of education, she now believed. The world is a big place to be, yet small in a way if you really want to be involved. She remembered how Linda would always be very happy anytime she came back from her numerous tourist trips which had taken her to the USA, Japan, Israel and Australia and almost all Eastern and Western European countries. Even to come out and socialise inside Vienna City has always been a problem. Just imagine, only this evening she came out, she had witnessed a lot, the *Wiener Linien* man's discrimination, the fat woman humanistic struggle to help and change the society, the magic of the breast-feeding by the Asian woman, this Kurdish demonstration and the last but not the least, this Kurdish history she had been lectured on by no other person than this orientated journalist of a man, John Nelson.

John Nelson reached down the wine bottle. His big hand went all the way around it. He poured the wine into the glass Lisa held out. He stared at her returning her grin and contemplating on what might had overshadowed her mind in this her long thought, he just decided to answer her last question, as firmly as he could.

"No . . . No, they never got their independence. In fact, they're one of the well known national groups which have no independence. They've got their own areas. Geographically, some are living in the northern parts of Iraq under the dictatorship regime of Saddam Hussein. Many others are living in Turkey . . . while many scattered all over the world" said John wistfully, cutting a piece of the red-meat with a fork, he picked it up and rolled it into his mouth. "Don't tell me you've . . . really don't know about the Kurds . . . they're everywhere in Vienna?" he asked.

"No! Not really, but what about them?" she replied, as though the mere mention of Kurds were painful. Her face changed immediately.

"Was anything the matter?"

"No, not at all" she shruggedly hesitated.

"What are you thinking about? I told you I read minds!" John jested.

He believed she had something in her mind that made her to change her face.

"Nothing" she lied. "I was just wondering what would've been the fate of that young girl if the police would've been late on her" she said, trying to keep anxiety and suspicion out of her eyes.

She had fallen in love with journalist John Nelson.

CHAPTER NINETEEN

"'The ideal population'; said Mustapha Mond, 'Is like an Iceberg Eight Ninths below the water line, one Ninth above"

===Aldous Huxley-from the book
'BRAVE NEW WORLD' pp 104.

Having acquired detailed information from *Fräulein* Lisa Egger concerning all the activities going on in and around the deportation prison camp since the Omofuma episode started, and with his vast range of interviews with all the other characters who were either directly or indirectly involved, journalist John Nelson pieced together his facts and wrote an exposé which appeared at the front-cover of the monthly *Augustin* newspapers and in various other newspapers and magazines throughout Austria and in many parts of Europe. The article which came with a portrait of gagged Omofuma and some of the pictures he had taken on the day he was tipped by his source about the police handling of the inmates peaceful protest; attached to it read:

AUSTRIAN IMMIGRATION POLICY PLAGUED BY RACISM AND RACIST OFFICIALS

OMOFUMA'S SCANDAL GROWS RESULTING IN NON-VIOLENT CIVIL DISOBEDIENCE IN THE IMMIGRATION DETENTION CAMP

AUSTRIAN AUTHORITIES REACTS WITH RACIST AND VIOLENT RESPONSES, ECHOES OF NAZI PAST

++

John Nelson was sitting comfortablely inside his office, with his legs on the top of his mahogany office desk. On the table was a complementary copy of the latest edition of the newspaper on which the article had appeared on. He took up his 'Camel-embrozened' coffee cup from its saucer with his left hand while his other hand was on the telephone, holding the handset firmly.

"Hi! Please, Judy, can you put me through with Dr. Lukas of the Interior ministry" he murmured to the company's receptionist and his personal assistance.

Judy heard the urgency in his voice.

"Sure, sir . . . Right away!" she replied from the other end of the inter-com extension and dropped her phone knot.

Judith Glasser, a slim, tall, blue eyed, blond-hair, who had been working with Nelson for the past three years; had never seen him so happy over any of his previous articles—even when he wrote award winning piece some months ago. 'I don't think it's about this article only! Something must be fishing that I have not known yet,' she thought as she glanced through the office address book—which contained private, offices and (even) hot-line-telephone numbers of Austria's 'who-is-who.' Or rather, possibly, he is one of those ghoulish people, who positively know how to make use of situations like these, getting on his way by embarrassing the authorities with his inquisitive journalism and still get away with it. That serves well for these God-forsaken officials who rather use their ass than their brains' she exclaimed to herself with a kind of beaming boisterousness. 'Let me put my money where my mouth is!'

She found and automatically dialled the number from her arm-shaped office tele-box. After a moment, a voice from the other end answered.

"Office of the ministry Interior, yes . . . please, what can I do for you?"

"Heeh thanks" replied Judith in her quiet pedantic voice. "Please, can you connect me to Dr. Paulus Lukas I'm Judith Glasser, from the *Augustin* press. I'm trying to get him for John Nelson . . . Ya! He knows him. Oh yeah, he'll be happy to chat with Dr. Lukas, if possible, right away."

"Hello! Is that Nelson?" greeted Dr. Lukas from his speaker phone.

"Oh, ja, *Guten Morgen*, Doctor! I don't think I'm disturbing your peace?" Nelson said, enjoying himself from the way Lukas's voice sounded from the phone with a trace of restlessness.

"Look, my friend, to tell you the truth, the last person I wanted to speak to now is probably you. I mean, for the embarrassment your exposé is causing around here . . . if you can understand me . . . especially for my own very self, John Nelson! Remember that it's not only the guilty that matters, it's also about the innocent," Dr. Lukas sighed, colour flamed up his face.

Nelson drained his coffee and smacked his lips, pouring himself another cup-full of his Cappuccino.

"Oh! Really I'm really sorry, Doctor" he said, smiling thinly to himself.

He spoke rather like a petulant small boy.

"As a matter of fact, I was really dismayed and dumbfounded when I saw you and the other officials present that day when these incidents took place. I mean, the brutalities and mal-treatments of these hungry prisoners by your men . . . have, you anything to say on that, sir?"

"Actually" said Dr. Lukas coolly and casting a nervous glance out to the corridor towards the Minister's office, "of course, I was present there but never in any way part of the immediate decisions taken . . . you know how these things usually go . . . And well, I didn't support those actions from the beginning" asserted Dr. Lukas, rubbing his chin thoughtfully. His tone when he spoke was persuasive and apologetic.

"Now, John, listen this is off record, agreed?"

"Not if it in anyway perverts justice, sir!"

"No, no, not really, I don't think that was the issue" assumed Dr. Lukas.

There was a kind of indignation in his voice.

"Then, I give you my word!" John said with a happy dulcet laugh. His right hand with a pen and a jotter ready to jot down everything and instantly putting on the recorder on his table, shifting and placing the handset's receiving piece nearer the recorder. Don't trust any journalist.

At that very moment *Fräulein* Lisa Egger, breathing rather heavily, breezed into his office. John had been waiting for her for their lunch date. She bounced brightly towards John. He motioned her to stop with his right hand. He greeted her with his eyes as he raised his fore-finger to his lips, signifying 'do not' speak and then he covered the mouth piece of the phone and wrote on the piece of paper on the table the name . . .

Dr. Lukas!

"Yes, go on Doctor, I'm all ears."

"Good! Right now, in front of me at my desk here is a dossier, I've just prepared. I was online with the Minister before your call came in . . . He has agreed to my plans, and I bet you, heads are going to roll over this matter" Dr. Lukas said.

He gave a sharp exasperated sigh.

"No culprit, I repeat, no culprit involved who'll not hear the music when it will start. Enough is enough. And enough of this mess. Every person would probably bear his or her cross" Dr. Lukas swore.

"If, I may ask sir, what is going to happen . . . what'll be the fate of these innocent prisoners?" John interrupted.

He shot a quick, horrified glance at Lisa who had by now comprehended fully, just how far her information had impacted.

"The only word, I have for the question now is that to no man will we deny justice . . . justice must be done!!!" murmured Dr. Lukas softly. "And please, if you could excuse me, I've a lot to do right now. I'll keep you informed about the goings. And don't forget everything I said is off record! See you later!! *Auf Wiedersehen . . . Tschüss!*"

John Nelson dropped his handset meticulously. He smiled his extravagant smile and explained as a matter-of-fact to Lisa that he was just chatting with Dr. Lukas from the Interior ministry who was the special adviser to the Interior Minister on security matters and that he had spoken on the phone with every individual concerned.

"Oh! Sweet ma'ma, I forgot" said John, with no indignation in his voice. "My secretary checked up that number you gave . . . I mean, which you said belongs to the Bulgarian Prof. Doctor . . . that performed the autopsy initially on Omofuma. I personally spoke to him" John uttered, lifting her up from his lap. John held himself very taut and rigid, and continued in his serious businessman voice. "By the way, he was able to confirm everything you said that appeared in the report. He didn't want to speak at first, citing confidentiality as his main reason. But when I told him I had spoken with his Austrian counterparts and explained to him how they had contradicted his results . . . by maintaining that Marcus Omofuma died as a result of heart attack. Then he told me every thing I wanted him to say, I meant, he comfirmed everthing I got from you."

"But these doctors must be out of their minds! How can such a system be allowed to exist at all?" *Fräulein* Egger said. "How can the public be certain that autopsies conducted by the police forensic institute in a case of extra-judicial killing are not modified to help the police? Look, I think I'm tired and exhausted about all these unscrupulous games being played by these disgruntled elements who called themselves doctors and experts" she said with red-rimmed eyes.

"Really" Nelson said.

She continued without looking at John who by now was jotting down some words in his handbook.

"But, one couldn't blamed them, anyway!" she shrugged. "It came as no surprise to me, when I read that on the dailies . . . I mean, about the Austrian side of the story . . . After all, they say old habits die hard" Lisa murmured, waving a scornful hand in the air . . . "As before, just like now. No changing at all."

"Easy! Easy!! Take it easy, ma'ma!!!" John said, in a conciliatory tone.

He stood and put his hand around her neck, held her closer and kissed her.

"I don't mean to get you or anyone annoyed. You couldn't take it personal . . . ma'ma!"

"No" she said. "It's out of question. You're acting on an invalid emotion."

She held up her fingers as John would've spoken.

"Of course, I'm not in anyway annoyed. In fact, I'm really enjoying the whole mess-up . . . If you would've been with me in the office this morning and see how our pompous commandant was wheeling around all the place . . . like he's being tormented by some evil spirits . . . And how happy I was watching all the while, you would've . . ."

Nelson whistled.

"Waooh! Up to that extent? The music had already started, even before the drummers cleans up their drums" Nelson said, with a happy strident laugh, "Just like the French always say: 'You can't make an omelette without breaking some eggs' . . . I think the heat is already on."

"Yeah it's really on, I tell you. Not only the commandant. As a matter of fact, with all his stupid and arrogant subordinates as well. I would like to see all of them go," Lisa remarked, giving John a quick lovely and conspiratorial look. "Nothing is ever settled until it is settled rightly" she said with a slightly twisted smile.

"Don't you think, as things are going now, that they would like to perish with some other people along with them? You know, the evil-doers don't normally die alone!" John stated with all seriousness.

"Look, I really don't think so" she shook her head and pointed towards the newspaper on the desk. "Look! With that constructive piece of yours and tensions and commotions that follow, I think they're already drawn to surface no more."

"Your commandant may be the mother of all fools in this world but he still knows his ways. He may still fight to the last as a wounded lion, and I'm afraid he would like to go with as many followers as possible."

"Leave him for me . . . I'll know what today will bring with it, but I still don't give a damn either . . . whatever comes out of it. The worst case scenario would be . . ." Lisa was saying.

"Now, listen cherry! I normally give a damn because I always want to protect my sources. One good turn, they say, deserves another" John smiled. "I am the type of man who always cares! You're a very big and trusted source and in a very good position for that matter . . . I'll not like to lose you or anything to happen to you."

"What do you mean?" Lisa queried, facing him defiantly.

"Well, what I meant, my sweet ma'ma, is that the police must like to know how these information—most of them too confidential—reached my desk, and if that is the case, trust the Vienna cops, they must track you and cause many problems for you . . . which means I'll have to lose you . . . . miss you," he corrected himself. "And that's never my way. And equally not what I bargain for! I believe in the school of thought that says principle must never be sacrificed on the Alter of expediency. So now you understand what I mean?" John maintained in the cleverness of his strategy.

He had been searching eagerly for an inner source at the centre of command in all the deportation prison camps in and around Austria because of the book he's writing on the Austrian immigration policies which is due to be published soon. Having been assured by Lisa that she had worked with the former commandants before Christian Gospel, he hoped she would be retained by any new commandant if the incumbent is no more, according to this off record tip from Dr. Lukas or that at least she'll remain within the corridor of power. That to him is very important to the progress of every investigative journalist like him. He had thought this overnight.

"You got me ma'ma?"

"Why! I clearly understood!" she agreed, nonchalantly.

"In that case, I can't stand losing you, my angel!" John spoke with all alacrity as he kissed her tenderly on the mouth. "I really believe we have to organize our meetings more secretly for now. I think it's better you stop coming over here to see me. The police, I'm sure, are already probing and nosing around to know from where these things are leaking. You could easily imagine our police, what they'll be up to and what they can do to anybody they catch. Please, you have to grope yourself with infinite precaution. I believe they might be tailing you if they knew what you're really up to . . ." journalist John Nelson advised professionally and rather cautionedly added, "your precious life and 'job' are most important to me, now I've got you my sweet ma'ma!"

"They can go to hell, for all I really care. I know I'm doing the right thing for the right purpose" Lisa smiled concretely. "And not when I'm doing it for my . . ."

"Put a shaimp on the barbie for the lady!" John complimented. "But, remember they can argue that you make the right choice for the wrong reason. Yet, one thing before the other, come on my angel. Let's get the hell out of here and smell some roses . . ."

As journalist John Nelson took her by the hand, leading her out of the office, Judith looked up from her computer, her eyes piercing from above her golden-rimmed glasses.

"I now know for sure, why he is so happy these days!" she murmured to herself and bent down to continue her work.

CHAPTER TWENTY

"Because you drowned others, they drowned you, and in the end those who drowned you will themselves be drowned."

===AVOs 2:6.

Dr. Lukas was in the office of the Interior Minister Dr. Alfons K. Schmidt, an old-fashioned retangular room. A large centre table with a red-coloured formican cover was first thing in sight. The Minister was sitting on the red embrozened leather rolling chair. On top of the table stood a family laminated photograph showing the Minister at the centre with his blond-silver hair and blue eyes, his heavily maked-up wife at his left, holding their one year old son in her lap, while their five year old daughter sat on her father's lap. And their two grown up children, a young boy of twenty and his elder sister twenty-two year old, stood on both sides of their parents. They were all in a happy and merry mood. Round the table were red roses. The surrounding walls were paper-coloured with the ruling party's redish symbol. Directly opposite where the Minister sat was a very big photo of the president of the Republic of Austrian, Dr. Hans T. Gestil glazed in a clear plastic while on the immediate stare of the visitor was that of the *Bundeskanzler* Dr. Stephan Blima. The floor of the office and surrounding corridor were all rugged in red, in accordance with the redishness of the ruling party's colour and symbol.

Dr. Schmidt stretched out his hand in greetings to Dr. Lukas who was still standing with visible emotions all over his body. Dr. Lukas made an attempt to defuse the tension by trying to smile his sun-shine smile but to no avail as Dr. Schmidt picked up the newspaper on top of his desk, waving it at the face of Dr. Lukas.

"Did you see this echoes of the Nazi past . . . I could understand if it was the extreme right party or even our centre-right coalition partner. You know I had the *Kanzler* on the phone this morning. At first, he talked politely and then he screamed at me 'how did it get this far? He said to me that we have to get tighter control over the police and the prison administration and the damn immigration . . . people—the *Fremdenpolizei*. You know that the law enforcement authorities are mostly in the hands of the right-wing and they would like to embarrass us as much as possible."

Dr. Lukas tried to suggest something but was cut off by the enraged Minister who continued in his arrogant, infuriating know-it-all attitude.

"The *Kanzler* demanded that I see him tonight and he wants me to bring a list of recommendations on how to improve the situation and get us out of the mud and on how to avoid this career-killing mess occurring in the future. He's also demanding a list of all the heads that should roll and recommendations for possible replacement; with special emphasis that we must suffused the police force and the prison department with officers who're affiliated to the party's doctrines and who has a natural affinity with the party and its numerous challenges, this was his own words" Dr. Schmidt stated. "And he wants a white paper on serious policy changes for Austrian asylum seekers . . . , so, Dr. Lukas, now you know the situation we are in?" Dr. Schmidt concluded as he strutted around his vast office.

Dr. Lukas responded by telling him.

"I've already compiled the dossier that has been demanded by the honourable *Kanzler,* and anticipated that there'll be a telephone call from the *Kanzler*. And the troubles we'll all be in. We've tried to start a media counter offensive, so, that was why I am arranging an interview with John Nelson, the reporter who wrote the exposé for the *Augustin* press. First and foremost, I believe we should ask for the resignation of the Prison commandant Christian Gospel or if that's not possible he would be transferred to a shitty little town in *Bregenzer Wald* where he could watch the cows shitting and all human incest he can take."

"Just be fast in whatever you thought is the best approach before is too late. Make sure you are going to the *Kanzler* with me."

Dr. Lukas thought to himself.

'Shit, he wants me to make the responsibility for the report in case our proposals backfire he'll have my head to chop'.

Speaking out aloud, he said.

"Certainly, I'll come with you but don't you want to have the *Kanzler* alone with you so he could say things he might not say in front of me . . ."

The Minister was in a very big thought as Dr. Lukas spoke, but he was able to shake his head in disagreement and insisted he should go with him.

Dr. Lukas smiled and replied.

"Don't worry I'll be there!"

He got up from his chair, shook hand with the Minister and left the office; saying to himself

"Fuck! Fuck! Fuck! He put me into the hot seat."

And he heard the words echoing in his ears:

'Because you drowned others, they drowned you and in the end those who drowned you will themselves be drowned'

But, he could not understand its full meaning yet.

++

Sitting in the coffee bar, sipping coffee and smoking his Cuban cigar, Dr. Lukas and Regina were reviewing his political situation. Regina took a drag on her cigarette, blowing 'Os' in the air with the smoke and said.

"My God, Paulus, you really walked in to that one."

Dr. Lukas slightly embarrassed retorted.

"What can I do, he's my boss and if he needs a fallen guy I guess it is only natural it would be me . . ."

Regina looking slightly amused.

"Dear doctor, I guess if it all brows up, we can move to some shitty little town in *Brengenzer Wald* and watch the cows shit along with commandant Christian Gospel and his men."

"I pray it doesn't reach to that or all my plans and my future would be in jeopardy" he poised.

++

Fräulein Lisa Egger was at the public phone booth, nervously trying to get John Nelson on the line. The phone rang a few times and finally, Nelson picked up and said.

"Ma'ma, Nelson's little boy!"

Lisa said. "Hold, the line for *Kanzler* Blima, please!

Nelson murmured. "No shit."

She answered. "Big shit"

Nelson replied. "Little Miss Muffit?" the code name he gave her for telephone conversation.

She responded with her own coded name. "Jack BeNimble"

Nelson said. "Hey! Babe, miss me?"

"More than you know" Lisa answered, giving a little lovely smile.

Nelson: "Anything in the pipe-line?"

Lisa: "I believe my boss is headed for *Brengenzer Wald . . .*"

Nelson responded: "Good, to watch the cows shit and the cousins fuck."

Then Nelson asked. "What about the hunger strikes?"

Lisa, finger-crossed, said somehow awkwardly.

"Some of them will be granted asylum. But I don't know much yet, because, the Austrians have hard time swallowing black skin . . . Poor souls . . . fucking poor souls!!"

"My dear are you saying that Austrians are racist?"

"Was Hitler German or Austrian, and is the Pope Polish or Italian. Self-explanatory I think!?

"Dinner as usual?" asked John Nelson.

"As usual" she responded. "I love you . . . I miss you!" she kissed and hanged up.

CHAPTER TWENTY-ONE

"Once a lion was devouring an animal and a bone stuck in its throat. The lion announced: 'To anyone who can remove the bone from my throat I will give a reward'.

A longbilled Egptian heron came and struck its beak into the lion's throat and removed the bone. The heron then said to the lion: 'Give me my reward'

The lion replied: 'Go and boast that you entered the lion's mouth in one piece and came out in one piece . . ."

===Rabbi Yehoshua. From the Book
"History of the Jewish people" Art Scroll History Series.

Comrades Andreas Volvaskov, Ogayan soyanov and Hyman Otta were ordered to be brought out from their cellar confinement where the ex-commandant had ordered them to be locked-up. O. C. Nico walked down hurriedly the aisle towards the cellar of the detention camp, his bunch of prison keys jingling as he moved.

From a distance he heard the hymn.

WE SHALL OVER COME, WE SHALL OVER COME, WE SHALL OVER COME SOMEDAY, OH! DEEP IN MY HEART I DO BELIEVE THAT WE SHALL OVER COME SOMEDAY!!!!!!!!! coming out of one of the dungeon in the basement.

He was instantly touched by the song. Being human, he thought about the situation he was in, wherefore he had to administer unreasonable punishment to innocent immigrants. Nevertheless, he always felt great admiration for the tenacity with which the inmates stuck to their plights and the circumstances. As he got closer to the cells, he began to ponder about his own predicament in that he's a gay in a very macho job, where he had to hide his sexuality. He wished he could stand up for his right as these prisoners persevered in spite of inhuman punishment meted out to them.

O. C. Nico opened Hyman's cell and that of Volvaskov and Ogayan, greeting them warmly as he shook their hands and patted their backs and he announced, triumphantly.

"Guys, you have won! You're officially being invited to have an audience with the acting prison commandant . . . and with due respect, you're asked to report immediately" he smiled happily at them.

"Amen and Amen!" Hyman uttered a little grin on his hunger strikened face as he inquired from O. C. Nico.

"Sir, what of the old commandant, what has become of him?"

"The old cargo is now looking for a house in *Brengenzer Wald*" he replied.

"*Brengenzer Wald*, what is that? And, where's that?" Hyman inquired in puzzlement.

Officer Nicole smiled.

"Let's put it this way, what's the least place in Africa that you would want to live in? Figure the answer yourself!"

Hyman smiled and nodded his head.

"I understand! It serves him well."

"Oh! Guys that's history now! It's an old story!" Officer Nicole said smilingly submmitted.

They entered into the office of the acting commandant Thomas Muller, a very short, stocky man, around forty-two years of age. Redish hair with flat features of a farmer. He was dressed in civilian clothes. A complete grey safari suits with a pair of black shoes to match.

"Gentlemen, you're all welcome! As you can tell I'm not in uniform. I've just been called away from my vacation to take over the running of this prison camp. My superiors had informed me that three of you along with others in this list," he raised a sheet of paper and showed them a list of names, "will be released as asylant. My superiors will also like me to inform you that . . . these actions are being taken not as a response to your hunger strike or civil disobedience but rather on the basis of the merits of your individual cases" he blatantly lied.

O. C. Nico who was standing behind the acting commandant, smiled and winked his eyes at the three freedom fighters and thumbed his index on the air for their new found freedom which he thought was over due.

Hyman, Volvaskov and Ogayan simultaneously exclaimed.

"Thank you, Sir!"

"You're welcome! It's not my doing, it was a decision taken on the highest level. We just want to carry on as if all these had never happened" the acting commandant maintained. "Do you have any questions, gentlemen?"

"Yes sir! Just one question" comrade Volvaskov smiled. "Please Sir, could you explain to us where and what is *Brengenzer Wald?*"

+++

Hyman Otta hurried his way back to their cell, running and shouting praises to the living God. He sang.

'You have given us victory we will lift you higher, Jehovah . . . We will lift Him higher . . . '

'The wall of racism fell down, the wall of racism fell down down, when the people of God, were praising the Lord, the wall of racism fell down down'

O. C. Nico was smiling as he silently sang along with him and happily followed them on their way to freedom. They reached their former cells and the officer inserted his keys to the key-holes of the heavily secured iron door and gently, he opened it widely.

Hyman breezed into the cell, jumping, shouting and dancing and embracing Koso, Kanombe and Eto the Rastaman who had become skinny like the *bone-ga fish* in the last few days.

"Hey! Start packing up 'my Niggers'" he shouted.

'Our God has delivered us as He delivered the Hebrews from the hands of the Egyptians . . . On the Mountain, in the valley, on the land and in the sea . . . Even in prison, even in suffering, even hardship, and even in hunger strike . . . Hallelujah . . . the Lord is our portion in the land of the living, our God is good forever more . . . our Lord is our portion in the land of the living'

Hyman sang with his fellow African brothers echoing.

He brought the song to a sudden halt, as O. C. Nico winked an eye at him and pointed at his watch.

Hyman happily repeated his orders.

"Don't you hear me very well 'my Niggers' I said you should all start packing for our day and time of deliverance has finally come . . . Today is the day of the Lord, may His name be praised forever and ever, Amend!!!!"

"Amen and Amen!!" echoed Koso, Kanombe and Eto. Yet, they were shocked by the news to the point that they remained dumbfounded.

Eto, who for once seemed so confused and tensed that he couldn't understand what was really happening, ran and stared towards the cell's door (still widely ajar) and saw O. C. Nico as he was enjoying a stick of cigarette. He stood for a moment in ultra confusion.

"Look, my friend, I don't have time to waste, you've only but five minutes, could you please, make it quick and save the fucking time for me!" officer Nicole said tapping at his shoulders. "Go for your God in whom you strongly believe in has surely set you free" he praisingly declared to the Africans, stooping his head inside their cell.

Meanwhile Koso—who as usual the most outgoing of all, seemed to withdraw inside himself and was looking for confirmation from Hyman, as he was busy and seriously packing and arranging his belongings inside his big travelling bag—stood astonishly and said to Hyman.

"Charlie Boy. Do you really mean . . . ?"

"Don't wait till the ark of Noah is firmly closed and don't be a doubting Thomas! There's no time for fiddling arguments anymore."

Hyman snapped at him, as he bent to zip his bag.

"You must put on the suite of armour of freedom and of our God and stop doubting and believe more."

"Ireman . . . it's confirmed by O. C. Nico himself. So be fast, man! Or, the Zion train will leave you" Eto said, as he helped Hyman picked some bags.

"But we're not celebrating yet, there still an unpleasant atmosphere awaiting all of us out there" Koso cautioned, knowing fully well that life is not all that easy for the African asylum seekers in Austria. "And now, we don't know . . . whatever would happen to Ojo Madukwem, Andrew Peters and Muhamet Wakil, the Afghan?" Koso asked in a more serious note, meaning their fellow inmates who were admitted in the AKH.

"Gee! Now you come!" Hyman smiled.

Emmanuel Obinali Chukwujekwu

They were already outside their cell waiting for O. C. Nico to lock the door.

"The acting commandant . . . you know the former one had been booted out . . . assured us that the three of them will be going home from the hospital as soon as they're fully recovered. Boy! Could you imagine that? Every 'Nigger' and all their well-wishers having the God-ordained freedom the same day and at the same time, isn't it marvellous in the eyes of both, men and God?" Hyman exclaimed, raising up and waving his hands in praises.

Hyman Otta pardoned Koso finally for being doubtful even to the last. And he pleaded with O. C. Nico to let him have a look of their cell room for the last time.

As he stepped inside the cell, a ghostly figure of Marcus Omofuma appeared before him and said.

"So my good friend, Hyman Otta . . . you and my other brothers and friends are finally walking in freedom. But I'm here to warn you . . . and please do not forget me in the coming battlesssss."

Hyman stood and stared blankly for a while. And when he turned, his face darkened and his eyes reddened like that of a wound lion.

CHAPTER TWENTY-TWO

"But I am afflicted and in pain, let Thy salvation, O God,
set me on high. I will praise the name of God with a song
and will magnify Him with thanksgiving."

===PSALMS 69:29-30.

Joseph Onyema, a Nigerian activist for African Rights in Austria, came out
of his apartment building in the *Leopoldgasse* in the 2nd district of Vienna.
He walked down *Obere Augartenstrasse*. He entered the tram 31 heading
towards *Schottentring* where he emerged. He jumped in the underground
U2 and disembarked at the *Schottentor* stop. He walked up the escalator,
passing many other passengers on his way and went over to where he
waited for the *Strassenbahn* going through *Währingerstrasse*. Onyema up
to this point had not noticed that he had been under surveillance by
members of the Vienna police special organzied crime unit.

African activists had become target of this unit because it made them
vulnerable to fabricated charges of organized drug rings.

In a moment, the tram arrived and Onyema found his way inside, taking his
seat at the back. The tram drove away and made a stop at the *Schwarzspanier*
tram-stop, opposite the Hotel Regina, near the *Votiv* Catholic church. In
front was the famous *Votiv Park*. Down the street at the back from where
the tram stopped was the *Afro-Asiatisches Institut Wien*.

He immediately disembarked. Adjusting his suit and tie, he walked down
a stone-throw away passing the *Landesgerichtsstrasse*. He finally made his
way into the *Willkommen* Chinese restaurant along the *Währingerstrasse*.

Emmanuel Obinali Chukwujekwu

As Onyema entered the restaurant, he still hadn't registered in his consciousness that the blue Volkswagen Golf, the same one that had parked outside his apartment building was now parked across opposite the *Willkommen* restaurant. The two men inside the car had the same boring faces as Adolf Eichmann.

Onyema passed a couple of customers and moved straight to the first floor of the restaurant, where he believed that he would find some Africans enjoying their lunch. Most Africans normally came here to have their meal, he was told by a friend.

The previous day, Onyema had attended a meeting of the African activists and the *SOS Mitmensch* who were jointly organizing a big demonstration on behalf of Marcus Omofuma.

Upon hearing African voices, the loudest of which belonged to Abraham Agu Okeke, an African asylum seeker from Nigeria, Onyema felt that his mission after all would not be in vain. He contentedly went to one of the empty seats and sat down.

+++

Agu Okeke had arrived from Nigeria to Austria, roughly a year ago. An average height and with a heavily built physique, Okeke comes from the Igbo tribe, a well-to-do merchant tribe from the Eastern part of Nigeria, formally called Biafra. The Igbos, were also known as survivors and self-sufficient people after all they went through during and after the Nigeria-Biafra war of 1967-1970.

As an asylum seeker in Austria where his status did not permit him to have an official job, yet without any social and financial support; Abraham Agu Okeke has an unofficial work as a self-employed 'car finder'. He used to travel to the villages, find cars or buses or trucks etc. that were displayed for sale and then had to also look for buyers, a kind of being a middleman. He depended on the commission from both sides, and that was how he used to make his living to help supporting himself in the ever increasing cost of Vienna's lifestyle—which currently ranked 17th in the world's high-cost cities.

Okeke used to look for his clients anywhere he could find them, including the various restaurants and night clubs where many Black guys frequented.

Abraham Okeke, having finished some businesses with a client of his, was relaxing for the day with a bottle of *Ottakringer* beer after a meal of fried rice and turkey parts when he looked up and saw a man in suit, standing in front of the table he occupied.

"*Nnm-de-wo . . . wanne m!* (Well done my brother)" the man, with the black suit, white shirt, red-silk tie, black pairs of shoes and silver-rimmed sunglasses, greeted, stretching out his hand in handshake. "I know you don't know me, but I'm Joseph Onyema from the Association for Human Rights and Democracy in Africa (AHDA). You might be thinking why do I come straight to your table but something in me told me you can help me out" the man asserted.

"And what exactly can I do for you?" asked Okeke, who was somehow embarrassed by the fraudstar's approach the man had applied. "And, by the way how did you know I'm an Igbo man?"

"Oh! Really . . . one can see you're a typical characteristic of an Igbo man . . . I mean, for any person who knows the Igbos very well" Onyema assured, a trace of pride in his voice. "Of course, you even resembled General Chukwuemeka Odimegwu Ojukwu, the former Biafra leader and a well known war warrior. And fortunately enough, I'm also an Igbo man, a patriotic Biafran if you say so" Onyema murmured proudly, flashing a gap-toothed smile. "Now, you believe I can recognise my brother wherever I see one, just like the Jewish will be proud to recognise their fellow Jews wherever they go."

"Damn me! *Nwanne mmadu!* You're an Igbo man for sure . . . a damn, son-of-the-soil, for that matter!" Okeke exclaimed, as he rose from his chair and embracing Onyema . . . in a Black—brotherhood manner. "Please, forgive me for being rude . . . could you sit down, please brother . . . what can you take?"

"I don't really know if I'm in the mood to take anything now. I'm on my way to . . ."

"No brother. Absolutely no," Okeke shook his head in disagreement. "You may be on your way to even heaven or hell but you must take something first with me before going. We Igbos don't normally eat alone, you must remember that. So just a little and it would be well for both of us, you know. 'Man no die man no rotten!" Okeke slangly insisted.

"*Aha Nwanne m* . . . as you insisted, then let me have a bottle of coke."

"You don't take a beer?" inquired Okeke with a bright grin on his face. "Are you a woman? Because I took it that coca-cola is really woman stuff . . . if you get what I mean. Let them bring a bottle of beer or guiness?"

"Thanks, but really, I'm not in the mood for beers this afternoon, I'm on my way to . . ." he was saying as he raised his brown leather briefcase and placed it on his laps.

He carefully opened it with its set numbers and extracted some posters and flyers and placed them on top of the table.

"Actually, you must have heard about our Black brother who recently died at the hands of the Austrian police, while being . . ."

"No, I haven't," said Agu Okeke, looking quite astounded. "Incredible. Where, when and for what?" he demanded worryingly.

"You can't pretend that you're here in Vienna and haven't heard of this terrible news that's booming all over radios, televisions and news dailies . . . such an international news, that even CNN is aware of" Onyema said, his face frowning in angry consternation.

"Forgive me brother, but I'm not always in Vienna. I use to go to . . ."

"Now you come again, no part of Austria or round Europe that the news is not heard. In fact, it's now old news. Well, of course, I know many Blacks do not care for news but their stomach. Anyway let us forget about that. Now that you've heard it, can you help me to distribute some of these posters and flyers to others of our brothers and to anybody that seem interested" he picked one up from on top of the table, turning it over, an enlarged photo portrait of Omofuma appeared before both of them.

"Oh! Oh!! Oh!!! . . . No, no, no that can never be, that can never happen. Tell me it is not true" Agu Okeke bitterly cried aloud, even to the hearing of the other clients inside the restaurant. "You mean this was the guy that got killed by the police? It can't be!" he screamed again, this time even louder.

There was a sharp reaction from other customers, both Whites and Blacks who were all busy eating their meals. Every one of them turned in the direction where Okeke and Onyema sat. Many of the Black guys left their tables to ask what was happening. As Onyema's prediction came out, none of the Africans inside the restaurant—numbering about ten—have heard of the news—and they all professed to that.

Tears were dripping down the cheeks of Okeke as he started sobbing.

"I knew this guy very . . . very well, believe me my brothers. We were in the asylum camp together. We ate and drank in the same table at the *Traiskirchen* asylum camp. Oh! now I could remember, he was arrested and sent to the *Rossauerlände* deportation camp almost after our interviews . . . I mean, that was several months ago . . . You can't really believe what it's like over there in the camp, with their poor and unhealthy food but we all seemed to be happy then because beggars have no choice. Yet, after all those painful experience, these people eventually got him killed . . . this poor guy. Oh! It's only God who can judge!" Okeke sobbed.

He digged inside his pocket and took a handkerchief, whipping his face with it, and murmured.

"May his soul rest in perfect peace, amen."

"Amen and Amen" echoed the other Black guys and Onyema who was by now really sorry he brought this agony to this young man.

He felt sorry like one who had brought the news of the sudden death of a young and beautiful wife to her husband.

"So, you really know him?" Onyema asked rather sympathetically.

Okeke, unshaved and with red-rimmed eyes answered and said in a very deeply and emotional tone.

"I think I knew him more than a mother would've known her son! He was a very good friend indeed . . . He was like a younger brother to me. Brother . . . Sir, please, tell us in details, how did it happen?" he demanded, cleaning his eyes with the handkerchief.

As Onyema began to retell the story of Omofuma's death, the echoes of the conversation were being overheard by the two police officers sitting in the unmarked police car outside the restaurant, and was also being recorded by two other undercover police agents, a man and a lady, who were initially ordered to monitor Onyema and his activities inside the restaurant. Both of them had come in like any other customer and made their way upstairs and sat at the table beside Onyema and Okeke. During the conversation one of the policemen in the unmarked car had told another officer on the police walkie-talkie to put a tail on Abraham Agu Okeke.

Onyema finished his story. Okeke felt very upset as his eyes had become red like an animal that had been freshly cut by a snare. Even like that of a wounded lion which is the real meaning of his name *Agu* (lion).

Agu Okeke promised Onyema he would be willing to help in organizing the demonstration and asked to be given more posters and leaflets to help distribute to others. Onyema was very happy about his acceptance. He immediately extracted more posters, leaflets and flyers of different sizes and gave them to Okeke who without wasting time started distributing them around various tables and to various customers, both Whites and Blacks, including the couple, undercover agents.

As Onyema left the restaurant happy that his labour of locating the restaurant was not really in vain, there were now two unmarked police cars. One started up and followed him while the other stood behind, waiting for Abraham Agu Okeke.

CHAPTER TWENTY-THREE

"Our nettleson task is to discover how to organize our strength into compelling power so that the government cannot elude our demands. We must develop, from strength, a situation in which the government finds it wise and prudent to collaborate with us. It would be the height of naiveté to wait passively until the administration had somehow been infused with such blessing of goodwill that it emplored us for our programs. The first course is grounded in nature realism; the other is childish fantasy"

===Martin Luther King Jr. (1929-1968).

Opposite Hotel Regina, Abraham Agu Okeke had disembarked from the tram 38. He stood and glanced through a map booklet in his hand. A middle-aged man passed and gave him a suspicious glance. He wanted to ask the man how he could connect his way to where he was going, but the man's attitude made him to change his mind as he approached a taxi driver who immediately parked behind him. The driver spoke with him at length, pointing straight down the street. He thanked the driver and walked down the street with high spirit. There were not many who thought as he did. Since that very moment Onyma had showed him that poster of late Omofuma inside the restaurant, he had vowed to himself that he must be part and parcel of both the planning and execution of the coming demonstrations in his honor. 'He lacked malice, but the police behaviour this time around were growing like a malignant disease, which must be stopped by all means or they would wipe out the whole Black community in Austria within few years', Okeke thought, as he stopped to look at a sign post. He saw the building immediately, on the *Türkenstrasse* 14, the *Afro-Asiatisches Institut Wien*. A very mighty three story building, which was painted in a beige colour with the institution's logo proudly displayed on a flag hoisted on the top as it flapped in the wind.

Okeke looked at the building narrowly before he entered. Passing the main entrance gate, on the right side was the security cabin. The steps were directly on the left side. There were two or more elevators moving up and down the main building. Near the steps were toilet cabins for men and ladies. In the first floor occupied the mini-student hall where the meeting was going on. And beside the hall were a restaurant and a bar which were built for students.

Abraham Agu Okeke finally trudged his way down the hall and seated himself at the far back, nodding and waving to some people in greetings.

+++

Sabina Rudas was standing in the middle of the hall, talking about the demonstration, the aims and the objectives. Sitting all around her, listening intently were many human rights activists, both, Blacks and Whites, belonging to *SOS Mitmensch*, the Association for human rights and Democracy in Africa (AHDA), Amnesty Internaional (AI), Association for Human Rights of Immigrants (GEMMI), the Nigerian community in Austria and the African Community in Austria. Also sitting around among these group of individuals were comrades Hyman Otta, Koso Osei, Andrew Peters, Ojo Madukwem, Prince Eto, Jean Kanombe, Andreas Volvaskov, Ogayan Stoyanov, Wakil Muhamet and of course, Joseph Onyema who was actually one of the main organizers. There were also representatives from various Black African churches in Austria. Occupying the rear-row seats were journalist John Nelson and his camera man Mr. Preiter while *Fräulein* Lisa Egger sat somewhere in the corner with a disguised long brown hair-wig and attire and with her good friend Linda whom she had invited along.

And the last but not the least, were police agents of ranks and files who were fully represented.

"We've decided to gather everybody here tonight because more than anything else we would like this demonstration to be multi-racial. I'm looking forward to getting your imparts about how to proceed. Personally, I think my organization believes that the message we should get across is that the inhuman treatment meted out to Omofuma is a symptom of racial discrimination and something very wrong in the Austrian society. The demonstration needs to reach out to Austrian society at large to stem the tide of growing racism. We should not allow the authorities to paint every Black man and Black woman as non-human and as drug dealers and use that pretence to destroy them . . ." Sabina Rudas was saying, moving about, as she gesticulates with great emotions. "I'd like to call on Hyman Otta, an African asylum seeker who had just been released from the deportation prison camp, and who had successfully conducted a hunger strike and a sit-in action with many other inmates in the detention camp in honor of Marcus Omofuma, their former roommate in the prison" she asserted, and turned her head, staring directly at Hyman Otta, she said.

"Please, Mr. Otta, take the floor."

As Hyman stood up, there was applause from the crowd. Tears rolled down from his eyes and he used the back of his right hand to wipe away the tears. He flagrantly edged his way forward to the centre of the table where Sabina Rudas and many other organizers were sitting.

From where he sat, journalist John Nelson recognized him immediately and was eager to listen attentively to what this wonderful oriented African was about to say. He got his writing materials ready, moving a little closer and switched on his recorder.

Fräulein Lisa Egger, who had witnessed the Africans being interviewed while imprisoned and equally had heard about this vibrant young African both from her sacked hard-liner boss and his officers and her newly founded lover boy, journalist Nelson, fascinatedly straightened from where she was to get whatever he has to give as she secretly eyed John Nelson, smiling gathered all over her face.

"Firstly, I would like to thank everybody here today. Could we all please stand up for a minute of silence for the soul of Marcus Omofuma" he pleaded.

Without hesitation, everyone stood up and observed a minute of silence.

Observed!

Hyman went on and described in details to the audience their predicaments and their sufferings with the late Omofuma inside the prison. He also mentioned about the hunger strike and the demonstration that resulted in him and his two friends being silenced in their prison cellar for some days. At that point, he used the opportunity to introduce his fellow former prison inmates to the audience as he called out their names one after the other while they only stood up from their seats, bowed their heads to the crowd, who were responding by giving them heavy rounds of applause.

"I would like also to use this golden opportunity to thank journalist John Nelson of the *Augustin* press for his persistence in reporting, and his courage in helping us, particularly for his daring interviews of the . . ."

John Nelson was by this time busy, jotting down in his handbook. He looked up and somehow embarrassed, stared at Lisa Egger who encouraged him with the wink of an eye to stand up. There was another round of applause.

"Once again" Hyman said, his eyes taking in the audience. "Thank you for having me here. Please, let's not allow the memory of Omofuma to fade away! Thank you and May the Almighty God bless all of you for being present here today!"

After Hyman had spoken many other activists and speakers came who gave their view points in the content of the demonstration. Agu Okeke was one of them. He had spoken at length and had aroused the hostility and suspicion of some of the participants—a delegation from the Nigerian Embassy, who has been handling of the issue, the luke-worn approach of the incumbent Nigerian Ambassador in Austria towards the death of Omofuma. He also accused the Embassy on the way it has been drown into issuing Nigeria travelling documents—TC—indiscriminately, even to non—Nigerians, because of being bribed by the Austrian authorities, who always believed that even a man from south America as far as he is a black, would easily obtain his papers from the corrupted Nigerian officials in the Embassy. Okeke also echoed the belief of many Nigerians living in

Austria, that if the Embassy had not issue the TC, Omofuma might be alive today.

A lady member of the organizing committee was later selected by the organizers and she was asked to compile the list of those that would speak during the course of the demonstration.

Finally Joseph Onyema gave his reports about the distribution of the posters, the flyers and the leaflets. He asked that more materials be printed, so that he and his colleagues who were assigned for the distribution would be able to reach out to more people. He asserted that their distribution networks spread across Austrian other cities including Graz, Linz, Innsbruck, etc. He also outlined the full procedure of the demonstration to the audience. The precise time the protest would start, the routes the demonstrators would take and where they would stop to speak during the course of the demonstration.

"I advise each of us to stuff his or herself with energetic food and drink for as it seems the journey will not be an easy one. It will even surpass the Israelites journey through the wilderness" Onyema uttered jokingly in his magniloquent style. "And, do not forget ladies and gentlemen, that the demonstration must be free of violence. Let everyone be warned before hand. Thanks and more blessings to each of you."

As the meeting peacefully came to an end, Agu Okeke in his usual friendly and inquisitive manner quickly approached Hyman and his friends to thank and get first hand account on what really happened to his friend Marcus Omofuma from their own perceptive. He sat with them for a few minutes listening attentively, but their discussions abruptly came to a halt when comrade Volvaskov spotted the four undercover agents shadowing Okeke and some other activists. On their way out, Agu Okeke asked.

"How are you sure they were there because of us?"

"Because I am a naturally suspicious man and besides, it's my job. I'm paid to be suspicious, my friend!" comrade Volvaskov declared emphatically.

++

About a week later the big demonstration finally took place. They started gathering as early as 8 o'clock in the morning at the *Kettenbrückengasse-Naschmarkt* area. By 10 o'clock, a rainbow coalition of people from all work of life—mostly White Austrians, mix-married couples with their mulatto children, Black Africans and immigrants from across the world had assembled themselves. A television station estimated of forty thousand people.

Many of the demonstrators marched with their mouths covered with adhesive tapes distributed by the organizers in symbolic gesture to the method of death employed against Omofuma by the authorities. Among the special group of people fully represented at the demonstration, were group of Austrian punks. All of them had their mouths masked by adhesive tapes and were dressed in complete black attires.

Beside the police surrounding all the areas, there were also a flood of national and international journalists, including, John Nelson and his *Augustin* crews; the CNN, the BBC, the ABC, the ORF, TFI international and many other media houses. Leaflets were being distributed to the journalists and among the protesters.

The demonstration started at 12 noon promptly and proceeded down the *Naschmarkt* towards *Dr.-Karl-Lueger-Ring.*

All down the route of demonstration the anti-riot police units had the protesters boxed in on all sides, including overflies of helicopter surveillance.

At the forefront of the procession were the police escort riders with their big motorcycles, followed by the police cars with sirens and flashing lights.

At the head of the demonstration side of the line, an activist chase car moved slowly. Behind was a white VW van filled with musical and broadcasting equipments, with giant loud speakers and microphones on top of the van. The two sideways of the van were widely opened. Apart from the DJ, there were other women and men singers, who sang along and always descended from the vehicle wherever the procession stopped.

Behind the van was a group of mixed-raced activists carrying a mammoth banner spread across the front-line which was used as brocade in between them and the heavy police quards, on the banner in black letters against a white background was boldly inscribed:

WE WILL NEVER FORGET THE MURDER OF MARCUS OMOFUMA

Behind the people holding the big banner was a multi-cultural group of students, housewives, workers, diplomats, union representatives, politicians mainly from the Green party, and migrants, both, asylum seekers and 'legal' immigrants.

At the centre was a group of Africans beating different types of drums. Immediately after the drummers and trumpet blowers was another group of Black asylum seekers led by Abraham Agu Okeke. This group comprised Omofuma's friends and colleagues who had either been with him in the *Traiskirchen* asylum camp or in the *Rossauerlände* deportation prison camp; which were the only two places Omofuma had been to through his short stay in Austria. Among people in this 'gang' were Hyman Otta, Koso Osei, Prince Eto, the Rastaman, comrade Volvaskov and others.

Then followed by the rest of other demonstrators carrying different posters, placards and gagged portraits of Omofuma, all with different slogans.
As the procession moved on slowly, the first port of call was at the Balkan airline ticket office. There was a spontaneous outburst of shouting, rock throwing as they attempted to breach the police line to enter the airline's office but they were forced back by the overwhelmed police re-enforcement units. Even though they were repulsed by the police, they succeeded in breaking the show case glass window of the office.

The demonstration moved again through *Ringstrasse* towards *Schottenring* and stopped once more at the police headquarter, near the *Schottentor* round about. In front of the building many of the demonstrators laid rites and lit candles. Some human rights activists eulogized Marcus Omofuma, blaming the police for his untimely death.

The protesters left and made their ways directly to the *Schmerling Park*, the Parliamental park, and again a brief address by the organizers, criticizing and condemning the government asylum policies took place. Leaflets were been distributed at every corner and every route the protesters passed by the activists.

The procession finally came to a halt in front of the Austrian Parliamental building as everyone assembled together to listen to the closing speeches from different organizers. While the speeches were on, Abraham Agu

Okeke and his group were busy dancing and singing many African war songs—mainly in Igbo dialect.

'*Nnzo wu Nnzo wu Enyimba Enyi'* . . . '*Anyi ga me, Anyi ga eme, Anyi ga eme yi ha egwu'* (We're going to show them wonders).'

As they sang and danced, what Okeke and others did not knew was that many of the photojournalists milling about the crowd, taking pictures of most of them, were undercover policemen.
One of the journalist singled Agu Okeke out because many of the younger protesters seemed to be drown to the group following him. The undercover cop journalist from a phoney newspaper requested an interview from him as John Nelson made an impromptu appearance at the side of Agu Okeke to interview him as well.

"Do you mind if I interview you, sir?" the cop journalist asked mannerly.

"Of course, I don't mind being interviewed. It's an honor!" Agu replied.

"Did you know Marcus Omofuma personally, sir?"

"We were in the asylum camp together" Agu said emotionally.

He went on to describe his relationship with Marcus and how he felt when he first heard the news of his death as well as his role in organizing the demonstration and how he would mobilize many more people to attend subsequent protest and so on.

"Please, sir, could you describe in details your reasons for coming to Austria for asylum?" asked the fake-journalist. "Why did you come to Austria and not to other . . ."

"Well . . . actually, my problems were complex in nature, which I wouldn't like . . . to state here for some reasons," said Agu Okeke confidently, "I'm still under the jurisdiction of the *Bundesministerium* and the application of my asylum are still on course . . . if you understand me . . . so I don't think it is wise to speak about my problems publicly."

"If you wouldn't mind, sir, how did you leave your country?" said the cop journalist, already aware that John Nelson was somehow suspicious of his integrity as he motioned to his cameraman to take more snaps of Agu Okeke.

"I've told you I can't comment on anything concerning my asylum. I would like to go if that's all you want to know" Agu replied aggressively, having doubts within himself as to while this journalist is so concerned about his personal particulars.

"Hi, I'm John Nelson from the *Augustin* publishers. What were your expectations when you left your country to Europe?" the *Augustin* reporter first introduced himself to Agu before posing his questions, like a professional he was.

"Of course, as one that was running away to save his dear life, I expected to be very welcomed and sheltered" Okeke asserted, recognizing John Nelson for the first time.

"And were you sheltered in Austria if I may ask?" interrupted Nelson.

"And why Austria in the first place, why not another land?" added the cop impersonated journalist insistedly.

"Firstly, I wasn't . . . I didn't have any country in my mind when I left my country. As I said before, one that's trying to save his life doesn't have to choose where to go and where not to go . . . It happened, I saw myself in Austria . . . Hey! Man that was a long story to tell" Okeke snapped at the fake journalist and asked angrily.

"Have you ever been in some deadly situation that warrants running for your life?"

"Of course, no," the undercover agent said curtly.

"Then, you've no idea what I went through and you'll never understand! I think that you're one of those lucky journalists that haven't been to war-torn countries, you would have got some nasty experiences" Agu Okeke frowned and turning to John he said. "And to your question sir, I was not sheltered and so were many other asylum seekers like Marcus Omofuma, who we were all remembering today by doing this demonstration in his honour. The asylum policy in Austria, I'm sorry to say, is mainly designed to discourage, intimidate and render immigrants completely useless and unproductive. The Austrian authorities I believe do not really welcome the idea of people coming to seek for asylum here but because of the existing international law on asylum, which unfortunately for them, Austria is a signatary to, and which they claim in the eyes of the world to be championing. Can you imagine a situation where an asylum seeker is not entitled to do any type of work, yet the police will arrest and detain anyone who has . . ."

"Who is dealing on drugs?" cut in the undercover agent journalist impatiently and unprofessionally, "was that what you're trying to say?"

John Nelson, embarrassed by these unorthodox journalistic questions, immediately confirmed in his mind, what he had been assuming.

"No, sir" replied Agu Okeke promptly. "Not exactly what I was saying was that the police have special power to put in prison anyone that does not possess a *Meldezettel* . . . I mean, a police registered address, showing you got an apartment to sleep in. And to state the fact, I believe this Austrian asylum system was deliberately devised by the authorities to encourage and force some of us immigrants to engage in some petty crimes . . . so that we will be branded as criminals and be blackmailed in the eyes of the world. We all are human beings, and as human, we will all agree that a living man must eat, must change his clothes and that he must equally have a place to put his head, being legal or illegal."

"Thank you for the opportunity, Mr Okeke!" John Nelson smiled, jotting words on his handnote.

"Thank you too, sir!" replied Agu Okeke happily, shaking hands with the cop journalist first and then facing Nelson. "And you especially sir, for your exposé which caused a great political turmoil among the ranks and files as well as the powers that be. And which helped us in many ways to bring together the gathering for today" Okeke asserted and added jokingly. "Actually, sir, you look like and remind me of Roger Colen, the *New York Times* reporter for Germany, Austria and Switzerland who also reports for the International Herald Tribune and who recently wrote an exposé for the *New York Times* magazine about Jörg Haider which I really took pleasure in . . ." Okeke assured.

"I'm flattered by this remark, sir!" journalist John Nelson expressed with admiration.

+++

At the rear where the demonstration was officially coming to an end at precisely 8:30 pm, Joseph Onyema was reminding the departing protesters through his hand-held megaphone as Abraham Agu Okeke, Hyman Otta, Jean Kanombe, Koso Osei, Andrew Peters, Prince Eto and many other demonstrators were busy posing for photographs:

"DON'T FORGET IT IS AN ISRAELITES JOURNEY. THE BATTLE CONTINUES."

EPILOGUE

Barely three weeks after the demonstrations—for there had been two or more mini-protests on behalf of Marcus Omofuma—the Austrian police in conjunction with the ministry of Internal affairs launched an operation to arrest as many Black Africans as possible under the guise of belonging to an alleged 'drug ring' and being members of a non-existing criminal organization.

The operation, which was code-named *Operation Spring* was purely designed to eliminate as many Black activits as possible from Austria and to discourage any further activities on behalf of Omofuma by the immigrants and the asylum communities.

More than 250 Black African immigrants were initially arrested on the 27th of May 1999 precisely and were flung into prison. These arrests took place in all the major cities of Austria—including Graz, Linz, St. Pölten, Innsbruck and Vienna among other cities.

The operation was timed to begin at 5:30 am and it was simultaneous and continuous throughout the day.

The police swept was so comprehensive that Black people driving their cars or walking down the streets were picked up instantly by special 850 Cobra police officers trained for the operation. Many apartments were bursted into by the heavily masked officers while many of the Black African immigrants were beaten and intimidatedly arrested.

The *Operation Spring* was also motivated as a formidable political force to blackmail and portray the image of the Black community ralling for more voters in the then coming national elections on the 3rd of October, 1999.

The ruling Social Democrats (SPÖ) and their conservative coalition partner (ÖVP) were being forced by the extreme right-wing party to show they could be tough on immigration and crime.

The problem with the *Operation Spring* was that nobody in the government or the Austrian society at large thought about the aftermath of their actions. People were sitting in prison not on the basis of evidence but on the basis of their colours and statuses.

Onyema, Agu Okeke, Kanombe, Koso, Eto, Peters and many others, were taken into custody in the course of the operation. The author of this book was among them and he wrote this and other manuscripts, while in detention prison camp.

THANKS BE TO GOD ALMIGHTY FOREVER AND EVER. AMEN! TO GOD BE THE GLORY.

EMMANUEL OBINALI CUHKWUJEKWU.
11/9/2002.